T0286898

Praise for *The Gift of Thorns*

As a human with a cacophony of desires clamoring for attention all the time, I am grateful for the words within this book by A. J. Swoboda. Swoboda not only helps us face the mirror of our own desires—and the thorniness of them at times—he comforts us with the One who is in the work of redeeming each and every one of them.

—**Lore Ferguson Wilbert,** author of *The Understory, A Curious Faith,* and *Handle With Care*

Through a breathtaking combination of personal vulnerability, biblical wisdom, and pastoral hope, Swoboda explains that too many Christians have been taught to ignore the desires of the heart, when in fact they should be attended to and then sanctified by Christ. Much like St. Augustine, Swoboda's theological reflections are his *Confessions.* Take it up and read with delight.

—**Nijay K. Gupta,** professor of New Testament, Northern Seminary

In *The Gift of Thorns,* A. J. Swoboda has comprehensively argued a faithful theology of desire, and it is prophetic, pastoral urgency that ignites his words. On every page, Swoboda invites readers to believe the truly good news of Jesus. "The flesh entices us into short-term enjoyment and relief that leads to long-term anxiety and death," he writes. "The Spirit invites us into painful faithfulness in the present leading to long-term life and peace." May many read his words—and follow this narrow road of desire into the fullness of joy.

—**Jen Pollock Michel,** author and speaker

In a world and culture that encourages emotions to be what shapes thinking and belief, more than ever do we need to pause and look at whether they are aligned with Jesus and truth. *The Gift of Thorns* gives us guidance to align our passions and thinking with the mind and heart of Jesus.

—**Dan Kimball,** vice president of Western Seminary, author of *How (Not) To Read the Bible*

In a poignant and personal "journey of homesickness," as the author describes the human life, A. J. Swoboda offers an examination of what motivates us at our core and asks the elemental question: Shall we surrender to our self-centered wants or to the One who, out of his own desire, created desire within us?

—**Joe Womack,** president of Bushnell University

What do you want? With pastoral care, cultural savvy, and winsome prose, Swoboda lays out a practical theology of desire that is wide ranging and easily accessible. He avoids unhelpful extremes that either deify or demonize human longings. In so doing, he draws us toward the sinless and empathetic King, who longed for us to the point of bearing thorns.

—**Joshua M. McNall,** associate professor of pastoral theology, director of the Honors College, Oklahoma Wesleyan University, author of *How Jesus Saves*

With deep insights from Scripture and honest personal inquiry, this book offers wisdom and hope for the longings and thorns we encounter. A thought-provoking understanding of how our relationship with desire shapes our very essence.

—**Amy Bragg Carey,** president of Friends University

In a day and age where every podcast and social platform has an opinion about my desires, this book stands as a prophetic voice amid the chaos. *The Gift of Thorns* is going to help aid Jesus followers not only to name their desires but to know what to do with them.

—**Andrew Damazio,** lead pastor of the
Rose Church, Portland, Oregon

With a mix of apologetic flare and contemplative aplomb, A. J. Swoboda has written a vital contribution to the new wave of work on the theology of desire, which is right at the heart of what it means not just to be human but also to be made in the image of God. By plumbing the depths of the mystery of the cross and its relationship to the longings of our hearts, he blows the dust off our current views of desire and brings fresh insight into what it means to be transformed through the life, death, and resurrection of Jesus. At the center of our desire to flourish is a paradox: we must die in order to be born again into the resurrection life. This book has a masterful grasp of the mystery not just of desire but of the gospel, which is the Christ of Gethsemane who prays, "not my will but yours be done," and him crucified.

—**David Bennett,** postdoctoral research fellow, faculty of
theology and religion, University of Oxford; research fellow,
Wycliffe Hall, Oxford; author of *A War Of Loves*

Through a wise, carefully researched, theologically sophisticated, and pastoral exploration of how our desires shape us, A. J. helps us answer Jesus' age-old question, "What do you want?" I welcome his voice as a trustworthy guide because I have seen the desires of his heart produce good fruit in life.

—**Randy Remington,** president of the Foursquare Church

THE GIFT OF THORNS

THE GIFT OF THORNS

Jesus, the Flesh, and
the War for Our Wants

A. J. SWOBODA

ZONDERVAN
REFLECTIVE

ZONDERVAN REFLECTIVE

The Gift of Thorns
Copyright © 2024 by A. J. Swoboda

Published in Grand Rapids, Michigan, by Zondervan. Zondervan is a registered trademark of The Zondervan Corporation, L.L.C., a wholly owned subsidiary of HarperCollins Christian Publishing, Inc.

Zondervan titles may be purchased in bulk for educational, business, fundraising, or sales promotional use. For information, please email SpecialMarkets@Zondervan.com.

Requests for information should be addressed to customercare@harpercollins.com.

ISBN 978-0-310-15328-3 (hardcover)
ISBN 978-0-310-15330-6 (audio)
ISBN 978-0-310-15329-0 (ebook)

Published in association with literary agent Tawny Johnson of Illuminate Literary Agency, www.illuminateliterary.com.

Cover design: Spencer Fuller, Faceout Studio
Cover photos: Shutterstock; GettyImages
Interior design: Kait Lamphere

Printed in the United States of America

23 24 25 26 27 LBC 5 4 3 2 1

To Morris.
Who taught me to look for the light.

He who wants a rose must respect the thorn.

—*Persian proverb*

CONTENTS

FOREWORD

Not long after I had given my life to Jesus, I asked a pastor and mentor of mine to baptize me. On a cloudy day we went outside the city to a creek. We sat on the bank of the creek and talked about what baptism means. Then we went into the water. I asked him to hold me down under the water for a few counts because I wanted this pregnant pause to mark that I was passing from an old life to a new one. I was longing, as A. J. writes, for my flesh—my sinful desires—to be washed away by the waters of baptism. The pastor baptized me in the name of the Father, the Son, and the Holy Spirit and held me down a long time after the third dunk. When it was over, we hugged and walked back to the bank.

In what will seem either like I am making this up or like a scene from a movie, suddenly the sun pierced through the clouds and shone directly on a tree behind us. We looked back to this unburning but well-lit tree, and then the pastor walked toward it. He broke off a branch, walked back, and handed it to me. It was from a thorn tree. He then spoke to me about thorns: about Paul's thorn in the flesh—something that stayed with Paul after his baptism—and about suffering and temptation. I took it all in. But I had no idea what he was talking about. I assumed that I, having had my sins freshly washed away, would walk in the sunshine of holiness from that day forward. I was wrong.

I was smart enough to do one thing. I kept the branch, with its five sharp thorns. Today it is in a glass case that sits in my study where I pray and write. It is a kind of relic to me, a moment when I was given a theophany in the form of a thorn. For years I did not understand what all this meant. Though I would experience joy, elation, and success as well as suffering, grief, loss, and failure over the next four decades, I did not have a clear sense of what that thorn branch meant.

Then I was asked to write a foreword for this book. I agreed because A. J. is my friend, a talented writer, and someone I deeply respect and love. But to be honest, when I heard it was a book about *desire*, I thought it was a niche subject. By the time I finished reading the last page, I was fully convinced that desire is at *the core of our spiritual formation and our very lives.* Though many years had passed since that soggy-turned-sunny day on the banks of a creek, I know now—thanks to this book—the importance of thorns and how they are a gift.

Two Questions

For many years, I lived with this narrative: "Desire, bad. Denial of desire, good." If I desired something, it was probably sinful. If I denied my desires, it was probably good. Something inside of me knew this was wrong, but I did not know why. All I knew was that inside me were countless desires swirling around, some ghastly and some godly. Dr. Swoboda is a master teacher who knows how to ask the right questions. There are two essential questions this book raises and answers: Why do strange desires lurk inside of me? And what does it look like for our desires to be formed in the image of Christ?

As to the first question, I had assumed that all of the strange desires lurking in me meant I must be an awful person. Thanks to this book, I see that every desire is pointing to something else. As A. J. writes, "What we assume to be a reservoir of lust may actually be a longing for intimacy."

The second question, *What does it look like for our desires to be formed in the image of Christ?* is, I believe, the center and purpose of this book. Christian spiritual formation is simply the formation of our lives into the image of Christ. This is why I have come to believe the central verse of Christian formation is this:

> And all of us, with unveiled faces, seeing the glory of the Lord as though reflected in a mirror, are being *transformed into the same image* from one degree of glory to another; for this comes from the Lord, the Spirit. (2 Cor. 3:18, emphasis mine)

This book brilliantly explains the essential role of desires in our formation into Christlikeness. As such, *The Gift of Thorns* deserves a place among the *essential books in Christian formation.*

This book is a guide to help us to know what desire is, why it is central to our lives, and how desires can be trained and shaped and ordered in order for us to live a good and beautiful—ergo, Christlike—life.

Honesty and Humor

To take on a subject like this, a subject that deals with very personal and painful issues, requires honesty. This subject cannot be approached without the author being vulnerable so the reader can be vulnerable as well. Vulnerability opens the door for the Spirit to enter and heal. For example, Dr. Swoboda writes about how, in his journals, he begged God, like St. Paul, to deliver him from a thorn in his flesh, which he (wisely) referred to as his X (for we all have an X or two). Yet he discovered, and leads us to discover, that our X is not something of which to be ashamed: "The X has marked the very spot where God has most intimately met me." The honesty in the book allowed me to be honest with myself, and I trust it will for you as well.

But to take on this subject also requires humor. This book is full of humor. I found myself laughing out loud at times. Rarely does this happen when I am reading a Christian book. The humor in this book takes on many forms, and often it is subtle and under-stated. There are so many passages in this book where I felt the anguish over our dark desires and how they harm our lives, but just when I needed it, some humor was offered to help me keep it in perspective. One of the funniest lines for me is this: "Thorns hurt. But they're a quiet gift. Of course, it's hard to appreciate that when they're in your side."

Quotable Quotes

The writing in this book is masterful. There are so many sentences that shimmer. A great sentence is one that cannot be improved. I found so many in this book that at a certain point I started writing the letter Q in the margin to remind me to go back and compile these quotes—a compendium of quotable quotes, a la C. S. Lewis or G. K. Chesterton. Once I started, the list grew longer and longer with each chapter. Here is a sample of just a few:

"We become the 'tapes' we most often play about ourselves."
"A perversion always implies a purpose."
"We desire more of the desires we follow."
"Desire and duty are the two feet of discipleship."

There are so many more (I wore out a brand-new highlighter in just this book), but I will stop here and let you, dear reader, highlight your own book.

Desire and Doxology, Healing and Hope

My favorite part about reading this book is that it indirectly stoked the fires of my desires for God and the things of God. I often say that when I read the writings of Hans Urs von Balthasar (quoted in this book), I am moved to *doxology*—to praise God spontaneously. I found that same feeling when I was reading this book. Countless times I had to put the book down and look to God and say, "Thank you, Lord, for this truth."

This book has also been healing for me. I found myself slowly healing from the poison of false narratives I have lived with for many years. We live, as Dallas Willard said, "at the mercy of our ideas." They run, and often ruin, our lives. Old wounds from my childhood were exposed as I read this book, which then offered me truths that set me free. I was especially moved by the sentence, "Jesus welcomes *all* of my childhood in his arms." Thank you, A. J., for that sentence alone.

I am not sure what forewords are for (and I refrained from the temptation of googling it). Nor do I know what makes a foreword a good one. All I know is that for you who are reading *this* foreword, I have only one *hope*. I hope what I have written here has kindled in you a desire to read this book, provided just enough of a sample as to make you hunger for more, so much so that you want this foreword to end so you can get right to it. If this is your desire, then amen and amen.

Finis.
James Bryan Smith

INTRODUCTION

In 2005, philosopher William Braxton Irvine published an academic volume about human desire entitled, appropriately, *On Desire*.[1] Central to his thesis, Irvine contrasted two figures: Roman Catholic priest and activist Thomas Merton and atheist philosopher and writer Bertrand Russell.

What could two such different men possibly share?

In his youth, Merton pursued a life of wanton licentiousness and earthly pleasure—anything but the saintly image Christian history remembers. Merton's eventual turn to Christianity seemed unthinkable even to those closest to him. What happened? As Irvine narrates, it was no reading of some compelling Christian intellectual, engaging church service, or witnessing family member who inched Merton toward faith. Rather, he experienced a sudden, unexpected awakening of desire. Merton recalls, "All of a sudden, something began to stir within me, something began to push me, to prompt me. It was a movement that spoke like a voice."[2]

This seemingly spontaneous desire stopped Merton in his tracks and upended his life's trajectory. Soon Merton found himself being baptized. New and exotic desires began blossoming from the soil of Merton's freshly converted heart. What would've earlier only hindered his youthful lusts now became his life's calling. Again, Merton reflects, "There had been another thought, half forming itself in the back of my mind—an *obscure desire* to become a priest."[3]

---

1. William B. Irvine, *On Desire: Why We Want What We Want* (New York: Oxford University Press, 2006).

2. Thomas Merton, *The Seven Storey Mountain* (San Diego: Harcourt Brace, 1948), 236.

3. Merton, *Seven Storey Mountain*, 239. Italics mine.

Irvine's research helps us appreciate that this quintessential tale of the making of a modern saint is owed almost exclusively to the supernatural awakening of desire—a desire, mind you, that never subsided, consuming Merton's every breath as a monk, priest, and activist until his untimely death. This desire inspired his attempts at rearticulating Christianity anew to the disenchanted, countercultural generation of the 1960s and '70s. All because of "an obscure desire."

Desires can lead to character, faith, and service. But they can also lead to self-centeredness, narcissism, and infidelity. Enter Bertrand Russell. By the early 1900s, Russell was revered as a leading figure in a vanguard of atheists challenging the religious climate of the century's turn. Russell's acerbic and scathing arguments against Christianity continue to serve as foundational texts for the "new atheist" movement of our time. And like Merton, it was the whim of desire that changed his life's trajectory.

Russell dearly loved his wife, Alys. But everything changed during an afternoon bike ride. Russell recounts an epiphany during a gentle stroll on a beautiful, sunny day:

> As I was riding along a country road, I realized that I no longer loved Alys. I had had no idea until this moment that my love for her was even lessening. The problem presented by this discovery was very grave. We had lived ever since our marriage in the closest possible intimacy. We always shared a bed, and neither of us ever had a separate dressing-room. We talked over everything that ever happened to us. . . . I knew that she was still devoted to me. I had no wish to be unkind, but I believed in those days . . . that in intimate relations one should speak the truth.[4]

---

4. Bertrand Russell, *Autobiography of Bertrand Russell: 1872–World War I* (New York, NY: Bantam, 1968), 195–96.

Following this "epiphany," Russell left Alys. After an extramarital sexual experience, he divorced his wife and married another. Russell's marital desire, quite simply, had blown away with the afternoon breeze that sunny day.

These two stories expose the sheer complexity of human desire. Like the wind in Russell's hair, desires come and go. Yet little has more bearing on who we are becoming than how we relate to our desires. Indeed, what a person does with their desires invariably shapes who they are, where they're going, and how and who they'll love. In other words, *how* we desire has as much consequence as *what* we desire.[5]

How, then, do we follow Jesus with such wayward and fickle desires?

Our longings are a central component of the human experience. Like my reader, I'm a man beset with many desires—some good, some bad, some questionable, some trivial. One afternoon, moved by sheer curiosity, I jotted down every particular want that came upon me over the course of a seemingly inconsequential one-hour faculty meeting at the university where I teach. I was surprised to discover a desire within for

+ a more fulfilling prayer life,
+ Jesus,
+ more coffee,
+ shorter faculty meetings,
+ pizza and fries,
+ sex,
+ updated sales numbers on a recent publication,

---

5. David Benner similarly writes that "the choices we make can be very important in our spiritual journey . . . *how* we decide can be as important as *what* we decide." David Benner, *Desiring God's Will: Aligning Our Hearts with the Heart of God* (Downers Grove, IL: InterVarsity Press, 2015), 17. Italics mine.

- to go home for dinner,
- better sales numbers for all my publications,
- more sex,
- an end to this faculty meeting,
- more time with my son,
- Jesus to return,
- a hug,
- time alone,
- a more fulfilling sense of calling,
- more friendships,
- and a pen with more ink.

I stopped there. This was only one hour. Much has been omitted for posterity's sake. One trembles to imagine what a whole day brings.

"Our life," St. Augustine once wrote, "is a gymnasium of desire."[6] No doubt, the tumult of our desires can be comical. But often they cast a long shadow over our life story. Not long ago, I was scheduled for back-to-back appointments with two students. The first was with a young, engaging, devout Christian student who processed her lifelong desire of becoming a missionary. She'd long sensed a call from Jesus to serve the poor and marginalized in the urban landscape. The next was with a Christian student who vulnerably confessed a lifelong journey with sexual desires he knew didn't align with the way of Jesus. By discussion's end, he had invited me into a long-term mentoring relationship exploring how he might follow Jesus in a body swirling with intrusive, unwanted desires.

My responses to these students left me curious. I offered seemingly contradictory counsel. I told one to follow her desire. I invited the other freely place his desire on the cross with Christ. Was this hypocrisy? This brought me back to Merton and Russell. What would I have told them to do with their desires? Truth be told,

---

6. Augustine, *Tractatus in 1 Johannem* 4.2008–9.

had I invited both students to simply "follow their hearts," something of the spiritual authority I'd been given in their lives would have been violated. These back-to-back appointments expose the sheer complexity of how we handle our own desires. And how we need wisdom to navigate them.

There are times when it's good to hope, with the psalmist, that God will give us the desires of our heart (Ps. 37:4). But there are also times when the desires of our heart are distorted and untrustworthy and deathly to their end. The Christian way isn't the uncritical pursuit of our desires *du jour*. No, the Christian call is to follow the One who made us out of his desire and gave us our own.

Unresolved questions tumble around inside many of us. Which wants do we obey? What longings should be crucified? Which are good? Or bad? What about those deep, cavernous, hidden, sometimes unspoken, churning, burning, unquenchable, and all-too-often unwanted cravings that we spend much of our lives forced to live alongside? We must open ourselves up to this kind of interrogation because, in the end, our relationship to desire shapes everything about who we're becoming—in the temporal and everlasting. Christian spirituality, among other things, is "what we do with . . . desire."[7] Indeed, laying our desires bare before the Spirit who "searches all things" (1 Cor. 2:10) is part of God's deep work in our lives. For if the trusted hands of the Great Physician aren't permitted to touch our unseen desires and wants, then our salvation remains cosmetic and performative. By ignoring our desires, we run the risk of doing great harm to others. And even greater harm to ourselves.

This might explain why desire occupied such a central place in Jesus' teaching ministry. Jesus often asked the blind, lame, and unwell, "What do you *want*?" So significant for Jesus was this question that of the 307 questions he's recorded asking in the Gospels,

---

7. Ronald Rolheiser, *The Holy Longing: The Search for a Christian Spirituality* (New York: Doubleday, 1999), 5.

it is one of the most repeated. The first words Jesus is recorded as saying in all four gospels are to Joseph in the temple courts: "Why were you searching for me?" (Luke 2:49). Equally important are the first recorded words of Jesus as an adult in John's gospel as two followers of John the Baptist come to investigate his ministry, saying, "What do you want?" (John 1:38). In both inaugural public statements as child and adult, Jesus interrogates the desires of those before him. John caps this off by revealing Jesus' first postresurrection words to Mary: "Who is it you are looking for?" (John 20:15). Philosopher Gil Bailie highlights the importance of Jesus' line of questioning:

> It can hardly be dismissed as merely fortuitous that the first words spoken by Jesus . . . in the gospels are: "What do you want?" It would not be too much to say that Jesus came into the world to help humanity come to grips with that question. We spend much or all of our lives wanting, punctuated only momentarily by fleeting moments of satisfaction, rarely pondering the implications of this gigantic fact of our existence or realizing that it is what defines our species.[8]

The testimony of Scripture doesn't always iron out our questions about desire. Sometimes, instead, it adds to their head-scratching mystery. Take, for example, the story of the demoniac in Mark 5. Jesus has crossed the Sea of Galilee, happening upon a demon-possessed man living among some tombs. As Jesus liberates the man of the dark spirits residing within, the demons begged not to be sent out of the area: "Send us among the pigs." Jesus consents, sending them into a nearby herd of swine who immediately rush to

---

8. Gil Bailie, *God's Gamble: The Gravitational Power of Crucified Love* (Kettering, OH: Angelico, 2016), 155. The quote is shortened for efficiency. Underscoring how desire is integrally tied to discipleship, James K. A. Smith points out that Jesus didn't ask "What do you know?" or "What do you believe?" James K. A. Smith, *You Are What You Love: The Spiritual Power of Habit* (Grand Rapids: Brazos, 2016), 1–2.

their cold deaths in the waters below. Unsurprisingly, the pigs' own-ers become angry, begging Jesus to leave their region. Again, Jesus consents, immediately preparing to depart. As he does, the liberated man begs to join Jesus' ministry team. For the first time in this story, Jesus does *not* consent. The answer is no. The man was to go to the town himself and tell of Christ's miraculous work in his life.

What's most unsettling about Mark's story are the desires of each of the three characters Jesus encounters: the man, demons, and townspeople. The demons want to be sent into the pigs. The townspeople want Jesus to go away. And the liberated man wants to follow Jesus. To our wonder we discover who does—and doesn't—get what they've asked for. The one character who doesn't get what he wants is the one who wants to follow Jesus. The ones who get what they want are those who either misunderstand or stand opposed to Jesus' mission.

Any reasonable reader may be left wondering why Jesus would consent to the desires of the demons and the townsfolk but not the man who desired to follow him. A crucial lesson about discipleship lingers underneath this story: following Jesus isn't a surefire way of getting everything we want. As we eventually find, following Jesus often entails experiencing a wounded desire. The desires of Jesus are mysterious, illogical, and perplexingly upside down. God desires, but his desires aren't like ours. Mark's short story isn't an anomaly. We learn at nearly every turn of the Gospels that Jesus refuses to bend his mission to the desires of those around him. He centers his entire existence not on our desires but on the desires of his Father. And he invites us to do the same.

John Henry Newman once wrote that "nothing is so easy as to be religious on paper."[9] Discussing our longings in the abstract isn't difficult. But we don't follow Jesus on paper. We follow with

---

9. From Newman's *Sermons, Chiefly on the Theory of Religious Belief*, 1844. Quoted in Gil Bailie, "On Paper and in Person," in *For René Girard: Essays in Friendship and in Truth*, ed. Sandor Goodhart et al. (East Lansing: Michigan State University Press, 2009), 179.

our lives. The blood, sweat, and tears that come from partnering with God's Spirit in the formation of our desires is a lifelong and arduous journey. The way of Jesus is the way of desire. To follow this way is to put our own desires under his, recognizing that our strongest desires aren't always the most important. Through desire we become missionaries, marry, follow Jesus, remain single, resist appetites, choose a career, and pick a church. And through desire we abandon truth, question our dearest friends, gossip, hurt one another, and give ourselves over to greed. Yet too little time is given to understanding how our desires are forged around Christ and his cross. If true—that we're disproportionately shaped by how we walk with the desires within—then what does it look like for our desires, like the rest of us, to be formed to the image of Christ?

The answer begins in the ancient story of Genesis.

In the origin story of Scripture, a serpent enters Eden. His desire? To deceive the first man and woman, subverting God's good creation. The serpent could do nothing to God and his glory. So he conceives another line of attack—an assault on those in the garden who reflect God's glory. Our forebears were tricked, resulting in a traumatic and disastrous rebellion against their Creator. Soon after, God "curses" the serpent for his trickery. But the humans could not sidestep the consequences of their decision. For the woman, the glories of childbearing would become exceedingly painful. Rather than walking side-by-side, the man would seek to rule over the woman. And for the man, work would become toilsome, anxiety-ridden, and counterproductive. Life would be marked by sweat, fret, and unsettledness, not the joyous and flourishing trust God had envisioned. And the man would work the land to his own travail.

There God offers a promise: "The land will produce thorns and thistles *for* you and you will eat the plants of the field" (Gen. 3:18, emphasis mine).

For the first time, thorns are introduced into the story of creation. As we'll discover, the theme of thorns pops up time and again. If we watch long enough, the thorns will teach us. We'll get to that. In a metaphorical and literal sense, these thorns and thistles represent a world in which things don't go the way they should. But we mustn't miss the author's inspired word choice. What are the thorns *for*? What does the postfall disappointment, difficulty, and toil lead to? What's the reason for thorns? Well, the thorns will be . . .

. . . for you.

No one would question that a postrebellion world is a world of thorns. The land doesn't do what we want, our bodies don't do what we want, our jobs don't fulfill us like we long for them to, and our relationships don't meet all our desires. Ours is a world of thorns. But what if, for a moment, we considered these intentional inconveniences built into our everyday existence not as bugs, but as features—not as problems, but as gifts. What if, indeed, the thorns are *for* us?[10]

Pay close attention. Light will break through. For, in the end, the fact that a humanity beset with sin and rebellion *doesn't* get all their desires, whims, and wants very well may be the greatest gift they've ever been given. Those thorns, they aren't just for us.

One might say the thorns lead us to salvation.

---

10. For the astute biblical reader, reading this particular passage about the thorns being "for us" may not seem to be the most natural reading. Indeed, I'm aware that what I am proposing may not stand as the most common reading. Still, I am convinced that the author of Genesis (intentionally or not) was recording something that would (and could) only be understood in light of what was to come—as my reader will see.

Part 1

THE WAR FOR
OUR WANTS

Chapter 1

GOD'S DESIRE

Immediately following the Boston Marathon bombing on April 15, 2013, a manhunt to apprehend the culprits that killed three and injured dozens was unleashed on the eastern seaboard. Arrests were soon made. The criminals have since been tried and sentenced. Following their trials, news stories emerged detailing how authorities had prosecuted the men. Prosecutors used the internet search histories of Dzhokhar and Tamerlan Tsarnaev to establish intent that they had, indeed, been plotting an attack for some time. In the end, their online searches for bomb-making instructions became a pivotal angle in the legal case against them.[1]

A new legal precedent was being born. Stories like this have become a normal part of the digital landscape. When Ashley Madison—an online website catering discreet meet-ups for extramarital affairs—was hacked in 2015, a list of those who had searched the site was leaked by hackers. The secret desires of thousands were laid bare in the public domain. The results were disastrous and heartbreaking. Trust, lives, and marriages were shattered. Multiple people (including a pastor, a theologian, and a well-known nonprofit executive) took their own lives out of shame and embarrassment.

Our internet searches reveal much about humanity—the dark,

---

1. On the bomber's relationship to their internet activity, read Michiko Kakutani, "Unraveling Boston Suspects' Online Lives, Link by Link," *New York Times*, April 23, 2013.

odd, and spectacularly peculiar. Consider, for example, that one of the most searched for phrases on International Women's Day according to Google Trends is "When is international men's day?" Or the time one popular internet pornography distributor revealed that, after an errant tweet accidentally and inaccurately informed those on the island of Hawaii of an inbound nuclear bomb, visits to their site during and after the event skyrocketed. Something similarly odd transpired as the city of San Francisco learned their NBA basketball team would beat the team from Cleveland. Pornography downloads in the region plummeted 21 percent as downloads simultaneous spiked in Cleveland by 34 percent.[2]

What's to be learned? Apparently, humans are prone to cope with impending disaster through escapism and fantasy. And as one group of people is being celebrated, the other group wonders when *they* will be celebrated next.

Humans are a tragically odd bunch. Not only do our search histories reveal much about our longings and wants, but they have become a vulnerable point of exploitation. An entire desire economy—powered by an iPhone in the hand with its near-omniscient algorithms hidden within—has been constructed to fulfill our every desire, quantify wants, and monetize longings.[3] Those in power not only know our desires; they're doing what they can to reshape them. Have you ever been in a conversation with someone about a product or place and soon thereafter see an ad for said product or place on your phone? Our phones are watching us. We're being spied on. This is Silicon Valley's cheap version of prayer. Just say the word, and thy want will be healed.

This is the new world of "globalized desire" where—as William

2. Gus Turner, "After the Cavaliers Lost the NBA Finals, Cleveland Fans Watched a Lot of Porn," *Men's Health*, June 16, 2017, https://www.menshealth.com/sex-women/cleveland-cavaliers-fans-porn-nba-finals-pornhub.

3. I borrow "desire economy" from Daniel Bell, *The Economy of Desire: Christianity and Capitalism in a Postmodern World*, The Church and Postmodern Culture (Grand Rapids: Baker, 2012).

Cavanaugh says—"everything is available, but nothing matters."[4] And this is just the beginning. Given that there were 361 million internet users in 2000 and 5.5 billion by 2022, our internet searches will likely ignite legal battles for the foreseeable future.[5] What will happen to them after we die? Can they be made public after our death? Do they die with us? Is it illegal to search for certain things?[6] These pressing questions will be hashed out in the courts of law and opinion for years to come. But one thing remains certain: the transcripts of our desires are currently being housed in an air-conditioned data center out in the desert. This is nothing short of terrifying. "On our crowded planet," Alexander Solzhenitsyn prophetically foresaw, "there are no longer any 'internal affairs.'"[7] Everything is now being recorded.

Our moment presents a unique opportunity. Whether remaining hidden or becoming exposed, we can learn about ourselves by attending to what we desire and long for. Furthermore, we cannot expect to be liberated fully into our God-given glory *without* looking into the transcripts of our desire. To paraphrase Jesus, we can clean the outside of a cup and still remain wretched and malformed inside.[8] The desires of our hearts—to which Jesus was undoubtedly referring to—constitute a critical and essential component of our "insides." Holistic transformation remains out of reach without curiously and lovingly examining them.

For years, I've been invited to journey alongside women and men who have endured a gnawing struggle with an addiction to

---

4. William Cavanaugh, *Being Consumed* (Grand Rapids: Eerdmans, 2008), xi.

5. "Internet Growth Statistics," Internet World Stats: Usage and Population Statistics, https://www.internetworldstats.com/emarketing.htm.

6. A debate continues to swirl: Does searching for something constitute a crime? See Lee Rowland, "When Does Your Google Search Become a Crime?," *ACLU* (blog), May 13, 2015, https://www.aclu.org/blog/free-speech/internet-speech/when-does-your-google-search -become-crime.

7. Aleksandr Solzhenitsyn, *Warning to the West* (New York: Farrar, Straus and Giroux, 1976), 48.

8. Matt. 23:25–26.

pornography. Often, when walking alongside someone through this crucible, I ask them to recount where they are, what time of the day it is, and what they are doing when they are most prone to return to their self-destructive pattern. In some instances, I ask them to name the particular types of pornography they find themselves drawn to. Oftentimes this becomes the first time an individual will lend reflection to such exposing questions. We don't often want to think about our dark desires. We'd rather erase them and move on. All too common the person walking in a cycle of pornography addiction has quickly erased their search history to protect against exposure, shame, and reflection, taking little (if any) time to ponder the actual nature of their unwanted desires.

What if true transformation requires looking at those desires rather than turning away? "Fantasies are road maps," writes Jay Stringer.[9] A Christian psychotherapist focusing on sexual restoration, Stringer directs his professional energy to those with sex addictions (often pornography). His book *Unwanted* details how addicts often erase their internet search histories after falling into unwanted sinful patterns. However, Stringer insists, healing invariably includes paying attention to what we look *at* and look *for*. In these desires, we can identify the very place where Christ wants to meet and heal our hearts. Desire can actually be a signpost to the places in our souls that most need love. What we assume to be a reservoir of lust may actually be a longing for intimacy. "Pornography searches expose lust," Stringer writes, "but far more they reveal the dimensions of our lives that await love."[10]

We would rather shamefully look away from our desires than examine them with holy curiosity alongside the healing hand of the Holy Spirit. But this has been the human response since the beginning. We cover rather than confess. And this way of being is

---

9. See the introduction to Jay Stringer, *Unwanted: How Sexual Brokenness Reveals Our Way to Healing* (Carol Stream, IL: NavPress, 2018).

10. Stringer, 42.

often only heightened and exacerbated in too many Christian communities, which ultimately leaves us pseudo-transformed. Darkness isn't eradicated through denial. A different path is needed.

Jesus invites us to know our desires intimately. The truth will set us free. Pretending won't. And ignoring our desires only empowers them.

God has much to teach us through the transcript of our desires. But we can't begin there. If one's internet searches illuminate our hidden desires, then the Bible serves (in the words of Catherine Dunlap Carter) as a kind of "*incomparable* record of human desire."[11] Sacred Scripture diagnoses the human condition better than any. But that's not where Scripture begins.

The Bible begins with God's desire.

The Bible begins with God. Not you. As such, the Bible isn't primarily about you. Nor is it about its human characters—be they kings, prophets, patriarchs, or disciples. One character from the beginning of the story is found at the end: God. To be sure, a cast of human characters step on and off the biblical stage. But they appear more or less as cameos, extras in a quickly changing sequence of scenes. Put another way, the Bible is no ensemble. This is God's story.

While the Bible describes a dizzying record of human desires, they aren't central. The Bible tells the story of God's desire.

This is accomplished through words. Why? Words are how we learn the desires of another. A parent learns to listen through the disheveled grammar and word scrambles of their children to ascertain needs. A spouse attunes their attention toward the other to hear the heart's needs. Children, hopefully, mature to listen

---

11. Katherine Dunlap Cather, *Educating by Story-Telling: Showing the Value of Story-Telling as an Educational Tool for the Use of All Workers with Children* (New York: World, 1918), 119. Italics mine.

to the directions of a parent, teacher, or coach who knows what's best. By listening carefully, we hear an author's intent in their latest book. Without words, desires remain unknown, unrevealed, and unheard. Words can often serve as the grammar of desire.

For biblical authors, every word mattered. Note, for example, how few different words are contained in the first two chapters of Genesis: 282 to be exact. Rather than roll out a breathtaking array of new and exotic vocabulary, the human author repeated, recycled, and reused the same words over and over, squeezing out new meaning with each use. Hebrew scholar Robert Alter once argued this was the distinguishing accomplishment of Hebrew culture. The Sumerians, Egyptians, and Babylonians offered antiquity gifts of architecture, politics, and culture. In these realms, Israel was "meager," according to Alter. The Jews, on the other hand, gave the world the gift of words. Alter wrote,

> In literary art, the ancient Hebrew writers . . . eclipsed their neighbors, producing powerful narratives that were formally brilliant and technically innovative and poetry in such texts as Job, Isaiah, Psalms, and the Song of Songs that rivaled any poetry composed in the Mediterranean world. I have no idea how or why this level of literary achievement came about. The Hebrew writers were clearly bent on promoting a new monotheistic vision . . . with their literary gifts.[12]

Every jot and tittle of biblical literature is carefully chosen, intentional, imbued with timeless purpose and transcendent luminescence. Yet as its readers discover, biblical literature teaches not only through what's explicitly stated but also in what's implicitly assumed. God teaches through words. But God also teaches

---

12. Robert Alter, "A Life of Learning: Wandering Among Fields," *Christianity and Literature* 63, no. 1 (Autumn 2013): 100.

through the silence and gaps between words.[13] That is to say, we learn by what's spoken and by what remains unspoken. If words can be the grammar of desire, then the Bible is the grammar of God's desire.

We begin with the Bible's first words: "In the beginning, God made the heavens and the earth" (Gen. 1:1).

What can we learn about God's desire from this first line of the Bible? One may remember the first line in Charles Dickens' *A Christmas Carol.* The story begins, "Marley was dead, to begin with." This is distinctive Dickens. In one fell swoop, the author whisks his reader into two basic assumptions in the span of one sentence. First, there's a character named Marley. And second, this Marley is dead. No explanation. We are simply confronted by a flurry of assumptions.

The first sentence of biblical literature utilizes a similar technique by heaving two big assumptions in the reader's lap. First, notice that the Bible doesn't begin with some logical argument for God's existence. There's simply no clear, open-and-closed case for why someone *should* believe a Creator God exists. The Bible doesn't begin with debate. The Bible simply begins with a "God who is there."[14]

Why is this assumed? This is due, in part, to the religious context of the ancient world. Everyone worshiped some spiritual being or entity in antiquity. Atheism, in its contemporary form, wouldn't exist until the early-modern period. The ancient world had no purely secular readers. As such, no argument was necessary to prove the existence of a spiritual being. Admittedly, the Bible remains a stumbling block for many modern readers for this reason.

---

13. "Biblical gaps" are explored in Meir Sternberg, *The Poetics of Biblical Narrative: Ideological Literature and the Drama of Reading* (Bloomington: Indiana University Press, 1987), chap. 6.

14. D. A. Carson, *The God Who Is There: Finding Your Place in God's Story* (Grand Rapids: Baker, 2010).

The Bible's contemporary readers come with a vastly different set of assumptions than its ancient readers did. Ancient readers came spiritually interested and open. Modern readers often come skeptical and suspicious.

At the university where I teach, I teach a course entitled "Introduction to Biblical Literature" that boasts an astounding diversity of students. Some are Christian. Some are not. Time and again, my nonreligious students are invited to read a book that doesn't share their assumptions about life. One particular student couldn't get past this first line in Genesis. He didn't share the Bible's assumption. In one submission, he admitted his growing frustration:

> The Bible is full of assumptions. But so am I! The Bible assumes there's a God before I get to the text. But now I see that I assumed there wasn't a God before I came to the text. We stand toe-to-toe.

He earned an A for his honesty. But this reveals one reason the Bible comes off as offensive to modern readers: it doesn't share our assumptions. In his enlightening book *Unapologetic Theology*, theologian and historian William Placher discusses why it's challenging in the Western, post-Christian, post-Enlightenment, secular world to be a faithful Christians in the public square. The belief that a God *actually* exists is, at our cultural moment, not a shared assumption. And religious assumptions in Enlightenment cultures have been deemed the great unforgivable (and unforgettable) sins.

Placher goes on to point out that behind the prevailing modern skepticism about God is, well, a hidden assumption—an assumed *dis*belief in God. Placher contends that the church—in an effort at garnering respectability in the post-Enlightenment West—has paid the price for respectability by playing along and killing the Christian witness. "One reason seems to be that Christianity cannot criticize our culture very effectively," Placher contends, "because it has already accepted many of the assumptions of that culture as the price of intellectual respectability."[15] It is believed that Pascal once said Christians are to live "as though God actually exists."[16] Christian or not, everyone starts with assumptions.

Genesis 1 also assumes that God has a name. In the Bible's opening two chapters, God is said to have two names: *Elohim* (Gen. 1) and *Yahweh* (Gen. 2). Two names. Two chapters. While appearing insignificant, we must remember that the gods of antiquity often withheld divulging their names to the human inhabitants below. One may remember Paul in the New Testament arriving in the ancient city of Athens. There, he makes note of a statue bearing an inscription: "To AN UNKNOWN GOD" (Acts 17:23). Inscriptions to nameless gods were quite common in antiquity. Statues and idols would often omit the name of the gods they represented.

Why the anonymity? Simple: If the gods revealed their names, they were liable to be called upon, spoken to, and woken up. Knowing the name of your god gave you power to call upon that god. Comparing the biblical account of Noah's ark with the flood from the ancient *Gilgamesh* epic, the divine response is vastly different. In the Bible, God responds to sin and injustice in the world. In *Gilgamesh*, the gods respond angrily because humans have disturbed their slumber. They were furious for having been woken up.

In a world of anonymous gods, the earliest chapters of Genesis revealing *two* names for God would have come off as shocking. Apparently, this God desires to be called on—even known. Perhaps this adds to the weight of Jesus' prayer in John: "I have *revealed your name* to the men you gave me" (John 17:6 NET, emphasis mine).[17]

---

15. William C. Placher, *Unapologetic Theology: A Christian Voice in a Pluralistic Conversation* (Louisville: Westminster, 1989), 12.

16. As quoted in Eugene Subbotsky, *The Bubble Universe: Psychological Perspectives on Reality* (London: Palgrave Macmillan, 2020), 258–59.

17. Van Kaam, Adrian, *The Tender Farewell of Jesus: Meditations on Chapter 17 of John's Gospel* (New York: New City, 1996), chap. 7.

In the first two chapters of Genesis, God has already doxxed himself, giving humans a name which they can call upon. This God isn't unknown. Nor does this God want to remain unknown.

This God has a name. It's almost like God wants to be wanted. Or as A. W. Tozer wrote, "God is waiting to be wanted."[18]

———

The early chapters of Genesis assume a great deal about *how* the world came into existence. Stories like this—about the beginning of the world and the universe—are not unique to the Bible. Every ancient culture existing around Israel believed (as did Israel) in some kind of creation story about the world's origins. These are called "cosmologies." Ancient cultures based their sense of national identity on these stories they told themselves about how everything came to be. These kinds of cosmologies and origin stories were common among Babylonians, Egyptians, Sumerians, and Mesopotamians.[19] One distinguishing mark of many of these cosmologies was some colossal clash wherein the gods went to battle in a cosmological war. To the winner went the spoils—in our case, the realm of earth below.

In stark contrast, the ancient reader would have immediately noticed that Genesis doesn't begin with a cosmic war. It begins with, "And God said, 'Let there be light'" (Gen. 1:3). We see no bloody battle, intergalactic skirmish, or divine power grab. God simply spoke. And everything *became*. Consider this from an ancient point of view. In a diverse religious world of gods seeking to win power through war, imagine how stirring it would have been

———

18. Quoted in John Eldredge, *The Journey of Desire: Searching for the Life You've Always Dreamed Of*, expanded ed. (Nashville: Nelson, 2016), 59. The quote is slightly modified for writing flow.

19. An exhaustive examination of ancient cosmologies is found in Kyle Greenwood, *Scripture and Cosmology: Reading the Bible Between the Ancient World and Modern Science* (Downers Grove, IL: IVP Academic, 2015).

to hear that this God of Israel created only to divest and give power to the humans he'd made—to name, rule, and fill the earth. The God of the Bible doesn't war for power. He already has it. And he begins sharing his power with his human creations by the end of the second chapter.

This matters because people often become their cosmologies. Put another way, we become the stories we tell ourselves about ourselves. For homework, go and ask any trained therapist if this is true. When a culture believes its existence resulted from cosmic wars and battles, it's bound to become a warring people.[20] If we believe we are genetic mistakes, we will see little meaning in life. If we believe we exist because our ancestors lucked out in some primal game of survival of the fittest, then that's what our societies, cities, and systems will look like. We become—my counselor tells me—the "tapes" we most often play about ourselves.

This is what makes the creation story in Genesis so prophetically redemptive. God didn't strike a rock to create. God spoke and every rock came to be. Over all his creation he incessantly called the things he made "good . . . good . . . very good." This God loves what he made.

We aren't lucky. We are loved. God made us because he desired us. And he only makes good stuff.

Most conversations about creation in Christian circles obsess over the "how" of creation: How old is the earth? How many years ago did God make the universe? How could God create in a literal seven-day period? These are important, fascinating, and pressing conversations. But I think more pertinent for a conversation about desire is the "why" of creation. As Auguste Comte famously wrote in 1985, we'll never find out what the stars are made out of. His point? We can study the stars, but we can't study *why* the stars.

---

20. A core theme throughout William P. Brown, *The Ethos of the Cosmos: The Genesis of Moral Imagination in the Bible* (Grand Rapids: Eerdmans, 1999).

This has been called "the question" by many scientists. Although scientific inquiry can help us see what exists, it can't, with much explanatory power, explain why it exists. Science, able to explain the properties of stars' existence, can't explain their reason for being.[21]

As did Comte, some have attempted a guess or two. Some are quite comical. For instance, novelist John Updike suggested that if there were a God, he most certainly decided to create the whole cosmos out of boredom. John Horgan, author of *The End of Science* and *Rational Mysticism*, was struck by his own epiphany: "If there is a God, He created this heart-breaking world because He was suffering from a cosmic identity crisis, triggered by His own confrontation with The Question. . . . God is as mystified as we are by existence."[22]

Admittedly, these are challenging questions for anyone, not just scientists. But this uncovers another angle in which the biblical story confronts our modern, secular, scientific assumptions. "God made the world," the ever-wise Elie Weisel said, "because God loves a good story." That sums it up quite nicely. God did not create the cosmos because he *had* to out of compulsivity or necessity. Nor did he create the world out of boredom, sadness, a need for companionship, or some existential crisis. God, in love, created out of desire. Everything exists because God desired it to exist. As the ancient author of 1 Clement would reflect, "[God's] breath is in us, and when he so desires, he will take it away."[23]

We exist by divine desire. That's our cosmology. We were and are wanted. This remains the whole purpose of creation. "Desire is the good and beautiful momentum behind the artistry of

---

21. Although some attempts have been tried. See, for example, Lawrence M. Krauss, *A Universe from Nothing: Why There Is Something Rather than Nothing* (New York: Atria, 2012).

22. John Horgan, "Science Will Never Explain Why There's Something Rather Than Nothing," April 23, 2012, https://blogs.scientificamerican.com/cross-check/science-will-never-explain-why-theres-something-rather-than-nothing/.

23. See ch. 21 of 1 Clement in Michael W. Holmes, ed., *The Apostolic Fathers in English* (Grand Rapids: Baker Academic, 2006).

Genesis 1," Jen Pollock Michel reflects. "No compelling obligation stands behind these words [of "let there be light"], no shrugging sense of duty, only the heartbeat of heaven and the desire of God for humanity."[24] For this very reason, Avivah Gottlieb Zornberg appropriately titled her commentary on the creation story *The Beginning of Desire*.[25] This desire is what the whole story is about. In fact, Paul Hooker has beautifully paraphrased the opening chapter of John's gospel:

> In the beginning was Desire,
> and Desire was with The Infinite,
> and Desire was The Infinite.
> Desire was the crown The Infinite wore,
> and Desire made The Infinite Beautiful.[26]

Likewise, we desire because God desired. God loves giving life. God is a *begetting* God. Few things lay nearer to the Creator's heart. And again, we mirror the Creator. As God desires our world into existence, we desire in this world as well. As humans live into their vocation of birthing and flourishing and making, we mirror God's nature in the world. As Eugene Peterson wrote, all those *begats* in the biblical genealogies are how humans most closely participate with God's creative nature: "Every birth is kerygmatic."[27] Our creativity preaches the creative longing of God.

---

24. Jen Pollock Michel, *Teach Us to Want: Longing, Ambition & the Life of Faith* (Downers Grove, IL: InterVarsity Press, 2014), 31.

25. Avivah Gottlieb Zornberg, *The Beginning of Desire: Reflections on Genesis* (New York: Schocken, 1995).

26. Paul Hooker, *The Hole in the Heart of God: Stories of Creation and Redemption* (Eugene, OR: Resource, 2021), 7.

27. Eugene Peterson, *Christ Plays in Ten Thousand Place: A Conversation in Spiritual Theology* (Grand Rapids: Eerdmans, 2005), 58.

But does God really desire?

For a moment, reflect on two questions. First, who would you believe is the happiest being in the entire universe? Or who experiences more joy and happiness than anyone else? In the Christian tradition, the answer is God. The late theologian Marva Dawn, for this reason, always capitalized *Joy* in her writings.[28] Dawn was subtly reminding her reader that God is true Joy himself. Jesus is Joy in the flesh. Consider a second question: Who is the *saddest* being in the universe? Theologically, the answer remains the same. God is the saddest being in the universe. God's coming Messiah, for Isaiah, was "a man of sorrows, acquainted with deepest grief" (Isa. 53:3 NLT). No being in the universe experiences more pain and lament than God, who weeps over evil, injustice, and human sin. At every moment, God experiences pure joy and happiness alongside lament and sadness over the good and evil under the sun.[29] God experiences both at the same time.

God embodies perfect, sinless, and infinite emotion. This helps us see why humans are emotional creatures. Our Creator is emotional. All human joy and sadness derive from God's abundant joy and sadness. Underneath this is a key foundational biblical theme: the idea that humans are created in what Genesis calls the "image of God" (Gen. 1:26–27). To be truly human is to reflect our Maker.

Why, then, do humans desire? Humans desire because God desires. We can think of the biblical story as a double exposure photo, simultaneously representing God's desires and human desires overlapping. Just as ours is a world created, shaped, and crafted by a God who desires, ours is also a world that has been reshaped by human desire.

Indeed, God "wanting" and "desiring" is a key thread in the Old Testament. "I *desire* mercy," says God, "not sacrifice" (Hos. 6:6).

---

28. Marva Dawn, *Being Well When We're Ill* (Minneapolis: Fortress, 2008), 11.

29. I'm grateful to my friend Steve Overman, who over coffee asked me this rhetorical set of questions about God's emotions.

God's desire for his covenant nation to be of deep truthfulness is expressed by the psalmist: "You *desire* truth in the inward being" (Ps. 51:6 NRSVue). Even the pagan Queen Sheba declares, "Because God loves Israel and *desires* this kingdom to last forever, he has made you king over them so you can rule with justice and righteousness" (2 Chr. 9:8 NLT). New Testament literature is equally replete with texts about God's desire. Jesus, in calling his disciples to himself, called "those he *wanted*" (Mark 3:13). In closing his telling of Jesus' earthly life, John records the prayer of Jesus: "Father, I *want* those you have given me to be with me where I am, and to see my glory" (John 17:24). Peter expressly writes that God "does not *want* anyone to be destroyed" (2 Pet. 3:9). Paul underscores this, saying, God "*wants* all people to be saved" (1 Tim. 2:4).[30]

God is a desiring God. In some moments, the biblical authors even risk revealing God's desires when no human could have known them otherwise. In Genesis 6, for example, God surveys a world of wickedness and declares to himself, "My Spirit will not contend with humans forever, for they are mortal; their days will be a hundred and twenty years" (Gen. 6:3). At this moment, there's no human in dialogue with God. Scripture is disclosing God's desire. In another instance, God calls Moses to confront Pharaoh in Exodus 4. Moses responds that God would be better off sending his brother, Aaron. The text states that God wanted to kill Moses (Ex. 4:24). Again, no human could have known this. The text risks naming a divine desire even when no human appears present to have known it. Thankfully, God doesn't axe Moses. But these little moments show how Scripture voices God's otherwise unknown desires for the reader's benefit. By disclosing this divine self-talk, the desires of God are revealed for the world to see. God doesn't merely desire. God wants us to know his desire.

Building on this, Christian theology has long considered

---

30. Emphasis added to each of the Scripture quotations in this paragraph.

desire as an entry into reflection on God and his creation. Take the Trinity. In its essence, the Trinity is an eternal relationship between three coequal, coloving, cosubmitted persons. Theologians have often spoken of this relationship between Father, Son, and Spirit as a *condilectum*, or "equal longing." God is in and of himself a relationship of mutual love, service, and desire. The Christian life, then, is entering the Trinity's hospitable desire. Former Anglican Archbishop Rowan Williams believes that through faith in Christ, we are included in this love of the Father, Son, and Spirit. "The whole story of our incorporation into the fellowship of Christ's body," Williams writes, "tells us that God desires us as if we were God."[31] Williams isn't suggesting humans are divine beings. Rather, through faith in Jesus, we're incorporated into the Trinity's desire and love.

Then there's creation. The novelist Dorothy Sayers saw desire as the rationale for creation in her book *Mind and Maker*. "We find one single assertion, 'God created,'" Sayers wrote. "The characteristic common to God and man is apparently that: the desire and ability to make things."[32] This was mirrored by her contemporary G. K. Chesterton. Pondering as to why the sun rises time and again, Chesterton suggested that more is at work than just the cold laws of physics. In *Orthodoxy*, Chesterton argued that the world spins, the sun rises, and the oceans wave simply because God desires them to:

> It might be true that the sun rises regularly because he never gets tired of rising. A child kicks his legs rhythmically through excess, not absence, of life. They want things repeated and unchanged. They always say, "Do it again"; and the grown-up person does it again until he is nearly dead. For grown-up people

---

31. Rowan Williams, "The Body's Grace," in *Theology and Sexuality: Classic and Contemporary Readings*, ed. Eugene F. Rogers (Oxford: Blackwell, 2002), 311–12. Italics original.

32. Dorothy L. Sayers, *The Mind of the Maker* (New York: Harcourt Brace, 1941), 44.

are not strong enough to exult in monotony. But perhaps God is strong enough to exult in monotony. It is possible that God says every morning, "Do it again" to the sun; and every evening, "Do it again" to the moon. The repetition in Nature may not be a mere recurrence; it may be a theatrical encore.[33]

For Chesterton, God gleefully declares over creation, "Do it again; do it again." This desire pulsates, animating every fleck of creation—a desire that led Abraham Kuyper famously to declare, "There is not a square inch in the whole domain of our human existence over which Christ, who is Sovereign over all, does not cry: 'Mine!'"[34] God wants creation. So much so that sixteenth-century Pietist theologian Jacob Boehm would call creation a "concentration of desire."[35]

The doctrine of God's desire matters because it lies at the heart of some of our most vexing theological questions. Each semester, I make space for students to ask whatever questions they've got—the existence of aliens, who Cain's wife was, if marijuana is okay, if angels are sexual beings. I keep a folder. Every year without fail, I'm asked, "Why would God still want this world knowing how bad it would turn out?"

In considering this question, my hunch remains that some may feel uncomfortable about the fact that God desires. I suspect this is because we assume that God desires because he lacks. But this is disastrously misguided. "Not to have," wrote Wallace Stevens, "is the beginning of desire."[36] That's true—for humans. Unlike God,

33. G. K. Chesterton, *Orthodoxy* (New York: Lane, 1908). The text has been shortened for efficiency.

34. Kuyper, "Sphere Sovereignty," in *Abraham Kuyper: A Centennial Reader*, ed. James D. Bratt (Grand Rapids: Eerdmans, 1998), 488

35. Cynthia Bourgeault, *The Holy Trinity and the Law of Three: Discovering the Radical Truth at the Heart of Christianity* (Boston: Shambhala, 2013), 98.

36. Wallace Stevens, "Notes toward a Supreme Fiction," in *The Collected Poems* (New York: Vintage, 2015), 401–32.

the human experience is marked by what Augustine called *rerum absentium concupiscentia*, a "longing for absent things."[37] But this is our experience. God's desires are different.

How? Human wants are birthed from lack. Divine wants are birthed from love. God didn't create Eden because he needed more carrots or lettuce or fig trees. He didn't fill it because he frantically needed to be loved or affirmed by creation. God isn't egotistical, narcissistic, or in need of an emotional pick-me-up. Rather, God desired friendship, relationship, and intimacy with his creation—a desire arising from an uncreated and eternal perfection.

Humans desire and create out of lack. God desires and creates out of love, not deficit. God *desires* to create, *desires* to sustain, and *desires* to bless a world out of sheer love and joy that they might enjoy face-to-face relationship with him.[38]

My students' question haunts me: Why would God *still* desire to create all of this while knowing the wreck of pain and hurt it would become? The question, as all do, hides some assumptions: that God knew what would come of this world, that he has power to do something about it, and that things are not the way they are supposed to be. Admittedly, I share these assumptions. God did

---

37. Many others have written about this. Gregory of Nyssa wrote about what he called the "disposition of desire," which was the very thing that prompted humans to desire relationships with someone outside themselves. Even Plato wrote that "love is always the love of something and that something is what it lacks" in his *Symposium*.

38. Philosopher James Sire wrote, "God is totally unconstrained by his environment. God is limited (we might say) only by his character. . . . Nothing external to God can possibly constrain him. If he chooses to restore a broken universe, it is because he 'wants' to, because, for example, he loves it and wants the best for it. But he is free to do as he wills, and his character (Who He Is) controls his will." James Sire, *The Universe Next Door*, 5th ed. (Downers Grove, IL: IVP Academic, 2009), 33–34. Another important examination of this is Michael Reeves, *Delighting in the Trinity: An Introduction to the Christian Faith* (Downers Grove, IL: InterVarsity Press, 2012), chap. 2.

know what would happen, God has power, and, to borrow the wisdom of Cornelius Plantinga, the world is "not the way it's supposed to be."[39]

I ask my class to reflect on these assumptions. It's revealing to me. In a class of Christians and non-Christians, there's *never* any debate as to whether our world is going the way it should. Even a brief consideration of the evils of genocide, rape, crime, racism, ecological devastation, sexual exploitation, sexual trauma, sexual immorality, lying, tribalism, greed, and abuse provides enough evidence for even my atheist students to agree begrudgingly. Ours is a world that leaves much to be desired. Everyone can see it. As Reinhold Niebuhr famously said, "The doctrine of original sin is the only empirically verifiable doctrine of the Christian faith."[40]

For my Christian students, there's a logic to this. God created a world that spun into cosmic rebellion through the first humans and has been demonstrably cattywampus since. God's desire—or God's will—has *not* yet been done.

For my students who do not believe in God, how can it be said things are not going as they should? Doesn't a *should* always imply desire, intent, or purpose? Years ago, I wrote an academic journal article arguing that the reality of climate change, species loss, and human exploitation of the earth are an argument for God's existence, desire, and intent. My claim was simple: an environmentalist's or climate scientist's claim that the environment isn't being treated by humans as "it should" assumes at the onset there's some "supposed to be" that is universally agreed upon. I stand by this claim. What many Christians wrongly assume is some progressive agenda is in actuality one of the most compelling arguments for the Christian narrative we have in the public square. Where does this

39. Plantinga, Cornelius, *Not the Way It's Supposed to Be* (Grand Rapids: Eerdmans, 1995).
40. Reinhold Niebuhr, *The Structure of Nations and Empires* (New York: Scribner's, 1959), 291.

should come from? Who says there is some way it was supposed to go?[41]

A perversion always implies a purpose. Any assumption that things in our world are not the way they're supposed to be implies a desire, a purpose, a meaning that gave rise to our world. Indeed, there's a way things are supposed to be. God desired something—and what we are doing isn't *it*. Sin, in its essence, is to subvert and rebel against God's glorious desires.

This remains the transformative glory of the gospel—that epic story of the quiet life, death, and resurrection of the first-century Jew called Jesus of Nazareth. Immersed in every last inch of this story is the good news that all human beings from all of eternity are wanted and desired by the Creator who handknit them. This gospel may very well make the most sense to the unwanted among us—like a foster child, a refugee, or the unwanted wife or husband. Or for my friend who found out late in life that she was conceived by means of a traumatic rape. Trembling at the thought of that she had been unwanted, she found hope in being wanted by the God who knew her and loved her from the foundations of the earth. In a world where the unwanted go unheld and the unheld soon die, the gospel is saving grace. We worship the God who desires the undesirable, who, as Paul writes, "calls into being things that were not" (Rom. 4:17).[42]

So if God knew how bad this world would turn out, why did he still make it?

As I began writing this book project, my wife and I received a long-awaited foster daughter into our home. We had longed for more children for some time. With one biological son, we'd faced

---

41. A. J. Swoboda, "Reconciling Creation: Spirit, Salvation, and Ecological Degradation," *Australasian Pentecostal Studies* 22, no. 1 (2021): 87–103.

42. For more on the human need to be desired, read chapter 3 of James Bryant Smith, *The Good and Beautiful You: Discovering the Person Jesus Created You to Be* (Downers Grove, IL: InterVarsity Press, 2022).

nearly a decade of excruciating infertility since his birth. Having had one child, a parent is all the wiser about what they're getting themselves into. We knew what we would be giving up receiving a foster daughter—the loss of sleep, alone time, and date nights; how much it costs; how much needs to be saved for college. Still, we said yes.

Not too long ago, our foster daughter returned to a family that has undergone miraculous healing. The whole experience has been the most painful experience of our lives. As she drove away, it dawned on me. A parent makes room for a child even in knowing how painstaking it will be. Why? Because that is love. That child is your beloved. Knowing what we know, we'd *still* have received our foster daughter and all that came alongside her. Why? She was worth it.

Why would God still want this world knowing how bad it would turn out?

The unfolding story of Scripture narrates a God who is aware of the pain to come. He's a God who sees—and *saw*. He knew the heartbreak that awaited. As does a parent, he knew how hard it would be. Yet he still desired us. Glory to God. Gospel. Praise Jesus. This—the fact that God knew and still took it all in—is, in the Christian perspective, *the* cornerstone of who we know God to be. A God of love would rather have rebellious children than have none at all. He wouldn't take it back. He never stopped wanting you. The mystery of the gospel is that God still desires us knowing what would come.

Let that hit your soul. And in so doing, as poet John O'Donahue would write, "May you know the urgency with which God longs for you."[43]

---

43. John O'Donahue, "For Longing," in *To Bless the Space between Us* (Doubleday, 2008), 35–36.

Chapter 2

HUMAN DESIRE

In the last chapter, we saw that the God of the Bible created the cosmos, humanity, and every last fleck of creation through desire. This act was not accomplished through war, coercion, or rearrangement of preexisting materials but through desire. Even now, God continues "sustaining all things" (Heb. 1:3) by his desire and powerful word. This chapter builds on one theme I've already hinted at: humans are creatures of desire simply by virtue of having been made by a Creator of desire. We reflect our Maker.

Historically, Christians have had an awkward dance with desire. For some, even speaking positively about desire is tantamount to blessing lust, baptizing sin, and affirming rebellion against God. In her award-winning 2018 book, *Teach Us to Want*, Jen Pollock Michel recounts an exchange perfectly capturing a common Christian skepticism toward desire: "When I told [a friend] I was writing a book about a theology of desire, we're apt to wonder, 'Theology of desire? But isn't that an oxymoron?'"[1] Desire, Sean McDonough surmises, has been so colored in a negative light that it is essentially "guilty until proven innocent." So guilty, he continues, that if "you see Desire hanging around a street-corner, you can assume it's up to no good."[2] And it was far less common to

---

1. Jen Pollock Michel, *Teach Us to Want: Longing, Ambition, and the Life of Faith* (Downers Grove, IL: InterVarsity Press, 2014), 23.

2. Sean McDonough, "The Fall and Fallenness in the New Testament," *Trinity Journal* 40 (2019): 189. Desire is capitalized in the original text.

encounter positive Christian teaching on the topic of desire before the last few decades. Sadly, damage has been done. The church's discomfort with desire has projected a distorted vision for those outside of it. As one seeker friend confessed to me, "Christianity is like the suicide of desire. Why would I want that? It'd be the death of what makes me, *me*."

Indeed, many Christians seem "perplexed by desire and what it says about who we are as human beings."[3] But why? I suspect this lingering discomfort for Christians has two sources. On one hand, it's due to a widespread misunderstanding that Christianity and desire are either odd bedfellows or, worse, irreconcilable enemies. And on the other hand, it's rooted in a misplaced belief that Christianity somehow entails only the annihilation of one's desire; as though desiring itself is sinful. In so doing, Jason Brown laments, "The Church has ceded all of desire to the world . . . taking the position that the way to God is to rid ourselves of our desires."[4]

Given how central repentance, holiness, and self-denial are to Christian spirituality, one could uncritically presume that Christianity and desire are inherently hostile. But does this hold up? To Scripture? Or to the way of Jesus? As we'll see, these ideas are as half-baked today as they ever were. Not only this, but they're detached from reality and dangerous to the human soul. We were made to desire. To be desire*less* is inhumane.

The goodness of desire is one of the most important theological contributions of Christianity. Compare Christianity, for a moment, with Buddhist spiritualities that envision maturity as "letting go" of life's worries, concerns, and desires into a state called "detachment." One goal in Buddhism is freedom through the relinquishment of

---

3. Jonathan Jameson, "Erotic Absence and Sacramental Hope: Rowan Williams on Augustinian Desire," *Anglican Theological Review* 102, no. 4 (2020): 575.

4. Jason Brown, "Tinder and the Theology of Desire," *Holyscapes* (blog), August 3, 2021, https://holyscapes.org/2021/08/03/tinder-and-the-theology-of-desire/.

desire. To pursue this goal, Buddha is said to have abandoned his wife and child. This helps explain why the biblical narrative has often proved a stumbling block to Buddhist readers. If life's goal is detachment from desire, what's to be made of the God of Scripture who gets jealous? For a Buddhist, a jealous God has desire and is far too attached. But this illustrates a key difference between Christian and Buddhist approaches toward the good life.[5] The Gospels reveal Jesus as fully involved, present, and invested in the world's suffering to seek and save the lost. Jesus aim wasn't detachment. Jesus's aim was incarnation.

The Christian way offers so much more than a blind denialism or disembodied detachment. A Christianity that seeks to dissolve desire is, in fact, more Buddhist than Christian. To its credit, whatever desire deficit disorder the church has experienced is slowly being healed. In recent years, a welcomed renaissance of Christian reflection on the topic has emerged. And with it, a conviction that desire itself isn't our problem. Desire, in fact, is God's gift. As the ever-wise C. S. Lewis writes in *The Weight of Glory*,

> It would seem that Our Lord finds our desires not too strong, but too weak. We are half-hearted creatures, fooling about with drink and sex and ambition when infinite joy is offered us, like an ignorant child who wants to go on making mud pies in a slum because he cannot imagine what is meant by the offer of a holiday at the sea.[6]

With signature wit and wisdom, Lewis believes the human problem is that we are "far too easily pleased." Lewis's point went against

---

5. My use of the plural *approaches* and *spiritualities* is intentional. We must be keenly aware that there is not one definitive approach toward either Christian or Buddhist faiths with which they can be compared. I am speaking in broad-sweeping terms.
6. C. S. Lewis, *The Weight of Glory and Other Addresses* (San Francisco: Harper San Francisco, 2001), 26.

the grain of popular Christianity of his time, as it might our own. Lewis appears to aim his frustration at a church and a world he believes desires too little—that we don't desire *enough*. This is good news for my seeker friend who thought becoming a Christian meant the suicide of his desire. I responded to his confession, "At what point did you buy into the idea that Christianity was some hospice where desires go to die?"

He looked strangely at me. But his wheels were turning. The way of Jesus isn't a hospice for desire. It's the hospital for desire where it can be healed, restored, and resurrected to its original design. And, Lord knows, much healing is needed.

Something is wrong. In recent decades, we've had to come to terms with an epidemic of tragic proportions: the rise of deaths by despair and suicide.[7] All the more devastating is how common these deaths have become among teenagers and even children. What's happening? No doubt, a simultaneous clash of cultural and global disruptions—from COVID-19 to underemployment to the breakdown of social connectivity to global injustice and strife— have made mental health a distant dream for many. Such a moment has put unimaginable pressure on mental health professionals— especially, I'm told, in trying to spot signs of despair proactively. My colleagues in the counseling department tell me that one diagnostic tool mental health professionals use to identify depression in patients is by asking, "What's one thing you desire to be doing in ten years?" Having a complete absence of desire can be a telling sign that deep, unsettled sadness has taken residence in one's heart.

---

7. For a theological and pastoral response to the epidemic, see Matthew Sleeth, *Hope Always: How to Be a Force for Life in a Culture of Suicide* (Carol Stream, IL: Tyndale Momentum, 2021).

Depression can often manifest itself as a loss of desire.[8] We are wired to and for desire. Without desire, something of our God-ordained glory is lost and the landscape of our lives devoid of relationship, purpose, calling, and hope. Desire, the great theologian James Houston contends, is "the throbbing pulse of human life."[9] Desire forges culture. Desire helps. Desire harms. Desire builds. And it destroys. Desire births, and desire kills. Every crevice of the realm of humanity is drenched with desire. "Desire is primal," contends Michel. "To be human is to want."[10] As the philosopher Avivah Gottlieb Zornberg writes, "The cycle of desire is present in all dimensions of life, intellectual, interpretive, [and] emotional."[11] Oxford philosopher William Irvine further speaks of desire in totalizing terms:

> Desire animates the world. It is present in the baby crying for milk, the girl struggling to solve a math problem, the woman running to meet her lover and later deciding to have children, and the old woman, hunched over her walker, moving down the hall of the nursing home at a glacial pace to pick up her mail. Banish desire from the world, and you get a world of frozen beings who have no reason to live and no reason to die.[12]

But what exactly is desire? I was perplexed to discover in my own research that desire remains a relatively underexplored

---

8. Some believe depression to be humanity's evolutionary adaptation to an inability to attain desires. See Randolph M. Nesse, "Is Depression an Adaptation?," *Archives of General Psychiatry* 57 (2000): 14–20.

9. James Houston, *The Heart's Desire: Satisfying the Hunger of the Soul* (Colorado Springs: NavPress, 1996), 7.

10. Michel, *Teach Us to Want*, 29. From the Reformed tradition, John Piper has called the heart a "desire factory." John Piper, *Future Grace: The Purifying Power of the Promises of God* (New York: Crown, 1995), 277.

11. Avivah Gottlieb Zornberg, *The Beginning of Desire: Reflections on Genesis* (New York: Schocken, 1995), xiv.

12. William B. Irvine, *On Desire: Why We Want What We Want* (New York: Oxford University Press, 2006), 3.

academic discipline. One philosopher went so far as to say his colleagues have become "bored" with the topic.[13] Scholars have struggled to define desire. Defining desire, it seems, is akin to nailing Jell-O to the wall.

At the same time, desire has enjoyed exploding interest on the popular level. Scads of publications about "getting everything we could want" have been noticeably flooding our airport bookstores for decades. There's a reason. In consumer cultures detached from traditional religion, where life's goal is grounded in the present alone, desire achievement becomes everything. You only live once, they say. Better "get yours." Jokingly referred to by some as "wantology," the popular study of wants has been undertaken by the likes of Arlie Hochschild and her widely read *New York Times* article "The Outsourced Life."[14] Today, a whole cottage industry of thought leaders cleverly maps out ways for the masses to name and attain their every want. This is has become the philosophy of *carpe Diem* ("seize the today"), or what Dallas Willard calls the "sensuality of the moment."[15]

Yet, it would seem, the need to reflect on desire will only grow given the sudden rise of new digital technologies. Artificial intelligence is a prime example. Many are arguing that increasingly complex, humanlike robots and machines should have built-in humanlike emotions.[16] Could this include desires?

The blurred line between humans and machines is reflected in how people speak of them. For instance, when the satellite *Cassini* cataclysmically plunged to its death on Saturn, observers and journalists initially called it "*Cassini's* suicide." The response from scientists, psychologists, and sociologists was quick. Doug Gillan,

---

13. Timothy Schroeder, *Three Faces of Desire* (New York: Oxford University Press, 2004), 4.

14. Arlie Hochschild, "The Outsourced Life: Intimate Life in Market Times," *New York Times*, May 5, 2012.

15. Dallas Willard, *Knowing Christ Today* (Grand Rapids: Zondervan, 2009), 49.

16. Nico H. Frijda, "Emotions in Robots," in *Comparative Approaches to Cognitive Science*, ed. Herbert L. Roitblat and Jean-Arcady Meyer (Cambridge, MA: MIT Press, 1995).

a psychology professor at North Carolina State University who researches the overlap of human and technology, warned against such attempts at anthropomorphizing robots and machines. He called "*Cassini's* suicide" a "bad analogy."[17]

It may be too broad a question to ask, "What is desire?" We must be more precise: What is *human* desire? Desire encompasses a good deal. No doubt, it includes our values, motives, aims, purposes, emotions, attractions, and attachments.[18] But desire, more than anything, is the orientation of one's entire life toward something. One philosopher, Timothy Schroeder, has come as close as any to defining desire by calling it "purely a matter of being motivated to attain an end."[19] In this light, desire is one's drive to attain something. But even in ironing out this definition of desire, Schroeder admits to a glitch in the purely secular view of desire. Desire isn't unique to humans. Animals desire too. He writes, "Cats can desire to drink fresh water, dogs can desire submissive behavior from those below them in a pack structure, owls can desire dark sleeping places, and so on."

If humans are mere products of natural history, then the study of desire is nothing more than that of evolutionary impulses toward our species' survival. But Schroeder, among others, admits humans have some desires animals do not. (Keep in mind Schroeder isn't writing from a distinctly Christian perspective.) Unlike the brute beast, humans can resist their glands. A dog may desire this or that food or a particular kind of back scratch. But fish don't crave respect. Ants don't march against injustice. Amoebas don't long for forgiveness, equality, or equity. "Only humans," Schroeder admits, "have *certain* desires."[20]

---

17. Marina Koren, "Scientists Don't Want You to Call Cassini's End a 'Suicide,'" *The Atlantic*, September 15, 2017.

18. This list is framed by Alan Padgett, "Discipleship of Desire and the Hunger for Justice: Wisdom from Luther and Wesley," *Word & World* 4, no. 4 (Fall 2022): 391.

19. Schroeder, *Three Faces of Desire*, 11.

20. Schroeder, *Three Faces of Desire*, 9. Italics mine.

This brings us to Genesis 1 and 2. Welcome to Eden—or "delight" in Hebrew. In these chapters, we're told of God's glorious creation: the light, stars, moon, insects, grass, trees, animals, fish, and humans. This is God's world of *shalom* and interdependence. In this garden, God places humans. We learn they are creatures of desire. Sin doesn't make human desire. Just as human work, sex, and the need for rest aren't consequences of sin, neither is human desire. Desire was an original feature of the human person. We were made with an inborn desire for relationship, sex, worship, naming animals, eating, gardening, and vocation. Desire is part of our primal existence.

These two ancient chapters have much to teach us about our desire. Yet, sadly, we often overfocus on how desire is corrupted following the rebellion of Genesis 3. There's a good reason to focus on sin's corruption. In so doing, however, we never feel fully at home in the good desires we've been given. Put another way, we tend to focus only on "original sin" after Genesis 3 without giving proper attention to "original desire" in Genesis 1 and 2.[21]

Our near obsession with the corruption of desire has led to an ignorance of God's intention for desire. What follows is an attempt to remedy this. In broad terms, I want to suggest that God gave us three core original human desires. Humans have the desire to help, rule, and long.

Let's look at the details. Humans, first, are made to help and be helped by one another. In Genesis 1 and 2, the sea, sky, and land creatures are described as being made "according to their kinds" (Gen. 1:25). A biologist would look at this and call it the emergence

21. Others who draw on this category of original desire include Kenny Damara, *Divided Desire: Restoring Lost Connections in the Global Village* (Eugene, OR: Resource, 2013), 145; Alberto Albacete, *God at the Ritz: Attraction to Infinity* (New York: Crossroad, 2002), 120.

of species, or "speciation." God created the various species to reproduce and flourish for future generations. God even gives the animals a calling and vocation. God—the divine biologist—gives a directive to the animals: "Be fruitful and increase in number and fill the water in the seas, and let the birds increase on the earth" (Gen. 1:22).

The animal kingdom has its marching orders: reproduce, flourish, teem, and fill creation in all their splendor. At that point, humans had not yet been made. This commandment to the animals is God's first in creation specifically given to something God has created. And it's not to humans. God's first command is to the nonhuman creatures. Animals, as such, aren't the dumb creatures devoid of agency or decision making that modern, Western culture imagines them to be. Animals have a vocation. And a relationship to God. And a command they are explicitly told to obey.

To equip these sea, winged, and land creatures for this vocation of "filling" the earth, God creates them simultaneously in pairs. These male and female pairs reveal one of the glorious dimensions of God's design work. As a dimorphic (two-sexed) species—created to flourish through sexual oneness with the opposite sex—God has built in a need for each animal. That is, they need someone different from themselves to do what God has commanded them to do. The animals *need* each other to fulfil God's command.

Humans, incidentally, share this quality with the animals. However, one fundamental difference remains between animals and humans. We're told Adam existed first and by himself. The humans are not initially created in a pair. In Genesis 2:15, God created Adam, giving him the dual assignments of caring for God's garden and naming the animals. As did the animals, Adam had a responsibility to fulfil God's command faithfully. But something was unfinished. The text reads, "But for Adam no suitable helper was found" (Gen. 2:20). In naming the animals and working the garden, someone was missing. God names Adam's predicament:

"It is not good for the man to be *alone*. I will make a helper suitable for him" (Gen. 2:18, emphasis mine). The difference between animals and humans is simple but critical. Animals were originally created in pairs ("according to their kinds") at the same time. But in the human kingdom, the first man was created *before* the first woman. They were not created immediately in pairs.

Later, after creating the woman, God instructs them as he'd done with the animals: "be fruitful and multiply" (Gen. 1:28). In God's wisdom, the world has been made in such a way that the commands of God demand community, relationship, and intimacy. The creatures God made could not do what he had told them to do all alone. They needed another. The garden environment assumes a built-in need for community.

God then puts the man to sleep and creates the glorious woman. But let's pause. It's reasonable to believe that the "firstness" of the man's creation likely provokes some emotional responses in the reader. For some, Adam's firstness has been interpreted to mean he is somehow better or best. But any Western assumption that the man's firstness is the same as being best reflects our bias projected upon the text.[22] In the biblical imagination, first does not mean best. If first meant best, then we must be prepared to admit the jellyfish are "better" than humans, given their creation before humans. To say nothing of the fact that literally every man in all of history (except for Adam) came from a woman. I came from a woman. Jesus came from a woman. Does this somehow mean my mom is more important than me? Or Mary better than Jesus?

Something crucial is going on. Keep in mind, sin has yet to infect the world. Human rebellion wouldn't happen until the next chapter. In fact, up to this point, God has declared every single

---

22. On our ideas of "firstness" in contrast to the biblical ideas of "firstness," see E. Randolph Richards and Brandon J. O'Brien, *Misreading Scripture with Western Eyes: Removing Cultural Blinders to Better Understand the Bible* (Downers Grove, IL: InterVarsity Press, 2012), 12–14.

creation as "good . . . good . . . good." Then comes a surprise. In a world before sin, there's a "not good." As God said, "It is *not good* for the man to be alone" (Gen. 2:18, emphasis mine). This "not good" isn't the result of sin or rebellion or disobedience. The serpent hasn't even been introduced yet. Something in Eden is incomplete, left undone. Man was alone. He needed help. Which is remarkably interesting. The first image we're offered of God-created masculinity is not—as too many believe—an exercise in self-security, independence, and brute strength. Man in his original, God-created, prerebellion state was alone, dependent, and in need of help, just as God wanted him. The first image we are given of a man is that of someone in need of help. God created men to be vulnerable.

Of all the creatures God made, Adam is the only one described as experiencing "aloneness." He desired a mate. And he was made without one. Unlike any in the animal kingdom, Adam was made without his partner. Adam, it appears, is the one being created by God to experience a divinely orchestrated unfulfilled desire.

This simple observation has reverberating implications. It's not uncommon in Christian subculture for someone experiencing aloneness to be told they "just need God." Or "more God." Or "more time with God." Adam's experience shatters these shallow recommendations. Adam had unmitigated, perfect, unending access to God in Eden. He had a life-giving job. Adam enjoyed all the food his heart desired. He likely shared communion and friendship with the animal kingdom. He had the whole world in his hands. Yet Adam was alone. Apparently, one can experience a real, true, and abiding relationship with God and still experience the existential crisis of aloneness in a sinless world.

It's almost like Adam was made to need more than just God.[23]

"It is not good for the man to be alone." These are God's words.

23. Single-handedly, the best treatment on this is a quiet blog post found at Sam Jolman, "You Need More than God," *SamJolman.Com* (blog), June 27, 2016, http://www.samjolman .com/you-need-more-than-god/.

They aren't to be tinkered with. God doesn't say, "It is not good for the man to be *unmarried*." Too often, we misapply God's words and prescribe marriage and sex as the fixes for loneliness. But this is merely symptomatic of a church that has idolatrously made marriage the goal of the Christian life and a secular world that has cast sexual freedom as the singular pathway to fulfilment. No, the answer to loneliness is deep and real relationship and community in God's good garden—not marriage and sex isolated from covenant community. Thus, our primary human vocation is oriented toward human relationships of which sexual union can be a part. All under God's rule and reign.

God isn't belittling or shaming the single among us. A human can be married and alone. So too can a human be unmarried and experience their blessed belovedness in community. If the goal of human life is marriage, we must be prepared to admit Jesus was a failure in the same breath. The most fruitful man in human history was a single guy from Nazareth. Singleness is not a Christian synonym for aloneness.

We were made by and for God. But in so doing, God created within us a need for deep and abiding relationships with others. Our desire and longing for community are hardwired into us. The first human came into this world unmarried. And any human redeemed by Christ will enter the next unmarried. Friendship with God precedes sexual union. And it will—Lord willing—follow it.

Still, Adam desired a helper—for which God never displays a wink of disappointment or hurt feelings. God desired Adam to desire another. There's a reason the woman is called, in Hebrew, *ezer kegnedo*—or "a helper."[24] Again, don't twist the language. The woman and the man were to walk side-by-side. She isn't "the help" the way a slave or maid "helps." The phrase "suitable helper" is most

---

24. Robert Alter, *The Hebrew Bible: A Translation with Commentary* (New York: Norton, 2018), 19.

often used about God himself or when an army was reinforced on the battlefield. She's not being told to bake or fold laundry. She's Adam's protection. This is why, at Jewish weddings, the bride marches around the groom seven times. She's an army guarding him.

In an ancient patriarchal world, it's notable how vulnerable Adam is portrayed and how powerful the woman is described. And, by extension, how in need of help the first humans turn out to be. A physician friend pointed me toward an anomaly in medicine. It turns out that humans are the only mammals in all of creation that need help in their birthing process. What's called the "obstetrical dilemma" is a well-documented mystery that humans, of all creatures, are in more need of help in their vulnerable moments than any other. Humans are a vulnerable species, made to need help. When we refuse the need for help, we refuse our humanity. Later in the storyline of Scripture, Jesus critiques the church in Laodicea for this very thing: "You say, 'I am rich; I have acquired wealth and *do not need a thing.*' But you do not realize that you are wretched, pitiful, poor, blind, and naked" (Rev. 3:17, emphasis mine). To need nothing is inhuman. To be needy, holy.

We need God—desperately. But we also need food, air, water, relationships, and companionship. We were created by God to desire God and those things God created us to desire.

Humans, second, are created to rule. Upon forming Adam from dust and the woman from his side, God speaks. This time, God gives humanity their first commandments—a proverbial syllabus—which serve as the framework for their existence in the garden: "Be fruitful and increase in number; fill the earth and subdue it. *Rule* over the fish in the sea and the birds in the sky and over every living creature that moves on the ground" (Gen. 1:28, emphasis mine).

Much is gained by patiently taking in all the notes and flavors of God's instruction here. Note, for instance, that God directly instructs humans to "be fruitful and increase in number." This command shapes the human vocation of reproduction. Humans are physically built to reproduce. But this work of bearing and raising children is designed to take place in the nourishing context of a community called "marriage." Some creatures in creation are asexual, reproducing alone. Think amoebas. But animals and humans are different. Again, as a dimorphic species, God has placed the vocation of reproduction inside the boundaries of the intimate social relationship of covenant.

Even more, God created sex—the path toward reproduction—enjoyable. Anecdotal experience dictates that sex can, from time to time, be quite the rewarding experience. Indeed, if our Creator gets the credit for making our body parts, then he should get extra credit for the sexual pleasure they have power to provide. Clearly, if God is the maker of the human body, then neither sexual desire nor enjoyment should be deemed sinful in themselves. These are God's creations, blessed, holy, so long as they burn within the covenantal relationship God has placed them. If God commanded humans to reproduce, then he also gave us the *desire* to reproduce. In sheer brilliance, God incentivizes the command with a splendid reward.[25]

This call to fruitfulness isn't limited to having children. Why? Fruitfulness, in the biblical narrative, doesn't require sexual union. As I mentioned above, the most fruitful person in human history was a virgin man: Jesus of Nazareth. And even he came from a virgin. Some theologians have often wondered if the Great Commission at the end of Matthew's gospel and its call to Jesus' disciples to "go into all the world and make disciples" (Matt.

---

25. Desire undeniably is intended to propel us toward action. As Willard writes, the "primary role of desire is to impel us to action." Dallas Willard, "Beyond Pornography: Spiritual Formation Studied in a Particular Case," *Journal of Spiritual Formation and Soul Care* 9, no. 1 (2006): 9.

28:18–19) partially represent a maturation of the command to "be fruitful." The church is now called to fill the world with God's grace and wonder through Christ's gospel—a gospel Paul would say "is bearing fruit" throughout the Roman empire.[26] We now, says John the Baptist, "produce fruit in keeping with repentance" (Matt. 3:8). Clearly, fruitfulness isn't only about the capacity for physical reproduction.

Being fruitful means making something of God's world—to nourish culture, invent new foods, cultivate environments, make families, plant trees, and develop a flourishing life on this little planet. We call this the "cultural mandate." Just as God brought the world from chaos to order, humans mirror God's creative pattern. "Inasmuch as creation stands unfinished," theologian John Navone writes, "God continues to call us from chaos to cosmos, from formlessness to the resplendent form of God's true images."[27] We're not only made to do this—we're made to *desire* to do this. This is seen in God giving Adam the responsibility of naming the animals whatever he wanted to name them (Gen. 2:20).

Every human has within a God-given desire to shape God's world—standing for justice, making babies, serving the poor, leading people to faith, baking, visiting prisoners, hosting a dinner, starting churches, leading nonprofits, being missionaries. This is "ruling."

I distinctly recall one of my first desires. I discovered in third grade that my school had a "student of the month" award. I was riveted. I *had* to win. My very identity hung on this. The day I sat in the front row at the next assembly and heard Clint Carlos's name called from the front was one of the most devastating days of my life. I wept in the bathroom. Even that early in life, I was an achiever. I've come to appreciate the little me. I was a "ruler."

---

26. Col. 1:16
27. John Navone, SJ, *Toward a Theology of Beauty* (Collegeville, MN: Liturgical, 1996), 45.

I wanted to make something of my world. It was in my blood. I wasn't the student of the month that month. But the wound awakened within me a desire—a force of nature, really—to show my teacher she had made a mistake.

I won the next month.

Ruling is in our blood. Still, there are boundaries. All ruling that humans undertake is to be done *under* God as Eden's owner. In fact, the very first activity God is described as doing in the garden is planting trees (Gen. 2:8). God is a gardener. And Eden is God's garden. This reframes the word *rule*—or *radah* in Hebrew. The sense here isn't that humans "rule over" creation. Rather, they "rule under" God. Why does this distinction matter? We often get tripped up by the word *rule* because it seems to imply some kind of taking advantage or abuse. God's command to rule isn't a hall pass to treat creation as a hotel room—trashing it because someone else will pick up after us. Humans rule for and under God. The humans care for the garden as the gardener desires it.

Nor does "ruling" permit humans to envision themselves arrogantly over or above creation. Humans have a knack for seeing themselves as the pinnacle of creation. But the creation story pokes holes in this arrogance. Notice what elements of creation that get their own day. The light gets its own day on day 1. The waters get their own day on day 3. The sea gets its own on day 5. Yet something shifts with the humans. They share day 6 with the land creatures.

Biblical scholar Richard Bauckham has convincingly demonstrated that the animals and the humans share a day as a way of accentuating the similarities between the two.[28] There are differences, of course. One is made in the image of God. One is not. But Bauckham is convinced the text invites us to see our shared

---

28. See Richard Bauckham, "First Steps to a Theology of Nature," *Evangelical Quarterly* 58 (1986): 229–44.

existence within creation and argues that the goal of this detail—
that we share a day with animals—is to instruct humanity in
the way of humility: "[Humans] are, from the perspective of the
scheme of creation, land creatures, though the rest of this account
of their creation distinguishes them as special among the land
creatures."[29]

Arrogance isn't allowed. Neither is naivete. Humans may be
land creatures, but they are land creatures with unique power and
authority. More than any creature, humans have the ability to
keep—or *break*—the peace of the garden. This human responsibility is seen in how Genesis 1 discusses food. Bauckham further
points out that God gives the "seed-bearing plants" (Gen. 1:29) to
humans and "green plants" (Gen. 1:30) to animals for food. Why
does God instruct humans about what animals were to eat? God
is reminding humans of their responsibility. They can't forget they
share with the animals. Even more, God is establishing boundaries.
Bauckham writes,

> Why does God tell humans that he has given every plant for
> food for the other living creatures? Surely, the reason is that
> it is the humans who need to know that the produce of the
> earth is not intended to feed them alone, but also all the living
> species of the earth. The clear implication is that the earth can
> provide enough food for all creatures. Humans are not to fill
> the earth and subdue it in a way that leaves no room and no
> sustenance for the other creatures who share the earth with
> them. God has given them [the animals] too the right to live
> from the soil.[30]

---

29. Richard Bauckham, "Being Human in the Community of Creation," in *Ecotheology: A Christian Conversation*, ed. Alan Padgett and Kiara Jorgenson (Grand Rapids: Eerdmans, 2020), 23.

30. Richard Bauckham, *Living with Other Creatures: Green Exegesis and Theology* (Waco, TX: Baylor University Press, 2011), 227.

Sadly, a look at creation reveals that the biblical command to rule has been treacherously misunderstood and disobeyed by humans. Humans throw plastic into the oceans, send our technological garbage to distant lands for others to pick through, produce toxins destroying air and soil, and consume more than our fair share. We haven't ruled under God. We've ruled over creation as furious enslavers. But our original intent was to rule with mercy. God gave humans the desire to rule. But that desire has boundaries that, when crossed, harm God's great creation.

The humans were to rule—God's way. But they were also told to have a sabbath day of rest. Over the years, sadly, I've engaged in far too many conversations with pastors' kids who hold deep resentment for the church for the simple fact that they see it as having stolen their parents from them. We are called to do the ministry of Jesus. But we are called to do it in the spirit of Jesus, honoring the boundaries, virtues, and heart of God. When we do the work God has given us without doing it the way God told us, we end up doing great harm to everyone: creation, our children, and the church.

Third, humans are imbued with a special desire and propensity to long. Part of this is our nature to love. Some of our wisest Christian thinkers have pondered this mystery. Philosopher Alasdair MacIntyre, for instance, extensively explores the myriad ways humans and animals share key similarities and essential differences in *Dependent, Rational Creatures*. As MacIntyre shows, one of the distinctive qualities of human beings is their moral nature and capacity to reflect God and his agency in the world.[31] Connected to this is the fact that we reflect the rhythms of God. The work

---

31. Alasdair MacIntyre, *Dependent Rational Animals: Why Human Beings Need the Virtues*, The Paul Carus Lectures (Chicago: Open Court, 1999).

of James K. A. Smith helps us understand humans as liturgical creatures—what Smith calls *homo liturgicus*. We are "desiring creatures" in that we are "liturgical animals" who are oriented by rhythm, habit, and liturgy.[32]

When I lecture through Leviticus, I call it "the book of parties." The biblical book that fleshes out God's holiness most extensively is also a book stuffed to the brim with invitations to feast and celebrate. I ask my students to consider that holiness may have less to do with being otherworldly and more to do with becoming human.

Humans were made to celebrate. Read Genesis 1. On day 4 of creation, God sets in the sky the sun, moon, and stars "to serve as signs to mark sacred times, and days and years" (Gen. 1:14). Humans wouldn't be created for two whole days in the scheme of creation. God is setting the cosmos up for a party even before humans are made from the dust. Humans have been divinely placed in a world in which they are rhythmically made to love God and celebrate his goodness. As Smith writes, "Humans are those animals that are religious animals not because we are primarily believing animals but because we are liturgical animals—embodied, practicing creatures whose love/desire is aimed at something ultimate."[33]

Humans are, Smith continues, "primordially and essentially agents of love, which takes the structure of desire or longing."[34] Less than being merely rational creatures, we are *longing* creatures. No doubt, among creation, humans uniquely build and form their lives upon practices and habits that reflect their desires and loves.

This is demonstrated by how Genesis situates the humans within the creation week. The seven-day creation rhythm outlined in Genesis 1 and 2 accomplished many feats. With each of the first six days, we're given the repetitive phrase that "it was evening and it

---

32. James K. A. Smith, *Desiring the Kingdom: Worship, Worldview, and Cultural Formation*, Cultural Liturgies 1 (Grand Rapids: Baker Academic, 2009), 40.
33. Smith, *Desiring the Kingdom*, 40.
34. Smith, *Desiring the Kingdom*, 50.

was morning—the first day." The same on the second day. And the third. In fact, this phrase is repeated in a nearly exact form for six sequential days. But something goes missing on day seven. There's no "it was evening and morning—the seventh day." The seventh day never finishes. And by extension, the first week of creation never fully finishes.

Ancient rabbis and modern commentators suggest the creation account is creatively erecting a signpost toward some future day when God's *shabbat*—his good rest and peace—would never end. Creation's unfinished first week is picked up in the Gospels, especially John. There, the apostle records that Jesus cries out "it is finished" (John 19:30) as he dies. What's finished? The only way we know is by looking at John's description of the resurrection morning, which ominously takes place on the "first day of the week" (John 20:1). John has been chewing on Genesis 1 and 2. In his death, Jesus has finished the first week of creation. And in his resurrection, a new week of creation has begun.

Built into the text is an invitation to long for the day when the rest never ends. Part of loving is our longing. Remember, humans are the one creature that wasn't created in pairs. The man was made first. Then the woman. In the book *Man in History*, theologian Hans Urs von Balthasar suggests this delay in God presenting the woman before the man is a paradigm for understanding the way God works in the world and in our lives. By providing the woman later, we see that humans are given a distinct capacity for longing. Balthasar writes,

> Even Adam, according to the legend of Paradise, although created in the fullness of God's grace, had an unsatisfied longing until God had given him Eve. Adam transcended and sought through the whole of nature—naming and hence knowing— looking for that which would bring him fulfillment and completion. He did not find it. It is strange that human nature,

obviously quite different from the animals which were already created two by two, has to *long* for the other.[35]

That experience of longing is unique to humans. Just as Adam experienced the unique human experience of longing, so do we. "God wanted Adam to know loneliness and absence," writes Dan Allender, "in order to enter the glory of presence and companionship."[36] The longing would be met. God, it would seem, did not simply desire to be known about. He wanted to be known as a loving provider. The gratitude in Adam's voice as he gazes at the glory of the woman says it all,

> This is now bone of my bones
> and flesh of my flesh;
> she shall be called "woman,"
> for she was taken out of man. (Gen. 2:23)

In the Hebrew text, the significance of Adam's words can't be ignored. He is singing a song over the woman. These are the man's first words uttered in the biblical narrative. And they are words of praise, undulation, gratitude, joy. His desire has been matched—God has seen and cared for his longing and want. Humans were made to love, to sing songs, to desire one another. Nothing in the text even comes close to the idea that his love was misplaced. He was created to desire her and the friendship and companionship that came through that experience. So we shouldn't be surprised to find that none of the other creatures in the creation account *sing* over their mates when they are created. They never experienced the same kind of aloneness that is rooted in desire which Adam did.

---

35. Hans Urs von Balthasar, *Man in History: A Theological Study* (London: Sheed and Ward, 1968), 84–85. Emphasis added.
36. Dan Allender, *To Be Told: God Invites You to Coauthor Your Future* (Colorado Springs: Waterbrook, 2005), 4.

We are longing creatures because we are loving creatures. We won't revisit it for a few chapters, but keep in the back of your head that there's something important about the one day in creation that never ended. Just as Adam's fulfillment was delayed, we long for something that we have yet to receive.

Chapter 3

SATAN'S DESIRE

Up to now, we've explored how God desires. We've also looked at humans as desiring creatures handcrafted by a desiring Creator. Along the way, we've considered some of the divinely orchestrated intricacies of human nature. We've called this "original desire," and it includes those innate, indigenous, hardwired particularities of human experience relating to what God created us to desire.

Yet the Bible doesn't conclude with Genesis 2—far from it. In Genesis 3, we move into what is often called "the fall." Here our shared history takes a dark turn. A serpent slithers up to the unsuspecting feet of our ancestors with a proposition: "Now the serpent was more crafty than any of the wild animals the LORD GOD had made. He said to the woman, 'Did God really say, "You must not eat from any tree in the garden"?'" (Gen. 3:1). Trouble is brewing. With each word, the reader can sense the spiritual temperature drop. As with all biblical literature, the text deserves to be read slowly with attentive minds and patient hearts. Though ominously absent up to now, a new character enters the scene. God desired. As did humans. Apparently, so does this "serpent." What's known about him?

The devil is in the details. Immediately we're told this creature was "made by God." (Gen. 3:1) The author's comment, for one, problematizes any notion that God and this serpent are equal enemies standing on equal footing. No hostility between them can be called a war of equals.[1] Any battle between them wouldn't be a fair fight. God is an eternal Creator. The serpent is a temporal creation.

Additionally, by the time we meet this serpent, he has evidently already undergone a rebellion. The text never irons out what happened before Genesis 3. But he's coming in hot. The deceiver has already been deceived. As such, Genesis 3 isn't *the* fall so much as *a* fall. A rebellion has already happened.

In Hebrew, he's called the *nakhash*. In most modern English translations, this is translated as "serpent" or "snake." Notice, however, that *nakhash* isn't a name. It's a title. The serpent's personal name is notably absent. This won't be the last time biblical texts intentionally omit a personal name. When Egypt enslaved Israel, for example, the Egyptian ruler is known simply as Pharaoh. Similarly, *Pharaoh* is a title, not a name. Egypt had *many* Pharaohs. It's interesting to consider who *is* named in Exodus 1. Unnamed is Pharaoh, but named are the midwives Shiphrah and Puah, who rescued the babies from Pharaoh's evil decree to have them all slaughtered. The names of the female heroes are to be remembered forever. Pharaoh, on the other hand, doesn't even get a name.[2] This kind of biblical trash talk has a point. The quiet women doing justice have names worth remembering. Pharoah is just one of many despot enslavers not worthy of being named.

If *nakhash* is only a title, then who is this character? Biblical scholars and theologians have debated this for centuries—with opinions as varied as they are odd. Some see the serpent as a personal force, an image of desire, a magical figure, or even a symbol for penis. Rather than read our own opinions between the lines of

1. This point has been most forcefully made in C.S. Lewis, *Mere Christianity* (San Francisco: HarperCollins, 2000), chap. 2.

2. Even the word *ha satan* in Hebrew is mostly adjectival, roughly translated "opposer" or "enemy" or "adversary." There remain, in fact, several characters who are portrayed as human satans—David is a satan to the Philistines (1 Sam. 29:4); Abishai is a satan to David (2 Sam. 19:23); Hadad is a satan to Solomon (1 Kings 5:4; 11:14); and Rezon is a satan to Solomon (1 Kings 11:23–25).

ancient Scripture, we would be wise to let the narrative speak for itself. Quite plainly, the New Testament appears to identify Satan (or the devil) as the "snake" or "serpent" (Rev. 12:9; 20:2). Echoing Genesis 3, Jesus casts the Devil as the "murderer" who was from "the beginning" (John 8:44). Through and through, a holistic reading of Scripture demonstrates that the serpent in Genesis 3 is, indeed, the devil, Satan, *el diablo*, or, simply, the enemy of our souls. John's apocalypse offers the clearest connection: "The great dragon was hurled down—that ancient serpent called the devil, or Satan, who leads the whole world astray. He was hurled to the earth, and his angels with him. . . . He seized the dragon, that ancient serpent, who is the devil, or Satan, and bound him for a thousand years" (Rev. 12:9; 20:2).

That Satan is described as what appears to be an animal in Genesis 3 is noteworthy. While the author doesn't consider the exact species of the *nakhash*—whether python, cobra, copperhead, or garter—worthy of inclusion, he's presumably not unlike other animals in Eden. As others have pointed out, it's striking that the woman dialogues with the serpent without any sense of surprise or embarrassment. This is merely conjecture, but one wonders if her lack of surprise is due in part to the fact that humans enjoyed relational intimacy with many garden animals. Humans could apparently talk to animals in Eden. In a world of *shalom* where humans and animals fellowshipped with God and each other, it wouldn't have stood out that a human could speak to an animal. Perhaps what's weird is that we can't today.

What's to be made of the fact that Satan can appear as an animal? Some modern interpreters have suggested that, since the serpent takes on a shape that looks like a penis, we're to believe the fall is tied to sexual desire (if you're really conservative) or patriarchy (if you're really progressive). But these are exegetical stretches. Fanciful interpretations like these both impose our modern sensibilities upon the text and ultimately reflect more about our own prejudices than those of the Bible. We shouldn't contort the Bible to our modern assumptions because Satan takes the form of a serpent. But we also shouldn't ignore this detail.

Jesus, as we already discussed, sends demons into a herd of pigs.[3] Evil—even personal evil—appears to have the capacity to be embodied, taking upon itself a physicality. If evil can take residence in serpents and pigs, we shouldn't be surprised that cultures, institutions, laws, and human systems can do the same. From the beginning, evil takes on bodies, cultures, even places.

He's also "crafty." The Hebrew author uses the word 'arum here. The same word is readily employed by the author of Proverbs to describe the "prudent" or "wise." The serpent was wise? Prudent? The author doesn't stop there. The serpent is "*more* crafty than the other creatures God made." What a profound statement about God's enemy. To caricature Satan as dumb, stupid, or a simpleton is to underestimate his power and cede him the upper ground.

More often than not, sadly, our imagination about Satan is drawn more from Dante's *Inferno* or Hollywood dystopian fantasies than anything else. Satan isn't dumb, stupid, or simple. And if he's more crafty than any creature God has made, one can only assume he's craftier (in some way) than we are. Paul even goes so far as to say that Satan "masquerades as an angel of light" (2 Cor. 11:14). He's brilliant. He's beautiful.

And there's a method to his madness.

———

Genesis 3 sets the stage for the rest of the Bible. The cosmic confrontation the serpent commenced in Genesis will be a repetitive theme throughout the New Testament. A full reading of the Gospels reveals a staggering array of moments where Jesus either teaches about Satan and the demons or outright confronts them.

———

3. See Mark 5:1–20

This is the case in John 8. Once again, Jesus has been debating a group of perturbed religious leaders about the nature of his own authority and ministry. Jesus says, "You belong to your father, the devil, and you want to carry out your father's desires. He was a murderer from the beginning, not holding to the truth, for there is no truth in him. When he lies, he speaks his native language, for he is a liar and the father of lies" (John 8:44).

Keep in mind to whom Jesus is speaking: leading first-century Jewish religious authorities. It's difficult to underscore how wildly offensive Jesus' teachings would have been to the ears of this audience. And they should be offensive to our ears. By uttering those words, Jesus is explicitly critiquing the religious thought leaders of his time. Who, for Jesus, have the devil as their father? The theologians. What a confrontation—for them and for us. It's easy for those of us in religious spaces to believe the devil does the majority of his work "out there" among those who hate God, sleep around, smoke marijuana, or never go to church. Or, in the largely conservative-leaning Christian world I inhabit, the liberals and progressives. But Jesus is confronting such religious claptrap.

Clearly, Jesus believed all religious spaces could be quickly transformed into environments wherein the devil could operate incognito. Consider Jesus' words to the future leader of his church, Peter: "Get behind me, Satan! You are a stumbling block to me; you do not have in mind the concerns of God, but merely human concerns" (Matt. 16:23). Indeed, being "religious" doesn't make one immune to lurking, devilish desires or powers.

Jesus describes Satan as a creature of desire. As we've noted, using "from the beginning" in John 8:44 is Jesus' way of linking his critique back to the creation story. Jesus is claiming that "from the beginning" the Devil has operated out of a certain set of desires. Yet, oddly, if we flip back to Genesis 3, we may be surprised to discover there's nothing explicitly said about the desires of the *nakhash*. Nothing. Nada. Zilch. Now we can appreciate the audacity of Jesus' claim in his original context. How could a thirty-year-old carpenter from Nazareth claim to know the first thing about the desires of the ancient serpent? How does Jesus know this information if he wasn't there? Who is this guy?

Jesus is implicitly claiming something about his identity. Jesus is audaciously claiming to know something about the events of Genesis 3 that the Pharisees and Sadducees (who knew the texts better than any other person) couldn't have known. Jesus is claiming something about himself by saying he has special knowledge of "the beginning." Jesus is claiming an authority, knowledge, and insight that these religious authorities could not have. One can only imagine how equally offended they would be at Jesus' claim, "I saw Satan fall like lightning from heaven" (Luke 10:18). Mere humans can't claim to witness "Satan's fall" firsthand, in real time. How could Jesus utter those words? It's ludicrous!

That is, unless Jesus is claiming to have *actually* been there. No wonder the guild of first-century theologians wanted Jesus dead. By sneaking in little theological offenses like this—claims to divinity and the like—Jesus was slowly moving up his date on the forthcoming Roman crucifixion schedule. More than anything, claims like these put Jesus on death row.

Don't miss the importance of his claim. Jesus claimed to know Satan's desires. He understood what drove him. The desire of God created the world. And the desire of Satan led to its rebellion. The devil is a wanting creature. He longs. He desires. Seen through the lens of Jesus, the biblical story goes out of its way to show that every major player in Genesis 1–3 desires. God desires. The humans desire. And Satan desires. Truly, ours is a world war of desire.

But what does Satan actually want?

Some have turned to the prophetic book of Isaiah to answer this question. The prophet identifies who he calls "the morning star, the son of the dawn," who had been "cast down upon earth" after saying in his heart:

> I will ascend to the heavens;
> I will raise my throne
>   above the stars of God;
> I will sit enthroned on the mount of assembly,
>   on the utmost heights of Mount Zaphon.
> I will ascend above the tops of the clouds;
>   I will make myself the Most High (Isa. 14:12–14).

Is Isaiah speaking of the Devil? Notice the words *ascend* and *raise* and *above*. Whoever Isaiah speaks of is clearly seeking in pride to become a god. No doubt, this *could* be Satan. But Old Testament scholars aren't so confident that Isaiah has Satan in mind. In context, Isaiah appears to be directly addressing the king of Babylon, whose policies and postures reveal a king with ascendent pride who seeks to rule the world. Isaiah could be speaking of two figures at once—both this king and Satan—as prophetic literature often does.

In John 10, Jesus contrasts his own work as the "good shepherd" with that of the "thief," who seeks to destroy what the good shepherd seeks to do. "The thief," Jesus teaches, "comes only to steal and kill and destroy" (John 10:10). This particular gospel section does not directly connect the "thief" to Satan. But there are undeniable overlaps between the two. Satan's desire is always to take what wasn't his, kill God's good creation and creature, and destroy the works of God. Furthermore, when looked at through the lens of original desire God gave humans, there's a haunting inversion. God wanted humans to long, help, and rule. But Satan's desires are the inverse. Satan desires to steal what we long for, to get us to kill who we are supposed to help, and to tempt us to destroy that which we were called to rule. His desire stands directly opposed to the desires placed in humans.

Paul's shorthand for Satan's desire is his *methodia*.[4] This is

---

4. For a thorough treatment of Paul's use of the word *methodia*, see ch. 3 of Marva Dawn, *Powers, Weakness, and the Tabernacling of God* (Grand Rapids: Eerdmans, 2001). Emphasis mine on Scripture quotations in this paragraph.

Satan's "method." Paul only uses the word *methodia* twice, both in Ephesians. Each time it is pejorative and overtly negative. Paul commands the followers of Jesus to "take your stand against the devil's *schemes*" (6:11). He further warns them to not be "tossed back and forth by . . . the cunning and craftiness of people in their deceitful *scheming*" (4:14). Many translations render *methodia* as "scheming." And, for Paul, Satan has a scheme—or, a *methodia*. And those who follow him share in his *methodia*. What's the method? "The role of this creature is that of seducer," writes Old Testament scholar Nahum Sarna, "laying before the woman the enticing nature of evil and fanning her desire for it."[5]

What does this mean? The work of the *nakhash* is built around stealing, killing, and destroying everything God is, has, and seeks to do. We hear Satan's method drip from the serpent's mouth as he talks to the woman: "Did God really say, 'You *must not eat from any* tree in the garden'?" (Gen. 3:1, emphasis mine). To catch the gravity of this, we must revisit God's original words. God had said humans were "free to eat from any tree in the garden" (Gen. 2:16). Only one tree was off-limits: "the tree of the knowledge of good and evil" (Gen. 2:17). Humans had near-total freedom. Given how expansive the garden likely was, they were invited to eat to their hearts' content. Had the humans simply said at that moment to the serpent, "No, that is not what God said," the fall likely would have been averted. But they accepted the premise of the question. Through insinuation—the serpent's mother tongue—humanity was deceived. Stealing, killing, and destroying was inaugurated.

What was the first trick of Satan? It was simple: he wanted to cast God in the minds of the first humans as a divine curmudgeon who simply wanted to keep them from all the good stuff. We hear lingering echoes of this insinuation in our hearts single every day:

---

5. Nahum Sarna, *Understanding Genesis: The World of the Bible in the Light of History* (New York: Schocken, 1966), 26.

God is withholding.
There's probably no God, so just have a good time.
God is deceiving you.
Your faith is keeping you from a fulfilling, enjoyable, liberated life.
You are missing out.

Ever hear these voices?

As many theologians throughout history have pointed out, Satan appears to be creating a kind of disruption—namely, a disruption in the realm of human desire. Before the fall, the humans trusted God's command. Now, it's in doubt. Is God just a lawmaker keeping us from living our deepest desires? Sadly, they listened. And so do we. This is step one of Satan's *methodia.* In one fell swoop, something of God's authority over humanity was handed to the entity of the serpent. This is why there remains an intimate connection between what desires we give ourselves to and who we submit to as our ultimate authority. If God has final authority over the garden space and all that is in it, then God has final authority over what in the garden we are permitted to desire and take. Desire and authority are inseparable. As the apostle Peter would reflect in his second letter, "those who follow the corrupt desires of the flesh" also "despise authority" (2 Pet. 2:10). The serpent undermines our trust in God's authority by awakening dark desires. The serpent seeks to cause us to *despise* God for his commands, to question God's wisdom, and to reject what God has said in the name of "freedom."[6] In so doing, we trade God's authority for our own— God's desires for our own. Immediately, "the eyes of both of them were opened" (Gen. 3:7).

---

6. Jonathan James has suggested that this represents *the* conflict between modern, secular culture and the Christian narrative. "In our age of autonomy and freedom," James pens, "seeing ourselves as contingent creatures is not an easy sell." Jameson, "Erotic Absence and Sacramental Hope: Rowan Williams on Augustinian Desire," 587.

I was eleven. An only child of divorced parents, I rarely enjoyed friendship with kids my own age. Loneliness was often my best friend. Since I was a relational amateur, when someone *did* offer friendship, I often became so clingy that I drove them away. Classic me. Earnest—if not desperate—for companionship, my little heart eagerly longed for any chance at friendship.

I met Reuben in Boy Scouts.[7] To my utter shock, Reuben invited me one day to come over after school. I didn't flinch. *Someone* wanted to play with me! I remember whispering to myself a little pep talk as we walked to his house: "Don't screw this up. Don't screw this up. Don't screw this up." I was good at self-talk back then. I remember the smell of his home—reeking of Marlboro cigarettes and some cute little dog who greeted me as I entered the door. The smell didn't bother me. I didn't care. I had a playdate.

First, we played in his room. While the object of our attention escapes my mind, the feeling of being wanted still pulsates through my veins. Someone saw me. Someone wanted me. Someone wanted to play with *me*. I played it cool, like I did playdates all the time. I hid my amateurism quite nicely. Then, like a rough cut in a movie, something shifted. Reuben looked up and quietly whispered, "Hey, do you want to see *something?*"

A cold awkwardness descended. The way his words landed was peculiar—the way you'd whisper if there were someone in the next room. But we were alone. I responded with an affirming nod. Of course I wanted to see something! Following him out into the living room, Reuben gestured toward a bean bag chair in the center of the room in front of the television. I sat down. I loved movies! Wrestling through a little brown box he'd brought out of

---

7. The name is changed to protect the anonymity of my friend—who, to his own credit, later asked for my forgiveness for what transpired.

his brother's room, he found a black VHS tape. He put it in and sat behind me. "Sit back and enjoy," he said.

He hit play.

At eleven, I was exposed to a whole new world—the world of hardcore pornography. There were body parts I'd never seen. Sexual experiences I didn't know were real. Today, at forty-two, though I can't remember my first-grade teacher's name, I remember nearly everything about those powerful images. The embodied memory within me of that moment included comfort, excitement, and shame at the same time. I remember feeling warm. I didn't blink for a second. Like my forebears, my eyes "were opened" (Gen. 3:7). Little did I know that my little body was being flooded with oxytocin and dopamine at unparalleled levels. A neuroscientist would probably say new neural pathways were developing in my brain that would set a trajectory for the rest of my life.[8] When the film finished, I just sat there staring at the screen.

I was a different child that night when I put my head on my pillow.

Given my parents' own pain, I withheld this story from them both. I talked myself through it, which, itself, would become part of my identity and role. "I don't need help. I'm fine. I'll take care of myself." The inhumanity of it all—when anyone must be their own "helper" through pain, shame, and confusion. This childhood experience paralleled other sexual trauma that set in motion wounds that would require years of work, counseling, prayer, and trusted friendship to heal and come to terms with. Effects linger to this day.

For any who experience any level of abuse, the stories stick with us. They may come from the distant past, but they remain in the present. And, always, behind stories like this is a plan. It never

---

8. Biophysiologist William Struthers at Wheaton has done marvelous work on the intersection of spirituality, pornography, and neuroscience. See Struthers, *Wired for Intimacy: How Pornography Hijacks the Male Brain* (Downers Grove, IL: InterVarsity Press, 2009).

just happens. There's intentionality. All abuse has a method and a scheme.

One of the serpent's most effective tools is the weaponization of our desires against us. In the book *Healing the Wounded Heart*, therapist Dan Allender describes how before an abuser undertakes their abuse, they must first perfect the craft of "grooming" their victims. They often begin by reading, studying, and knowing their prey. Allender writes,

> The first stage is the abuser's grooming through reading the needs and unique character of the victim. The grooming stage offers what has often been missed by one's primary attachment figures. It is a heartbreaking reversal. The abuser offers what is lacking in the relationship with one's caregivers to gain access to the heart. I have had to say many times during therapy that the abuser was a better picture of God than one's parents or other primary caregivers.[9]

The abuser's first work is to pay close attention to the felt needs of their prey. How did their parents ignore them? What wounds of loneliness or being forgotten linger within? How were they never touched or loved? Through craftiness, the abuser often meets us right where we have a need by paying attention to, noticing, and seeing us. Then they move toward abuse. Allender continues,

> This stage of grooming bears incalculable power. Whether the grooming period lasts a few minutes or months, trust is gained and access to the heart is assured. What is most diabolic is that the abuser sows seed that is often life-giving. God has created us to be studied, read, and interpreted, and the more accurate

---

9. Dan Allender, *Healing the Wounded Heart: The Heartache of Sexual Abuse and the Hope of Transformation* (Grand Rapids: Baker, 2016), 76.

and deep the reading, the more life-giving is the experience. It doesn't take long to be won by a careful reader.[10]

Abuse often weaponizes care. This is the very thing the serial killer Ted Bundy found worked with those he murdered in the 1960s and '70s. In most cases, Bundy lured women into his van by pretending to have a broken arm. He deceived by asking for help—original desire weaponized. He used the compassion of others against them. This is the *methodia* of the evil one. The serpent often meets us in that place we need to be met. He uses our desires against us. Notice the demonic exchange. Abuse trades in a real, God-created felt need or desire for something that fulfills the heart and longings of the abuser. This is why those who are abused often express how their abuse—evil as it was—provided some semblance of pleasure. The abuse provided something that was deeply needed: a caress, attention, being wanted, being chosen.

Looked at through this lens, Satan enters Eden having done his homework. The serpent knew God placed boundaries in the garden. And in speaking to the woman, he comes off as caring. *Throw off those boundaries. Be free. Get what's yours. God clearly doesn't have your best interests in mind.* He's suggesting he cares more than God does.

Satan is an abuser. And he wants to groom humans into his evil ways. There's only one problem for him. The Divine caretaker who made the humans has a love that is entirely, eternally, and endlessly perfect. The serpent could not give them anything they didn't already have provided for by the care of God. The humans had all their needs met: a garden, animals, creation, relationship with God, sex, food, everything! Satan couldn't attack on that front. So he was forced to take on a new approach. Satan was left with one option: arouse within the humans new and novel desires for the one thing

---

10. Allender, *Healing the Wounded Heart*, 74.

(the tree of knowledge of good and evil) God had instructed them they could not have. In a world where a loving God has met every imaginable need, Satan can only hope to arouse their wants. The serpent creates an artificial need—and, in turn, their desire for it. This is still the story. When we've got everything we need from a perfect God, the devil soon comes at us through our desires.

Satan always wants us to believe we need "more" than we have.

———

Was the tree of knowledge of good and evil bad? No, God created this tree. It was a good tree. Still, it *was* dangerous, and humans weren't to eat from it. Satan's appeal, then, was that the fruit of this tree was "good for food," "pleasant to the eye," and "desirable for wisdom." Notice that Satan's appeal to the humans is to take something that was good. The tree was good—just off limits for the humans. This is often how temptation works. We are tempted to take good, beautiful, and glorious things and use them in unintended ways. Food, sex, and pleasure aren't bad. But they can be dangerous, and their boundaries must be honored. Just because something is desirable and good does not mean it is for us. Satan is good at arousing human desire to use good things in ways God does not bless. This is why the ancient author of the *Shepherd of Hermas* said the "tree of knowledge of good and evil" aroused within humans something called "overcuriosity."[11] Satan was piquing interest.

The importance of this, in part, lay in us developing a maturing awareness that God can (and does) create good things that simply aren't for us. Just because something is beautiful and desirable doesn't mean it is for our desire's consumption. The temptation

---

11. *Shepherd of Hermas*, vision III, iii, 1, trans. Bart D. Ehrman, in *The Apostolic Fathers*, vol. 2, Loeb Classical Library (Cambridge, MA: Harvard University Press, 2003).

for more than what's been provided is how the serpent deceived the man and the woman—and how he often deceives us. There's a reason the Sanskrit word for "war" is "desire for *more* cows." Our world is ravaged by a desire for more. One could say it is the reason for most wars.

Humans had plenty. Yet the serpent aroused a desire for more. Upon believing this message, the woman "saw" and "took." Notice how these two words are used together: "When the woman *saw* that the fruit of the tree was good for food and pleasing to the eye, and also desirable for gaining wisdom, she *took* some and ate it. She also gave some to her husband, who was with her, and he ate it" (Gen. 3:6). We're surprised to discover that the man was standing right there, "with her." The text doesn't put the weight of all responsibility on the woman's shoulders. They both were there. The man was there too, watching, observing, and doing nothing. Yes, she *saw*, and she *took*. But he just passively watched.

This won't be the last time *seeing* and *taking* are connected in biblical literature.[12] When they are, something evil often takes place. For example, when King David observes from his Jerusalem rooftop the beautiful Bathsheba below, he sees and takes her (2 Sam. 11:2–5). And the prophet Samson sees a Canaanite descendent and takes her (Judg. 14). Achan does the same thing as he observes the glories of the Babylonian cape, seeing and taking it for himself (Josh. 7:20–21) Time and again, humans see and take what's not theirs. Perhaps Ariana Grande was reading her Bible when she wrote her famous song: "I see it, I like it, I want it, I got it."

One telltale sign of a world rebelling against its Creator is that its God-given limitations and boundaries are thrown aside. As Dallas Willard put it, "*I* will have what *I* desire."[13] Sinful humanity,

---

12. I would like to thank my friend Tim Mackie for repeatedly highlighting the connection between seeing and taking in his teaching work and ministry.

13. Dallas Willard, "Beyond Pornography: Spiritual Formation Studied in a Particular Case," *Journal of Spiritual Formation and Soul Care* 9, no. 1 (2006): 8.

in its newfound "freedom," seeks to take and conquer and steal that which it was not given. This is the essence of sin and the danger of unmitigated desire: seeing and taking what isn't ours. We see and take when we abuse or weaponize sexuality. Those in power see and take the lands and places of others. All of us see and take when we store up greedily and mercilessly hoard more than what's needed. It's the spirit of Julius Caesar who declared in the battle of Zela, "*Veni, vidi, vici*" ("I came, I saw, I conquered"). All sin, at its core, is the act of seeing and taking something that isn't given by God.[14]

This story of Genesis 3 can be read alongside Jesus' temptation in the wilderness in Matthew 4. There, Jesus comes face-to-face with Satan and faces three temptations: to turn stones into bread, to jump off a high place, and to bow down and worship Satan so he might have the nations. One of these temptations particularly parallels the Genesis 3 account: "Again, the devil took him to a very high mountain and showed him all the kingdoms of the world and their splendor. 'All this I will give you,' he said, 'if you will bow down and worship me'" (Matt. 4:8–9).

The serpent promises to give Jesus all of the kingdoms, or nations, if and only if Jesus bows down and worships Satan. Go back to the garden where the serpent makes a promise to the woman: "'You will not certainly die,' the serpent said to the woman. 'For God knows that when you eat from it your eyes will be opened, and you will be like God, knowing good and evil'" (Gen. 3:4–5).

The serpent promises, "You will be like God." But there was a catch. The woman had to obey the serpent's words to receive the serpent's promise. A thread weaves between these two accounts. What's the singular problem with offering Jesus the nations? All the nations and kingdoms were *already* his. What's the singular

---

14. Robert Jenson once quipped that this was Satan's method: "Above all, God gives himself among us, Satan's difference from God is unambiguously exposed. God gives. Satan can only suck reality into the vacuum of his own heart." See Robert Jenson, "Evil as Person," *Lutheran Theological Seminary Bulletin* 69, no. 1 (1989): 39.

problem with offering the woman to be "like God"? She had already been endowed with the image of God from the moment of her creation. By a simple question, he convinces her that she wasn't already like God through the mother tongue of the serpent: insinuation.

Both stories put the serpent's *methodia* on full display. He offers us the gift of something we already have in God. He often awakens our desires for something God has already provided for us. In short, he awakens our desires by insinuating that we are missing out. This is where our desire becomes most twisted. As Jen Pollock Michel writes, "And here is how desire becomes corrupt: wanting derails into selfishness, greed and demanding ingratitude when we've failed to recognize and receive the good that God has *already* given."[15]

There's a solution: awakening to the reality that there's no such thing as "missing out" when we are in Christ. As Paul wrote, "All things are yours" (1 Cor. 3:21). There is no missing out in Jesus. No, we won't be fulfilled *when* we get married because we are already fulfilled in Christ. No, we don't have to find our own identities because we already have names and love in the one who named us and made us. No, we won't experience true happiness when we get the job or the paycheck we want because we are already, now, full of the presence and grace of God.

When you begin believing you are missing out, look down. There's some snake at your feet. The serpent awakens our flesh by trying to convince us that we lack something. This is just his old bag of tricks.

Genesis 3 was a decisive victory for the serpent. But it was a *temporary* victory. It wouldn't be the end of the story. Just as the Bible

---

15. Jen Pollock Michel, *Teach Us to Want: Longing, Ambition & the Life of Faith* (Downers Grove, IL: InterVarsity Press, 2014), 84. Emphasis mine.

doesn't end with Genesis 2, it also does not end with Genesis 3. God does not wash his hands of the world and walk away. He has a healing vision for creation. And for each of us. Paul would later reflect, "He who began a good work in you will carry it on to completion until the day of Christ Jesus" (Phil. 1:6). This is as true for us as it is for all of creation. Despite the cataclysmic nature of Genesis 3—and the ensuing trail of bloodshed, evil, sin, and injustice—it's clear from the rest of the story of the Bible that God does not give up on creation. God begins the great reversal.

When we attend to the imagery associated with Jesus in the Gospels, it's clear the writers intend to cast Jesus as the eventual reversal of the trauma of Genesis 3. This is seen at a number of points. As he's being tortured on a Roman cross, Jesus is reported to have been given some "wine vinegar" (John 19:29) in a sponge by soldiers below. These same soldiers also "pierced Jesus' side" (John 19:34). Out of Jesus' side, John records, water trickles. There's little question John is up to something by highlighting a sharp contrast. In Jesus' first miracle in Cana, he was given water at a wedding and made it into wine. In his final miracle at the cross, Jesus is given wine, and out comes water. The cross appears to be a whole new wedding. How do we know? Because the last time a human was pierced in the side, it was Adam, and his bride was being created. At the cross, humanity pierces God in the side, and a new bride— the church—is given life. Adam would have had a scar in his side for the rest of his life. The second Adam will have his for eternity.

Reversals like this are all over the place—such as the resurrection accounts. As I pointed out in chapter 1, the first image of God in Eden is planting a tree as a gardener. At sunrise of the first Easter morning, a woman has come to the tomb to care for Jesus' body. Upon entering the tomb, she discovers that Jesus is gone. The tomb is empty. Heart racing and afraid, she exits the tomb. But she isn't alone. Standing outside the tomb is a man. She doesn't realize it is Jesus. John tells us that she mistakes this man in the morning darkness for someone familiar, "thinking he was the gardener" (John 20:15).

Easter preachers often make the mistake of chiding Mary for her comment. But they shouldn't. Mary wasn't wrong. She thought he was the gardener. And he was! The gardener is back. The Creator who planted the trees in the garden has now returned to die on a tree and resurrect in a garden. She won't recognize Jesus until he speaks her name. Upon hearing her name, she realizes it is, indeed, Jesus, her Lord. At this moment—as she hears her name, "Mary"—theologians say the clocks of world history change over from BC to AD. This is the most important moment of all time. As New Testament scholar Thomas Schmidt writes, "There is a curious and important detail in this story that really is the main point. Mary didn't recognize the risen Jesus until he called her by name. Everywhere that Mary went the Lamb was sure to go."[16]

He goes with us too—hidden, watching, present, with our name on his lips.

Or recall the story after the resurrection as two unnamed disciples walk to Emmaus. Just as with Mary, Jesus is with them, but they're unaware. Incognito Jesus approaches them to start a conversation. Not knowing it's Jesus, they invite the stranger in for a meal. As Jesus breaks bread and gives thanks, their "eyes were opened" (Luke 24:31). Luke doesn't miss a beat. Just as the first humans took the forbidden food and had their eyes opened, so now we can receive the food Jesus provides to have our eyes opened, back to God. Just as Satan deceived the world over food, Jesus heals it over food.

Indeed, if humans "saw" and "took" the food the serpent offers, God knows how to meet us. We are takers. And he knows how to heal takers. And he does so by beckoning us to come to him

---

16. Thomas Schmidt, *A Scandalous Beauty: The Artistry of God and the Way of the Cross* (Grand Rapids: Brazos, 2002), 70–71.

and eat. "Take and eat," he says at the last supper, "this is my body" (Matt. 26:26). There's no other way to reach a taker than to give a taker something righteous to take.

"The move from the kingdom of Satan," writes theologian Alan Padgett, "to the reign and realm of God involves, among other things, a reformation of our desires."[17] This is what Jesus is after. Jesus undoes Genesis 3. And with it, he begins the journey of restoring us to our original desires.

---

17. Alan Padgett, "Discipleship of Desire and the Hunger for Justice: Wisdom from Luther and Wesley," *Word & World* 4, no. 4 (Fall 2022): 282.

Part 2

THE DISORDERING OF OUR DESIRES

Chapter 4

FLESHLY DESIRE

ollowing the disaster of Genesis 3, everything would be inescapably changed. What once was a garden of goodness, intimacy, and trust descended into a world plagued by sin, selfishness, and distrust. Gloom and despair shone on God's good world. Almost immediately, as soon as Genesis 4, humanity constructs urban, city environments. Not that cities are bad—the final image of new creation will be a restored city with Christ at the center—but humanity's postfall urban development represents a society organized around *its* ambitions, ideals, and values. A world once centered on God's presence is being recentered. Ronald Rolheiser poignantly describes the results: "While rejecting God . . . [human beings] invariably set up certain ideals as normative—and then invest these ideals with an absoluteness that mimics and parallels every movement of religion."[1]

After humanity's banishment from Eden, their face-to-face intimacy with God was lost. Underscoring this, the Hebrew word for "banished" also means "divorce."[2] Humanity wasn't displaced solely geographically. Humanity was displaced relationally into a shattered world G. K. Chesterton called "a wild divorce court."[3] Everything was fractured.

---

1. Ronald Rolheiser, *The Shattered Lantern: Rediscovering a Felt Presence of God* (New York: Crossroad, 2004), 142.

2. Sandra L. Richter, *The Epic of Eden: A Christian Entry into the Old Testament* (Downers Grove, IL: InterVarsity, 2008), 112.

3. G. K. Chesterton, *What's Wrong with the World* (San Francisco: Ignatius, 1994), 88.

Yet, evicted from God's presence, humans continued to have the original desires they had been endowed with at creation. Humans still wanted to rule, help, and long. The divorce began to twist those desires. Unhitched from God's sustaining presence, human desires slowly corrupt, pervert, and invert. Our God-centered desires become human centered. This is represented by the moment the man and woman run into a tree grove to clothe themselves. An exchange has taken place. As Paul would reflect, humans now "worshiped and served created things rather than the Creator" (Rom. 1:25).

Humans were created to gaze into the face of the Creator of heaven and earth. Without God's face, we gaze into heaven and earth instead. Gerald May calls this phenomenon the "displacement of spiritual longing."[4] The deepest longings of human desire can only be truly satiated by God as the endless, infinite source of life and love, which can never be locally sourced. Created things let us down.

St. Thomas Aquinas, in the medieval church, often reflected on how human desire could never be entirely fulfilled outside of God. The result of the fall, Aquinas believed, was that human desire would be left searching for something to sustain it. It wouldn't find it. Dallas Willard describes this reality in modern terms:

> Desire is infinite partly because we were made by God, made for God, made to need God, and made to run on God. We can be satisfied only by the one who is infinite, eternal, and able to supply all our needs; we are only at home in God. When we fall away from God, the desire for the infinite remains, but it is displaced upon things that will certainly lead to destruction.[5]

4. Gerald May, *Addiction and Grace: Love and Spirituality in the Healing of Addictions* (New York: HarperCollins, 1988), 92.

5. Dallas Willard, *Life without Lack: Living in the Fullness of Psalm 23* (Nashville: Nelson, 2018), 134. Albacete similarly writes that the human heart "yearn[s] for infinity," but

This bears, in part, incredible explanatory power. In the volume *Theology of the Body for Beginners*, theologian Christopher West explores the nature of our own erotic desires. Within, West describes the difference between our deepest in-built longing for God (what he calls "Capital-E Eros") and the desires and joys of temporal life (what he calls "small-e eros").[6] Only God himself is infinite Beauty. No created thing can compare. And it is the beauty that all of our love, longing, desire—and even erotic impulses—is intended to point toward. When humans cut themselves off from living Godward and seeking expression in him, the human spirit must try to turn to lesser realities to find its sustaining meaning. West poignantly diagnoses the disease of post-Edenic life: we tend to look for capital-E love in lowercase-e places.

For West, this has reverberating implications for human sexuality. Broadly speaking, the Western, secular sexual ethic has heaped unimaginable pressure on one's drive for individualized sexual identity, expression, and self-determination—a journey that almost resembles a form of secular sainthood. The person who has "arrived" in the Western world is the one who claims to have discovered their "true" sexual self. But, as West contends, this search inevitably fails us. The temporal (sexuality in this case) cannot sate our need for the eternal. And as a temporal good, sex can't bear the weight of our desire for God. Nor can it replace God.

And anyone who has had it knows. Sex will eventually let us down—as Jack Kornfield aptly entitled his book, *After the Ecstasy, the Laundry*.[7] We never stay on the mountaintop for long. Searching for eternity in the orgasm always ends up disappointing us over the long run. This is precisely what Chesterton had in mind when he

---

without finding it, the heart eventually perverts all good. Alberto Albacete, *God at the Ritz: Attraction to Infinity* (New York: Crossroad, 2002), 120.

6. Christopher West, *Theology of the Body for Beginners* (North Palm Beach, FL: Beacon, 2018), 120.

7. Jack Kornfield, *After the Ecstasy, the Laundry: How the Heart Grows Wise on the Spiritual Path* (New York: Bantam, 2000).

suggested that the man standing in line at a brothel was secretly looking for God. Hidden behind all sexual immorality is a secret search for sexual immortality.[8]

Our search for eternity in temporal places also explains why human politics has, more or less, taken on a religious fervor in Western spaces. No longer do we merely vote for people or issues. Each and every political decision has the weight of all of history riding on its coattails. "History hangs in the balance," they say. "Democracy is on the verge of collapse." Every vote inches us closer toward utopia or civilizational collapse. In lieu of worshiping God, politics has become our new religion, policy its theology, and social media posts the new great commission. But can politics replace God's face as the sustaining force of society? Eric Voegelin, in his book *The Political Religions*, speaks prophetically of the danger of a politic without the reference point of the invisible:

> When God is invisible behind the world, the contents of the world will become new gods; when the symbols of transcendent religiosity are banned, new symbols develop from the inner-worldly language of science to take their place. Like the Christian ecclesia, the inner-worldly community has its apocalypse too; yet the new apocalyptics insist that the symbols they create are scientific judgements.[9]

Welcome to the apocalyptic political age.

Finally, consider the central place self-determined identity has been afforded in this moment. Freed from the shackles of blood and history—unmoored from anything outside oneself—the new

---

8. Sarah Coakley's reflections on Freud are instructive here. The Freudian view, she writes, makes sex primary and God marginal. The biblical vision turns this on its head. God is primary, sex marginal. "Desire," writes Coakley, "is more fundamental than sex." Sarah Coakley, *The New Asceticism: Sexuality, Gender and the Quest for God* (New York: Bloomsbury, 2015), 9.

9. Eric Voegelin, *The Political Religions* (Stockholm: Bermann-Fischer, 1939), 51.

human task in the late modern world is to become a fully determined self. "Be yourself" is the secular golden rule, the required catechesis for baptism into contemporary fulfilment. And while individualism benefits all of us in many ways, we shouldn't be surprised to see the rise of deaths by despair as a result of building a whole society on it. Individualism disciples us into individuals—people with no need for family, tribe, genealogy, or history. There's a real cost to this. With no one to define us but ourselves, we're damned to be by ourselves. The self-made have no need for others.

Again, a post-Eden world continues to desire—but this desire is misplaced outside of God's presence. And while we cram infinite meaning into temporal things, we'll be left wanting. Put another way, humanity has been losing face since Eden. It's no mistake that the Hebrew word for "face" (*paneh*) is also the word for "presence." This becomes a central feature of the Old Testament. There, time and again, people recoil at the idea of seeing God's face. Why? They know unholy people will die if they see God's face. As Teresa of Avila wrote, "How can I gaze into his omnipresent eyes?"[10] That is the theme of the Old Testament. How can a sinful people behold God's face?

They couldn't. It was too much.

What happens to human desire when it's divorced from God's presence? The New Testament's shorthand for this is "the flesh." English readers often presume "flesh" entails only our physical bodies: ligaments, legs, foreheads, and all. But that can't be the whole story. Our bodies—the skin and bones that comprise us—are emphatically declared by God in Genesis 1 as "good." Additionally,

---

10. St. Teresa of Avila, "He Desired Me So I Came Close," hosted online by the Sisters of Saint Joseph of Rochester, https://www.ssjrochester.org/filehandler.ashx?x=6673.

Paul calls our bodies "temples" with which we "worship" God.[11]
Flesh and body aren't always the same thing.

This is further reflected by the fact that the New Testament
employs different words for *flesh* and *body*. The body—the hard-
wiring of our bodily existence—is represented by the Greek word
sōma. Flesh, on the other hand, is represented by the word *sarx*, that
dimension of invisible, evil, rebellious desires within us. Sure, on
occasion, the word *flesh* can indicate "body" or "good human ability" in New Testament writings.[12] It's rare, though. The word *flesh*
can be used in different ways, just as the word *bald* can be used in
different ways—meaning losing one's hair or confidence. But *flesh*
most often speaks of that realm of sinful, evil desires within the
unredeemed person.

The flesh is where Satan appeals to and influences our desires.
Desire arises from two places within a person. In Paul's thought,
desire comes from either the flesh (*sarx*) or the Spirit (*pneuma*).
Paul most explicitly describes the difference in Romans 8 by
sketching out two kinds of people: those "who live according to the
flesh . . . [having] their minds set on what the flesh desires," and
those "who live according to the Spirit . . . [having] set their minds
on what the Spirit desires" (v. 5). Both kinds of people desire. What
distinguishes them, however, is the desire around which they orient
their lives. Do they center their existence on the desires of the flesh
or the Spirit? Paul refuses to cast the Christian (or any) life as one
absent of desires. Rather, the Christian life is one oriented around
certain desires.

Paul never claims the flesh will be silenced or annihilated by
conversion and baptism. Remember, Paul is writing to Christians.
He demonstrates in Galatians 5 that Christians will experience

---

11. 1 Cor. 6:19; Rom. 12:1–2.
12. For example, see 2 Cor. 4:11. A thorough examination of *sarx* in the biblical witness
can be found in Dallas Willard, "Spiritual Formation and the Warfare Between the Flesh and
Human Spirit," *Journal of Spiritual Formation and Soul Care* 6, no. 2 (2013): 152–59.

ongoing influences of the "desires of the flesh" after their spiritual
awakening: "So I say, walk by the Spirit, and you will not gratify
the desires of the flesh. For the flesh desires what is contrary to
the Spirit, and the Spirit what is contrary to the flesh. They are
in conflict with each other, so that you are not to do whatever you
want" (Gal. 5:16–17).

For the Galatian Christians, clearly, the "desires of the flesh"
still swirl within. In fact, Paul says the desires of the flesh and
Spirit are in "conflict" in the Christian. David Bennett describes
this as a "war of loves,"[13] Jay Stringer as "a civil war of desires,"[14]
and Augustine as "the old and the new, the one carnal, the other
spiritual—in their struggle tore my soul apart."[15] The Christian
experience to which Paul is giving language is, among other things,
a conflict of desire. This explains why Paul speaks of desires in
the plural and the Spirit in the singular. Even after faith, ungodly
desires can still swirl about the Christian. Yet, presiding faithfully
in the middle is the ever-sustaining, never-changing, fully present
Spirit who speaks life and peace to us. This provides some comfort,
sure. But for most of us, it feels like (in Augustine's words) being
"torn apart."

Lamentably, far too many Christians fall prey to the idea that
their battle against "desires of the flesh" after years of faithful discipleship and spiritual pursuit represents a failure in their Christian
life. Or we interpret the ongoing presence of the flesh in our lives
as a failure. But is struggling with the flesh a sign we are failing in
our pursuit of God? The answer is surprising. The ongoing presence of the war of desire between the flesh and Spirit is, in reality,
a sign of the Spirit's presence. How can we say this? Because before

13. David Bennett, *A War of Loves: The Unexpected Story of a Gay Activist Discovering Jesus* (Grand Rapids: Zondervan, 2018).
14. "Pornography and Our Stories of Desire," The Allender Center at the Seattle School, March 12, 2022, https://theallendercenter.org/2022/03/pornography-and-our-stories-of-desire/.
15. *Confessions* 8.

we followed Jesus and were indwelt with the Spirit of God, there was *no* conflict with the flesh. We unthinkingly followed the flesh. There simply was no conflict. Now, the Spirit is giving birth to godly desires. The battle itself, ironically, is the sign that we're walking in the Spirit. The absence of a battle is the concern. As Edward Welch wrote, "The battle is good. . . . It is a sign the Spirit is on the move."[16]

Think of it like marital conflict. When I'm asked to serve as the officiant in someone's wedding, I invite them to go through five sessions of marriage preparation. There are important principles to learn in advance. But more importantly, I'm spying on them. Over the years, I've learned the hard way some signs that marriage isn't a good fit for a couple. The most telltale sign is an absence of conflict in the relationship. If they claim they never argue, I get worried. Why? Conflict is a sign that real communication is taking place, and the tension that will inevitably exist in their marriage is being practiced in courtship. The presence of healthy conflict in a relationship is often a sign that good things are taking place. That's not to say that all conflict is good. Abuse, manipulation, and gaslighting is not good conflict. But true and good conflict is a sign of true and good relationship.

The conflict between Spirit and flesh within us is a sign that we're on the right track. As you reflect on these matters, consider this an invitation to ignore the serpent's whispers you've been hearing for years:

> *Why haven't you gotten past this struggle yet, you failure?*
> *If you were really mature, you'd be over this by now.*
> *After that, you can't seriously think you are a child of God now,*
>   *can you?*

---

16. Edward Welch, *Addictions: A Banquet in the Grave* (Greensboro, NC: New Growth, 2011).

Clarity is paramount here. To be certain, experiencing the flesh's desires isn't a sin. Following them is. By his tone, Paul is undeniably stressing the differences between the one following the "desires of the flesh" and the one following the "desires of the Spirit" in Romans 8. For Paul, the two create fundamentally divergent trajectories in life. The person seeking the flesh's desire is bound to a life of perennial "hostility toward God," which, without opposition, leads invariably to what Paul calls an "ever-increasing wickedness" (Rom. 6:19). We desire more of the desires we follow. As Shakespeare wrote in *Troilus and Cressida*, "Desire is boundless and the act a slave to limit." The cycle can be endless. But the one being governed by the desires of the Spirit will experience "life and peace" (Rom. 8:6).

Paul is mapping out a road to life and a road to death. We will either follow the desires of the flesh or the desires of the Spirit. Paul never gives us a map for a third way. Listen to the apostle John in his first letter: "For everything in the world—the lust of the flesh, the lust of the eyes, and the pride of life—comes not from the Father but from the world. The world and its desires *pass away*, but whoever does the will of God lives forever" (1 John 2:16–17, emphasis mine). John likely could have had Genesis 3 in mind. All three areas of the "world and its desires" overlap the temptations in Eden. "Lust of the flesh" corresponds to the serpent's lie that the fruit was "good for food." "Lust of the eyes" connects to the humans' "desiring the fruit." And "pride of life" overlaps with the desire for "wisdom." Still, notice that John contends that the world's desires will "pass away."

This is instructive on two fronts. First, the flesh's desires are not consistent, eternal, or transcendent. They fluctuate, arising at certain times of the day, burning off at others. This is in contrast to the Spirit, whose desires are consistent, don't come and go, and transcend moments of life. Put another way, the flesh entices us into short-term enjoyment and relief that leads to long-term anxiety and death, while the Spirit invites us into painful faithfulness in the present leading to long-term life and peace.

Second, good news drips from this teaching. The flesh *will* eventually "pass away." But not soon enough. The flesh is here for now. And there's no discernable evidence from any New Testament writer that the flesh will go away during our earthly lifetime. One would think (or at least hope) that upon following Jesus the flesh would go away. But it doesn't. The person regenerated by Jesus will have the flesh until resurrection. Until then, we cannot reform or change the flesh. The flesh doesn't repent. We cannot improve the flesh or make it better. Nor can it be cut out. The flesh won't submit. As Paul says, the flesh "does not submit to God's law, nor can it do so" (Rom. 8:7). In lieu of ridding ourselves of the flesh, Paul lays out another option: "Those who belong to Christ Jesus have *crucified the flesh* with its passions and desires" (Gal. 5:24, emphasis added).

Until glory, we crucify the flesh. This is one of the most brilliant gems of the Christian tradition. Crucifying the flesh isn't synonymous with desire going away or changing. Crucifying the flesh is hanging it on the cross with Christ. Crucifying the flesh doesn't change it; it *kills* it. This is a lifelong process. By the Spirit, we refuse to let the flesh have the final say, the microphone on the stage of our lives. We don't win by improving the flesh. We win by crucifying the flesh—an all-out, life-long, bloody assault on the desires of Satan that have corrupted our old selves. Christlikeness is found in the daily work of laying down our desires of the flesh for the sake of faithfulness to Jesus.

There is only one way to do away with the flesh. We must be crucified with Christ. Only at that moment when I finally stop striving will I find my relief and experience true transformation. That's grace.

Years ago, the Illinois Department of Natural Resources reported that over 17,000 deer are killed yearly by oncoming traffic on the state's bustling highway system. The director, a man named Paul Shelton, revealed that deer deaths spiked in late fall more than any other time of the year. Why? The bucks were in rut in November—ready to find a mate. In the heat of mating season, far less forethought was being given to personal safety among the deer population of Illinois. "They're concentrating almost exclusively on reproductive activities," Shelton reported, "and are a lot less wary than they normally would be."[17]

Desire unhitched from truth, revelation, and wisdom is extraordinarily dangerous for any species. When desire lacks a moral framework, it can cause us to disregard the well-being of ourselves and others. We were made with pulsating desires. But these desires need boundaries. Without them, we become what the prophet Jeremiah describes as the "wild donkey . . . sniffing in the wind in her craving—in her heat who can restrain her?" (Jer. 2:24). Controlled by these passionate desires, we act like the wild donkey—what Eugene Peterson describes as "unrestrained and purposeless except for one thing, the satisfaction of desire."[18]

The life of unhinged passion is a very real possibility for those who have not accepted the God-ordained boundaries around desire. What happens—even to our desire of longing—when it's separated from God's design, boundaries, and presence? Naturally, it doesn't go away. It often becomes unhinged. This is evidenced in the New Testament's teaching on *epithumia*, or "lust."[19] Our knee-jerk reaction to the word *lust* is likely negative. Lust is a sin, a vice. More often than not, the word *epithumia* is meant in the New Testament

---

17. Curry Pikkaart, *7 Habits of Highly Healthy People* (Maitland, FL: Xulon, 2007), 87.

18. Eugene Peterson, *Run with the Horses: The Quest for Life at Its Best* (Downers Grove, IL: InterVarsity Press, 2009), 115.

19. W. F. Arndt, F. W. Gingrich, and F. W. Danker, "Ἐπιθυμία," in *A Greek-English Lexicon of the New Testament and Other Early Christian Literature*, 3rd ed. (Chicago, IL: University of Chicago Press, 2000), 372.

to be understood in a negative light. For instance, Paul warns the church in Rome that if they're dead set on disobedience and false worship, then God will "give them over in their *epithumia* of their hearts to sexual impurity" (Rom. 1:24). Later in that letter, Paul instructs them "not to follow their *epithumia*" (Rom. 13:14). Jesus teaches in the parable of the sower that God's good seed is choked out by "*epithumia* for other things come in and choke the word, making it unfruitful" (Mark 4:19).

Lust—any disordered desire that consumes us to use someone or something for our own fleshly gratification—always has the power to destroy those it controls and those it impacts. Full stop. Some scholars even suggest an intimate connection between idolatry in the Old Testament and lust in the New Testament. David Powlison says, "If 'idolatry' is the characteristic and summary Old Testament word for our drift from God, then 'desires' (*epithumia*) is the characteristic and summary New Testament word for the same drift."[20]

The word is a compound melding *epi* ("above") and *thumia* ("desire"). *Epithumia* is a strengthened form of *thumia*. Lust is a strong desire for something God hasn't given us. But this is only one side of *epithumia*.

Perplexingly, *epithumia* is also employed to describe a strong desire for something good in New Testament literature. For instance, Paul says he has an *epithumia* to be with the church in Thessalonica (1 Thess. 2:17). Elsewhere, he says he has an *epithumia* to "depart and be with Christ" (Phil. 1:23). Even Jesus says he *epithumia*'s to go to the Passover feast (Luke 22:15). If we translated these instances into English as "lust," they would carry quite the head-scratching meaning. Paul "lusts" to be with Jesus and the church in Thessalonica? Jesus "lusts" to go to a Passover meal?

---

20. David Powlison, "Idols of the Heart and 'Vanity Fair,'" *Journal of Biblical Counseling* 13, no. 2 (Winter 1995): 36.

Is lust good or bad? It's complicated. Yes *and* no. A strong desire for something that isn't given to us by God is called lust; this type of *epithumia* is unequivocally sinful. But a strong desire for something God-given is called longing—the positive side of *epithumia*. Desire, when displaced from Eden, has a power to become perverted and distorted. In short, lust is longing without a seatbelt. The core difference between lust and longing is what's being desired. A strong desire, like a sharp razor, can take a life, or perform life-saving surgery. The goal isn't *less* desire, but cultivated and sanctified desire toward godliness.

Christians, I've found, often beat themselves up for the simple fact that they experience sexual desire or think about sex. But this illustrates a great misunderstanding of the difference between longing and lust. Lust *can't* be the same as having sexual desire or merely thinking about sex. The Bible itself invites us to see sexual desire as sacred. It even invites us to think about sex. Take the Old Testament writing of the Song of Songs. By and large, this wisdom book is a moment-by-moment depiction of two lovers passionately embracing in what's believed to be the first night of the marital union. No detail is spared. There are smells. Even tastes. By our contemporary Christian standards, the text is borderline graphic, speaking of certain body parts with verdant agricultural metaphors such as mountain regions and goats' hair. There's a good reason some Jewish communities do not allow it to be read by children until they are sixteen years old.

Yet this steamy biblical literature is publicly read in Jewish synagogues during the Pentecost season—every single year. If a desire for sexual longing and the thought of sex is a sin, then is God causing us to stumble (1 Cor. 8:13) by inspiring and including it in the biblical canon?

Of course, God isn't causing us to stumble because the thought of sex isn't a sin. Nor is sexual longing. In religious environments where we are told to never think of these things, this is a welcome point of healing. Silence is the worst teacher. God loves us enough to talk about the birds and bees and to show us the intricacies of sexual longing in its appropriate boundaries. In the Song of Songs, we are taught to think about sex with the wise guide of the truth and God's Spirit. This is its power. It shows us the *alternative* to our world of pornography. As Old Testament scholar Richard Hess wrote, "The Song of Songs is erotic literature, distinguished from pornography with its brutality and oppressive caricature of women. . . . [It] focuses on the shared love and total commitment that the couple enjoys."[21]

To desire and contemplate God's gift of sex through the scrutinizing eye of the Spirit is like dreaming of a sunset that God has made. Should we also cease longing for a good meal with friends? Is it a sin to contemplate the beauties of another? The Christian life is the crucifixion of our flesh, not our desire.[22] We nail the flesh to the cross, not our good desire. The enemy is lust, not longing.

The flesh calls us until our death. Early in marriage, I held out secret hopes that my new vows would magically wave my fleshly sexual desires away. I assumed "I do" straightened out those crooked parts of me. Soon I learned that expectations like this are dangerous and unrealistic—in marriage and in the rest of life. Not only did my flesh not go away, but in some respects, it became aroused. In my naivete, this myth of diminishing desire produced undue anxiety and shame of perceived failure. It also revealed my ignorance. As a result, I've had to learn to stop condemning myself for having

---

21. Richard Hess, *Song of Songs*, Baker Commentary on the Old Testament (Grand Rapids: Baker, 2005), 20.

22. David Benner writes, "Despite what you may have heard, Christian spirituality is not about the crucifixion of desire. Rather it is about the distillation and focusing of desire." David Benner, *Desiring God's Will: Aligning Our Hearts with the Heart of God* (Downers Grove, IL: InterVarsity Press, 2015), 77.

flesh. A healthy theology of the flesh reminds us that marriage (or anything else) will not and cannot reform or evolve the flesh. No amount of prayer, counseling, spiritual direction, or fasting fixes it. But that's okay. God doesn't invite us to change our flesh. God invites us to see that we are no longer enslaved and controlled by our flesh. We are now freed to serve the desires of the Spirit. In Jesus, the voice of the flesh no longer has the final say over our lives.

Around the time the New Testament was being composed and compiled, a series of spiritual writings were being penned detailing how the earliest Christian communities followed Jesus. One was known as *The Shepherd of Hermas*. For nearly four centuries, this spiritual vision was unique in its near-universal popularity and influence. Its widespread appeal, in fact, was such that many considered it worthy of inclusion in the New Testament. Though it didn't make the cut, many believed it should have, as evidenced by the fact that it was included in early manuscripts such as the *Codex Sinaiticus*. More than any other noncanonical writing, it's believed to have had a resounding influence on the earliest Christian communities that were tasked with the ministry of Christ in a hostile Roman empire.

The author—purported to be Pius, the brother of the first bishop of Rome—describes a man named Hermas, who experienced five "visions" about Christian living. The *Shepherd* is so significant historically because it offers the reader a bird's-eye view of some of the initial spiritual concerns the earliest Christians faced. One such issue was baptism. At the time, a theological debate consumed the church over whether someone could be forgiven for sins they committed after baptism. Bart Ehrman, a critic of the New Testament, goes so far as to suggest that the core theme of the writing is "what Christians can do if they have fallen into sin after being baptized."[23] Many held to a view that there was only limited

---

23. Bart Ehrman, *Lost Scriptures: Books That Did Not Make It into the New Testament* (Oxford: Oxford University Press, 2005), 251.

(if any) grace for these sins. This debate likely led Roman Emperor Constantine to be baptized only moments before his death.

In the opening vision, Hermas catches a glimpse of a staggeringly beautiful woman. Not long after, she ascends to heaven and calls out to Hermas telling him that God will judge him for having looked at her with desire. Then the author of *Shepherd* bursts into the scene. He says there *is* grace for second chances.[24] The door of grace is open. The God of grace that first saved us continues to save us through grace.

A story like this may seem trivial to modern readers. But the ancient tale illustrates one of the difficulties the early church faced around spiritual formation. The earliest Christians were quickly learning that while they had been saved and set free by the death and resurrection of Jesus, they still sinned. They lived in the same bodies as they did before they followed Jesus. The flesh hadn't left them.

The reality that our desires—particularly fleshly desires—remain with us after following Jesus is a central feature of the writings of the fourth-century Christian St. Augustine. Although he is one of the most influential theologians in the Western church, Augustine's route toward Christianity was a circuitous one. Raised by a Christian mother, Augustine set off for college in Carthage at the age of seventeen. There, he breathed the smooth intellectual air of the philosophers and began a life of intellectualism. As did many, Augustine also enjoyed the dark desires of sexual lusts of Carthage. Around this time, Augustine cast aside the faith of his childhood. Later, returning to the faith he'd left, Augustine would give witness to an ongoing struggle with unwanted, ungodly sexual desires throughout his subsequent writings. Given how consistently desire plays as a theme of Augustine's writings, one scholar has called him "the doctor of desire."[25]

---

24. Although, oddly, only one second chance. But it does raise an important ethical issue in the early church of what one does with sin after baptism.

25. Christopher West, *Fill These Hearts: God, Sex, and the Universal Longing* (New York: Image, 2012), 35.

Upon his own dramatic turn to Christ, Augustine famously wrote, "Oh, Master, make me chaste and celibate . . . but not yet!"[26] This is a man in a civil war of desire. And it is this kind of honesty that has attracted so many to engage Augustine's thought through the centuries. The apostle Paul speaks of his own similar inner conflict. In a letter to the Corinthians, Paul vulnerably describes what he simply calls "a thorn in my flesh" (2 Cor. 12:7). It is clear this thorn has brought Paul tremendous pain and difficulty—he goes so far as to say it has "tormented" him. Still, the nature of his thorn remains mysterious. Some believe Paul is referencing a sexual struggle. Others think he had some kind of struggle with addiction. Still others wonder if this "thorn" was some relational disturbance that hindered him or an illness. One scholar suggested to me that Paul was grieving not being one of the original twelve disciples. (This makes sense, given that the second letter to the Corinthians is largely about arguing that he was a legitimate apostle.) All this to say: the precise nature of Paul's thorn remains a mystery to this day.[27]

We do know, however, that by the time Paul writes this letter, the thorn has not been taken away. "Three times," Paul says, he "pleaded with the Lord to take it away" (v. 8). He pleaded to no avail. Nonetheless, Paul offers an interpretation. Paul believes God allowed the thorn to remain to keep him from "becoming conceited." That is, God has sovereignly allowed his thorn to remain to keep Paul from the sin of pride. Paul's attitude is instructive. Paul appears to see this thorn—whatever it is—as a gift. It is making him a deeper man of God.

My friend Tony has a similar story. He began following Jesus as a young gay man. Tony's conversion was powerful and

---

26. *Confessions* 8.7.

27. To add to this, there is a growing group of New Testament scholars who believe that Paul is actually referencing a time *before* he began to follow Jesus. I am not persuaded, but it does show that the topic is hotly debated in contemporary scholarship.

transformative. Still he found himself in the same body he was in before his conversion to Christ. His desires didn't up and disappear. Today, he is married to a beautiful woman and pastoring a church. Still, having walked alongside Jesus for years, those same desires that swirled within him the day he met Jesus remain. Yet, he reflects, these unwanted desires have served as surprising gifts to him. They are molding him into a man that desperately needs God every single day for every single breath as he submits his every desire to Christ. Through his thorn, God is leading Tony into increasing faithfulness, patience, and resilience. The Spirit hovers over the chaos of his desires. That thorn—those who know Tony would say—has made him the most patient, gentle, loving follower of Jesus they've ever meet.

Thorns hurt. But they're a quiet gift. Of course, it's hard to appreciate that when they're in your side.

Can God take away our unwanted desires? Sure he can. But Scripture, church history, and life suggests that this is not always guaranteed. Perhaps the longer we live with them—and find our humble confidence in God's grace—the more we start seeing the rose attached to them.

I identify so much with Augustine, Paul, and Tony. Like many, I'd love to say that Jesus rearranged my life to such a degree that my flesh was immediately gouged out—that the waters of baptism washed off my flesh. But they didn't. I've followed Jesus for three decades. And the same flesh, the same thorn that was in my side then is with me today. I haven't shaken it. But I have learned to listen more to the voice of the Spirit over the flesh. The thorns haven't gone away. But they have become less painful as I've lived with them. They've accomplished so much in me.

It's in the moments of my life when I am most vulnerable, most broken, most weak, that I can hear Jesus say to me as he did to Paul, "My grace is sufficient for you, for my power is made perfect in weakness" (v. 9).

Everyone born after Eden has a mysterious mix of desires, godly and fleshly. What do we do with our fleshly desires? Despite receiving a considerable amount of bad press in recent decades, one of the most relevant theological traditions from ancient Christian spirituality is the notion that we're all *born* sinful. Some call this "original sin." The basic idea is that we're all born with disordered souls into a spiritually fragmented world that systematically gravitates toward evil desires. As evolved and enlightened as we may think we are, we arrive in this world spiritually stillborn, predisposed toward rebellion. Our essence—in Paul's language—is "dead in your transgressions and sins" (Eph. 2:1). We're all born with flesh as a preexisting spiritual condition.

Because we're people with flesh, we build empires of flesh. At our present moment, powers lurk behind the cultural curtain seeking to awaken and reshape our desires into some graven and grotesque image. This empire of flesh has one rule: obey every desire. "The heart wants what it wants," Woody Allen proclaimed after leaving his wife for his wife's daughter.[28] The whims of the heart are it's sacred commandments. It's a vision Sigmund Freud—who saw repression of sexual desire as the cause of *all* evil (including Fascism and war)—would be proud of. The dogma of this empire has but one anathema: *not* obeying desires. Slowly and surely, we have been colonized into this empire's ways—learning its language and eating at its table—not by coercion or force but by titillation, suggestion, incitement, and provocation.

We're all formed by this empire, told from our earliest years that we're bound by the desires of our birth. In failing to resist, we're led into a great deal of dangerous self-talk. "I can never stop this."

---

28. Jeff Richman, "The Heart Wants What It Wants," Green-Wood, July 14, 2011, https://www.green-wood.com/2011/the-heart-wants-what-it-wants/.

"I was born this way." "This is just a part of who I am." "Nobody gets to pick their kinks." When we submit uncritically to this self-talk, we can be assured this empire has won us. Part of being a Christian is resisting the empire of flesh.

We mustn't forget that the early Christian church was born into an empire as well. Rome, the dominant global force of its time, had singularly global power to enforce upon people its rules and regulations. Rome believed it could use marriage and sex as political control. Men were given permission to marry whomever they wished. Understandably, this decree put many of the earliest Christians at odds with Rome. For the Christians, Rome couldn't have their sexuality. This confrontation was felt most by those early Christian women who had received from God the gift of chastity. A whole community of holy women—including Catherine of Alexandria, Margaret of Antioch, Barbara of Nicomedia, and Dorothea of Caesarea—resisted Rome's marital decrees with their very lives. Known to Christian history as the "Virgin Martyrs," they offered up their lives instead of allowing Rome to have either their bodies or their sexuality.

The Virgin Martyrs resisted by refusing to allow the empire to colonize their desires. Rome could take their lives. It could place them in prison. It could chain them up and put them in the coliseums. But it couldn't have their hearts. They desired Jesus. Jesus alone. Jesus above everything.

The Virgin Martyrs are a model for us. Their quiet witness reminds us that martyrdom isn't solely the sacrifice of a life. It's the sacrifice of everything—even our desires—to the way of Jesus. The empire hates these kinds of martyrs. It's telling of the empire that few groups in our moment are as misunderstood (and even vilified) than those who refuse to bend their knees to the idea that we are slavishly bound to our sexual desires. Countless friends of mine, men and women who wrestle with unwanted sexual desires, daily offer their bodies up onto the cross as an act of faithfulness to the

Spirit of God. These sexual martyrs are ridiculed by nearly everyone—by some conservatives for claiming to have such desires and by some progressives for not submitting to those desires. They will receive their crown of glory for their faithfulness to Christ.

We aren't bound to the empire or the desires it says we must bow to.

The Virgin Martyrs show us a way. As with the exiles of old, it's exhausting to daily face this empire as it pulls and tears at us, crouching at our morning door. But the longer we resist, the stronger we become. We won't give up. We *can't* give up. We must resist this empire, the one of which John says, "There will be no rest day or night for those who worship the beast and its image" (Rev. 14:11). This beast's empire bears no rest. But in Christ, there's rest.

The cross is a sabbath for our desire. Upon Calvary, our desires are welcomed to rest. There, our weary desires find their respite: "I don't have to follow my desires. I am free. I can rest them on the cross of Jesus."

The cross also frees us from beating ourselves up for our burning desires we know aren't of God. We didn't pick our flesh. And we don't have to hate ourselves because of it.

Rest your desire, friend. Because the empire doesn't own you.

Chapter 5

WANING DESIRE

We continue on. In writing this chapter, a peculiar news story about a Mumbai businessman named Raphael Samuel drew my attention. Displeased with life's outcome and angered by his own existence, Samuel sued his parents for having him. Samuel's legal argument was straightforward. He hadn't given consent to his birth. Thus, his begrudging existence wasn't his fault. Someone had to pay. He didn't mince his words: "I wish I was not born. . . . I'd rather not be here. You know it's like there's a nice room, but I don't want to be in that room."[1]

Few would disagree with Samuel's sentiment. Life *is* profoundly difficult. But are parents to blame for their children's pain? If not, who? Something of Samuel's litigiousness simmers underneath our cultural moment. Scripture resounds on the fact that God created us out of desire, not compulsion, coercion, or capitulation. But what if *we* don't desire us? Worse yet, what if life isn't satisfying or we don't want the life God wants for us? The prophetic lament of Jonah lends language to the existential angst many contemporary hearts nurture at present: "It would be better for me to die than to live" (Jonah 4:8).

Who's to blame? I see two options: someone is to blame (God, ourselves, someone else), or no one is to blame. Many believe the

---

1. Geeta Pandey, "Indian man to sue parents for giving birth to him," BBC News, February 7, 2019, https://www.bbc.com/news/world-asia-india-47154287.

second to be the most rational response. Remove God and no one is to blame. For a growing number, this line of thinking has coalesced into an emerging secular sensibility that seeks to dissolve the idea of God and any whiff of transcendent meaning. With no divine meaning or purpose, we're freed to determine meaning for ourselves. Eventually, this thinking meanders into the chilly lands of existentialism. "Man," writes Jean-Paul Sartre, the most famous existentialist of them all, "is nothing else but what he makes of himself."[2] More recently, this has been captured by the thinking of atheist Richard Dawkins in *The God Delusion*: "There is something infantile in the presumption that somebody else has a responsibility to give your life meaning and point. . . . The truly adult view, by contrast, is that our life is as meaningful, as full and as wonderful as we choose to make it."[3]

Maturity, in this vein, is marked by no longer needing anything (such as a God) outside oneself whom one can blame or rely upon. This secular eucharist of self-reliance is a powerful ideology—one that is giving shape to much of our moment. And, admittedly, these arguments have cultural sway and have proven seductively persuasive in the public space—over time metastasizing into cultural icons that impact millions. Cue in the iconic words of Tyler Durden in the 1999 movie *Fight Club*: "Listen to me! You have to consider the possibility that God does not like you. He never *wanted* you. In all probability, he hates you."

It's understandable why this is so attractive. On one hand, it alleviates the existential difficulty of conceiving of a God who desires our existence in a world of suffering. But all the more, a worldview devoid of a desiring Creator liberates us from our responsibility and accountability to someone outside of ourselves. Since no higher power exists, it's thought, we're "free" to do what we

2. Jean-Paul Sartre, *Existentialism and Human Emotions* (New York: Carol, 1990), 15.
3. Richard Dawkins, *The God Delusion* (London: Bantam, 2006), 403–4.

want. We become our own higher power. As orphans in a cold, free, meaningless universe, the world becomes little more than a Pleasure Island for our inner Pinocchios to discover the fetishes and frivolity that lay within. The only desire that exists is the desire within yourself. Leave God behind. Follow desire. You do you.[4]

The Western world appears at the present to be losing its desire for God. But this is not only a cultural phenomenon. There is, for many of us, a very personal dynamic to this. Many of us have lost a desire for God—something this chapter will explore. Even more so, it will explore how God invites us to reenter desire with the goal of experiencing God afresh. It's understandable why God desiring us could be so unsettling. If we aren't desired, we have less responsibility. The desire of one creature beckons a response from another. This is a parent's life. When my eleven-year-old bursts into my office wanting to shoot hoops in the front, I have two options: play or keep working. My crisis of decision is averted if I curate my life in such a way that there are never opportunities for him to ask. No desire, no decision, no hurt feelings.

This is why parents would often rather do nothing than do it wrong.[5] Absence guards against the wounding of desire. As a recovering introvert, I've long felt discomfort when someone expresses interest in friendship. Their desire for companionship threatens my introversion. Will I give up my own desire of reading dead theologians and the blessed bliss of silence, quiet, and alone time? Or open myself up to the dangers of relationship and all that comes with it: time, energy, vulnerability, and the possibility of hurt.

---

4. In his explosive thought, Charles Taylor contends that the late modern secular conscience has thrown off the old religious restraints and returned unrestrained toward hedonism: "In recent centuries, and especially the last one, countless people have thrown off what has been presented to them as the demands of religions, and have seen themselves as rediscovering the value of the ordinary human satisfactions that these demands forbade. They had the sense of coming back to a forgotten good, a treasure buried in everyday life." Charles Taylor, *A Secular Age* (Cambridge, MA: Harvard University Press, 2007), 627.

5. I'm grateful to my friend Michelle Watson, who often quotes this in her talks and conversations on parenting. Used with permission.

There's a certain freedom and diminished responsibility that comes with being unwanted, unseen, unneeded. When I'm not wanted, my introverted self is given free domain. In a way, desire demands both risk and response.[6]

God's desire threatens our individualism. We'll either return desire, or we won't. One can assume that a world without divine desire is safer, more predictable, maybe even more fun. But it's also more treacherous, inhumane, and stripped of the risks of love. A world without divine desire—to borrow the French anthropologist and ethnographer Claude Levi-Strauss—is a world of "floating symbols."[7] Things and people no longer have inherent meaning or purpose. Everything becomes what we desire it to be. Texts lose meaning; we give them meaning. Texts don't have meaning in themselves; they only mean what we want them to mean. The Bible eventually means nothing in itself other than what one projects upon it. Experiences don't point toward anything; they are what we make of them. Everything is up for grabs: sex, gender, justice, bodies, ideas, words. Without transcendent desire, nothing bears fixed, transcendent meaning in itself. In this world, people make themselves.

Still, remove God's desire and our desires become our gods—which is treacherous. It's a world where I'm not bound to love anyone I don't want to love. I can block, unfriend, even ghost the undesired. This language should remind us of whole populations that were annihilated in the Holocaust for being "undesirables."[8] It's a human only if I desire it.

---

6. Or as Sabatian Moore writes, "Risk is the refusal to forget desire." Moore, "The Crisis of an Ethic Without Desire," in *Theology and Sexuality: Classic and Contemporary Readings*, ed. Eugene F. Rogers (Oxford: Blackwell, 2002), 159.

7. Claude Lévi-Strauss, *Introduction to the Work of Marcel Mauss* (New York: Routledge, 2013).

8. Stanley Hauerwas contends that our undoing of God made space for the Holocaust in his *Unleashing the Scripture: Freeing the Bible from Captivity to America* (Nashville: Abingdon, 1993), chap. 16.

For many, desire for God has all but extinguished. We're like Adam in "The Creation of Adam" in Michelangelo's famous painting in the Sistine Chapel. God reaches out his outstretched arm in desire for his creature. The creature's response? Bent wrist, lazily stretched, haphazardly responsive, as if to mutter under his breath . . .

"Meh."

───────

To be converted is to return our desire to God. "God made us without our permission," Augustine wrote, "but he will not save us without our consent."[9] God created us through desire. But it's our reciprocity of desire to God's grace that inaugurates our transformation. Jesus calls us. But our response won't be forced. We follow willingly through desire. Anglican theologian and poet Thomas Traherne wrote about the dance of desire in our creation and our salvation: "Wants are the bands and ligatures between us and God. Had we not wanted, we could never have been obliged. . . . From eternity it was requisite that we should want."[10]

To be sure, one's desire for God looks different in different seasons. One's early faith can be marked by a tsunami of new and all-encompassing desires to love God—what J. I. Packer called an "arousal of affections God-ward."[11] I experienced this. Early in my own faith, I'd awaken at 5:00 a.m. to read the Psalms every day. My prayers were drenched in faith and boldness and fervency. I memorized books of Scripture. I shared my faith. I desired God with every atom of my existence.

───────

9. Quoted in John Amsberry, *More of You Through Prayer* (Bloomington, IN: AuthorHouse, 2009), 5.

10. Thomas Traherne, *Centuries of Meditations*, Cosimo Classics (New York: Cosimo, 2009), 33. This quote was pointed out in the introduction to Jessica Martin, *Holiness and Desire* (Norwich, UK: Canterbury Press, 2020).

11. J. I. Packer, *A Quest for Godliness: The Puritan Vision of the Christian Life* (Wheaton, IL: Crossway, 1990), 27.

Somewhere along the way, however, my desire changed. I still desired. But the excitement waned. I started waking up later.

This didn't mean my desire was dying. As you may remember from the previous chapter, a changing desire is not a dying desire. My desire was maturing. Marital love in a honeymoon looks different after fifty years of marriage. By sheer grace, prodigal desires will come home from time to time. When they do, be present. Enjoy them. The shy gift of felt desire is beautiful, enlivening, and breathtaking even if it doesn't always show its face. But for most of us, there will be times when we don't have the same felt desire for God we used to have. It's equally necessary to be aware and present in these moments. In walking through the shadows of desire, we need a resilient posture and a prayerful spirit. We'll need to surround ourselves with people who can guide, love, and support us toward God as desire has dissipated remembering that God desires us still in both experiences.

Desires change. But, as Paul wrote, love remains (1 Cor. 13:8). A distinctive mark of Christian maturity is one's ability to continue following Jesus when our desires have abandoned us. Experiencing a passionate felt desire for God isn't an unwritten prerequisite for God to continue in his love for us. That is to say, our commitment to Jesus goes beyond what we feel like we want today. The saints of old attest to this paradox. In Philippians 1, for example, Paul writes to a church from a prison cell and openly wishes to die and be with Jesus rather than live on for another day:

> For to me, to live is Christ and to die is gain. If I am to go on living in the body, this will mean fruitful labor for me. Yet what shall I choose? . . . I am torn between the two: I desire to depart and be with Christ, which is better by far; but it is more necessary for you that I remain in the body. Convinced of this, I know that I will remain. (Phil. 1:21–25)

Paul is torn between a desire to die and be with Jesus and the "necessary" thing of continuing his earthly ministry. It takes maturity to distinguish between Paul's "desire" (what he wants) and what he calls "necessary" (what's right). Paul's letter is a timeless witness to the fact that, from time to time, a good desire doesn't warrant our action to its end. Sometimes the necessary and the want are very different things.

We could call the "necessary" thing a duty. Duty is a powerful concept, often misunderstood. In short, duty is acting on principle apart from desire. Let me illustrate. A few years ago, I was invited to introduce renowned biblical scholar N. T. Wright at a major conference. In front of thousands, I publicly thanked Wright for writing a book that nearly single-handedly had rescued my faith in college. I introduced him. The audience stood to applaud. I sat in the front row. His lecture was mind-bending. But there remained one problem: his lecture went too long. An *hour* too long. I was in a pickle. Just after introducing my hero, I was given the unenviable task of having to loudly whisper from the front row that he needed to "wrap things up." Wright was generous, as predictable. In short order, he finished his talk. To this day, I still lament sending him conflicting messages of both gratitude that he'd rescued my faith and correction that he needed to get off the stage.

That was duty. I *wanted* to listen to Wright talk forever. But my duty required me to move things along.

Indeed, there remain moments in our lives when we follow Jesus out of desire. For the resilient Christian, however, there will also be moments when we follow Jesus out of duty—what Paul calls the "necessary." Sometimes we follow Jesus out of desire. Sometimes on duty.

The lens of desire and duty is an interesting way to look at human cultures.[12] Some cultures are desire cultures and others are

---

12. In fact, Dallas Willard argues that there's an inherent conflict between duty (what he calls "law") and desire. Willard, "Spiritual Formation and the Warfare Between the Flesh and Human Spirit," *Journal of Spiritual Formation and Soul Care* 6, no. 2 (2013): 155.

duty cultures. Take politics, for example: progressives, it's been said, fall in love with their candidate; conservatives fall in line with their party. Or consider intergenerational differences: my grandparents' generation, undertaking the fight against the Third Reich in World War II, upended their lives to fight in a global conflict. My grandfather Tex was a man of his generation. After being drafted to play basketball by the Chicago Bulls, he abandoned his dream to go and fight in the war following the bombing of Pearl Harbor—all out of a duty to his country. He didn't want to. He had a *duty* to.

When he was still alive, it was virtually impossible to get Tex to talk about the war. He never boasted about his duty or his stories. I couldn't help but notice how starkly this stood in contrast to my generation, which can't eat a good meal without taking a picture and boasting it on social media. Clearly, our generations are very different.

In the postwar era, there's been a notable shift away from duty toward desire. But in some ways, we're in an awkward space between duty and desire cultures. Increasingly, in issues of justice, environmental care, and inclusivity, there's an emerging absolutism and duty-bound ethic where right and wrong are seemingly viewed as ascendent moralities that are seen by many as being beyond question. Yet in the realm of sexuality, consumerism, and personal identity, we've been told that we're liberated to do whatever we want so long as no one is hurt. The result is a confusing mixture of duty applied in some realms and desire to others. Duty in the streets. Desire in the sheets.

Nonetheless, a shift appears to be taking place. On a cultural level, some are pushing back against some of the unquestionable absolutes the Western world has enthroned. For instance, Christine Emba's widely read *Washington Times* article "Consent Is Not Enough" made a thought-provoking case that the West's application of "consent" as the ultimate moral duty in sexual relationships has led to a near-complete loss of the meaning of sex. For Emba, all that matters now in the eyes of many Westerners is the consent of saying yes to sexual activity. Of course, Emba isn't diminishing the importance of sexual consent. Nor am I. But consent as the sole remaining duty in sexual intimacy sanitizes sex of its greater, glorious purpose. The duty of consent, Emba contends, should be the "floor" of our sexual ethic. We've made it the "ceiling."[13]

How, then, does duty serve us? A duty isn't an end unto itself. A duty helps us get somewhere. Rigid duty can be destructive. Think of the abused wife white-knuckling it through a marriage in the name of being faithful. Without the right goal, duty becomes what Thomas Merton called "bad asceticism."[14] This is why identifying the goal of duty is so critical. "Life is shaped by the end you live for," Merton wrote. "You are made in the image of what you desire."[15] We discern a good or bad duty by its goal, its end point. Duty as a goal can lead to rigid religiosity devoid of life. David Benner puts words to this:

> Despite how it is sometimes presented, desire is right at the center of the spiritual life. A sense of obligation may sometimes be enough to keep you going to church, but only desire will keep you open to God and still seeking when your experience in church is filled with frustration and is irrelevant to your deepest spiritual longings.[16]

Benner suggests that duty should always have a goal of awakening desire. But it shouldn't replace desire. A duty performed well can awaken desire. One way to understand duty is by thinking of

---

13. Christine Emba, "Consent Is Not Enough: We Need a New Sexual Ethic," *Washington Post* (blog), March 17, 2022, https://www.washingtonpost.com/opinions/2022/03/17/sex-ethics-rethinking-consent-culture/.

14. Thomas Merton, *Contemplative Prayer* (New York: Image, 1971), 15.

15. Thomas Merton, *Thoughts in Solitude* (New York: Shambhala, 1993), 55.

16. David Benner, *Soulful Spirituality: Becoming Fully Alive and Deeply Human* (Grand Rapids: Brazos, 2011), 15.

someone you know who is masterful at the piano. Almost always, in my experience, individuals like this had a caretaker who forced them to play piano as a child. Often, they hated playing the piano at the time. Yet they've come to love it as adults. This is the power of duty. With duty, the desire isn't always there from the beginning, but duty can help cultivate it. When we don't desire to live the way of Jesus, the duty of following Jesus can produce the same effect.

This was one of the main points C. S. Lewis bears in his final published book—a series of reflections on prayer called *Letters to Malcolm*.[17] Within, Lewis contends that any practice of duty, in and of itself, is the result of imperfection. Were we as humans fully righteous and sanctified, we wouldn't need duty. As one commentator on Lewis's works writes, "If we were perfect (as we will be in heaven), then goodness and righteous deeds would flow out from us as naturally as scent wafts from a flower. We would pray naturally and spontaneously out of our perfect, righteous hearts."[18]

For Lewis, duty plays a mediating role when perfection is not present. When desire is absent, duty can help structure our lives so desire might return. Desire *can* be the fruit of duty. And we can thank God for duty, for it saved humanity from sin. Jesus didn't desire to die. It was necessary for him to die. Cross is the duty. Resurrection is the desire. Duty, as such, is seen in those moments when we put aside a lesser desire to do a greater desire—trading the want for the "necessary." Desire and duty are the two feet of discipleship.[19]

---

17. C. S. Lewis, *Letters to Malcolm: Chiefly on Prayer* (New York: HarperCollins, 2017).

18. Tony Payne, "Fire Extinguishers," *The Briefing* (blog), August 6, 1991, http://thebriefing.com.au/1991/08/fire-extinguishers/.

19. Duty is often assumed to be the spirituality of the Puritan and desire the spirituality of the Pietist. But they are both needed. For an interesting study of the life of William Perkins, whose ministry brought desire and duty together, see Christopher Henderson, "Desire and Duty: The Spirituality of William Perkins," *Churchman* 131, no. 4 (2017): 307–23.

Again, the security of our identity is predicated upon God's desire, not our own. Relating to God hangs on God's perfect love for us, not (as some believe) on our perfect love for God. God's desire for us, furthermore, isn't dependent upon our felt desires for God. Our felt desires are fickle and unreliable. That doesn't undermine the crucial role desiring God plays in our formation. But putting all the weight of our identity on whether we are conjuring up enough desire for God sustains a false perception of our spiritual life. And it perpetuates an identity built on the self rather than the grace of God.

This couldn't have more bearing than when we compare our own desire for God with other people's desire for God. As an avid reader of Christian history, I'm often overwhelmed with "faith envy" in reading the writings of reformers and revivalists.[20] I always feel jealous after reading John Wesley: "Give me one hundred preachers who fear nothing but sin and desire nothing but God, and I care not a straw whether they be clergymen or laymen, such alone will shake the gates of hell and set up the kingdom of heaven upon earth."[21]

I want that passion. But I don't always have it. Encountering the pulsating desires of people like Wesley renews my reverence for them and leaves me doubly worried I'm failing. This isn't uncommon. In the shadows of our heroes, we often wish we had their desire for God, which seems to roar and glow, rather than our own, which seems to sputter and flicker. Unnamed and unseen, these envies of desire can linger a lifetime.

One of my students is a pastor's kid. He vividly described mornings in his household. He would wake up and find his father in fervent prayer in the dark twilight hours. My student's father is his hero. But he also acknowledged that this memory led to years

---

20. Barbara Brown Taylor, *Holy Envy: Finding God in the Faith of Others* (Norwich: Canterbury Press, 2019).

21. Quoted in Wesley Duewel, *Ablaze for God* (Grand Rapids: Zondervan, 2018), 107.

of self-condemnation. His passions seemed miniscule compared to his father's. Every day that he wakes up late, he fights against descending into a shame cycle that whispers that he doesn't desire God the same way his dad does. He is jealous of his dad's deep desire for God.

All envy, more or less, is a desire to be on the inside. In an obscure essay called "The Inner Ring," C. S. Lewis suggests that we spend our lives desperately seeking to enter into some mythical "inner ring" of those on some inside. Giving into this envy, life becomes a series of sequential moments of the gnawing sense that we're always on the outside looking in. Lewis writes, "I believe that in all men's lives at certain periods, and in many men's lives at all periods between infancy and extreme old age, one of the most dominant elements is the desire to be inside the local Ring and the terror of being left outside."[22]

That "desire to be inside" fuels much of our envy. Of course, the Christian faith has no inside group. "All have sinned and fall short," Paul writes, "of the glory of God" (Rom. 3:23). The divine fellowship can only be entered through faith. Even our most beloved heroes probably experienced spiritual slumps they didn't dare include in their journals. We spend our lives secretly judging the desires in our own hearts with the projected desires of others around us. No wonder we feel like failures. We must remember that our basis of adoption as children of God isn't on conjuring up enough desire. It's through faith alone. Our poverty of desire may come with great consternation, mean self-talk, and frustration, but our adoption as daughters and sons isn't built on the fluctuating level of our own desire.

I've had to come to terms with the fact that my desire for God comes and goes. This connects to two childhood experiences with

---

22. C. S. Lewis, "The Inner Ring," memorial lecture, King's College, University of London, 1944, https://www.lewissociety.org/innerring/.

the same familial figure. On one occasion, I asked him to read me a particular book. He wanted to read me a different book. After I won him over, he stopped, stared at me, and said, "A. J., you always get what you want, don't you?" I was seven or eight. That same figure would later respond to any moment I named my desire, "Well, A. J., now you know what it's like to want." Both responses were intended as lighthearted comments, but they stuck with me. Playing these tapes over and over in my head for thirty years has wounded my desire and internalized within me a belief that my desires were mostly bad and untrustworthy. "You always get what you want." *A. J., you're a selfish brat who always gets what he wants.* "Well, now you know what it's like to want." *A. J., your desires are bad, wrong, a mistake.*

Unintentional curses like these produced a toxic combination of shame and embarrassment that left the impression that I was bad because of my desires. As a result, I learned to hide my desires and to attune them to everyone around me. I rarely listened to my desires, and when I did, they came out so ferociously as to be destructive and harmful. This persisted into adulthood. To this day, I hate being asked what I want for my birthday or Christmas. I never know my desires. So I never have answers. In my malformed desires, I learned that one of the most powerful means to gain control and power was to withhold my desire from those closest to me.

I feel like I have a disability of desire. As a child, desires were hidden. As an adult, I oscillate between hiding my desire and withholding my desire as a power play—at great cost to those nearest me. But Jesus meets us in our desires. If he can heal our bodies, why can't he heal our desires? The healing of my desire has begun by actually listening to Jesus in Matthew 19: "Then people brought little children to Jesus for him to place his hands on them and pray for them. But the disciples rebuked them. Jesus said, 'Let the little children come to me, and do not hinder them, for the kingdom of heaven belongs to such as these.' When he had placed his hands on them, he went on from there" (19:13–15). Jesus welcomes the children. He wants all the children to come. He even desires our inner child to come to him. It's the adults who try to keep them away.

Today, I'm walking in healing by whispering to Jesus all those hidden desires I never knew or named when I was a child. *I need physical contact. I want a friend. I want a dad to play with. I wish someone wanted me right now.* Jesus listens. And Jesus responds. Jesus welcomes *all* of my childhood into his arms. I've learned that the healing of my desire comes as I allow the inner child to come to him battered and ashamed in all his brokenness. I have had to learn to ignore the rebuke of my inner adult who thinks this whole thing is a waste of time. That child and his desires deserve to be listened to, even if it's later than it should have happened.

"We must be transformed," writes Stanley Hauerwas. "We must be freed from our ill-formed desires, if we are to see that this is God's Son."[23] Thank God, Jesus can heal even retroactively. When we bring those deadened, shamed, and atrophied desires to Jesus, he touches them—raising them to new life. It's not difficult to sense when someone has placed too much weight on their ability to conjure up desire for God. I hear it when I ask my students about their relationship with God. Their responses reveal so much:

I haven't been reading my Bible very much.
I really don't want to pray—and I really don't.
I don't desire God all that much.

When we place the sole weight of our spiritual identity upon whether we desire undertaking certain activities for God, we're set up for failure. Our identity goes deeper than our fickle excitement. By basing our sense of self-worth exclusively on the depth

---

23. Stanley Hauerwas, *A Cross-Shattered Church: Reclaiming the Theological Heart of Preaching* (Grand Rapids: Brazos, 2009), 30.

of our desire for God, we end up replacing the Passion of Christ's death on the cross with our own passions. How quickly we turn a discipline into an indulgence. And how dangerous it is to place the load-bearing weight of our identity on how excited we are to read our Bibles from day to day. Losing a desire for a discipline isn't the same as losing a desire for God. We all experience desire loss—be it for God, church, doing devotions, prayer, you name it. We want it one day and not the next. We can all be collectively grateful that the essence of our identity are not merely the sum total of our unpredictable desires. God can—and does—hold us when we lose our desires. It's all grace. Or it is nothing at all.

———

The experience of losing one's felt desire for God is not a new experience. Evagrius Ponticus was a fourth century desert father who described what he called "acedia"—a spiritual lull and lethargy—in his writing *On the Eight Thoughts*. Charles Spurgeon writes about his own form of spiritual depression in a lecture he wrote entitled "The Minister's Fainting Fits." Even Mother Teresa was discovered after her death to have filled pages of her journals with grief and sadness that she had lost a desire to love God. These are our forebears. And even they experienced a profound loss of felt desire for God. Be it acedia, spiritual depression, or a loss of felt desire, we must choose to remember our identity in Jesus is founded more on who we are than what we do.

I would even go so far as to say that when we find our identity in God through Christ, we are permitted to enter new terrains of freedom to see God in the desires he has given us. Anyone who is serious about their life with God will, at some point, ask, "God, what do you want me to do with my life?" We wouldn't ask that question without some kind of desire. We *should* desire what God desires, what the New Testament calls "God's will." Should I get married?

Should I become a pastor? Should I become a teacher? Should I forgive that person? Should I foster that child? Questions like these are the initial sign that deep down, we desire to know and do what God wants for our lives. We wouldn't ask if we didn't believe God had something to say. Nor would we ask if we didn't care.

But we won't always get clear answers in a timely and sensible manner. Sometimes God responds quickly. But not always. These can be frustrating experiences. Yet, in moments when I've sought and not received a clear response, I've walked away wondering if perhaps the fact that I sought God's will is in itself some small part of God's will. We are often closest to God's will when we are wrestling to discern it. In fact, on more than one occasion, I've asked God what he wants and sensed a quiet question in return: "A. J., what do *you* want?"

Does God sometimes allow us to follow our desire? To follow what we want? Yes—but with boundaries. We should remember the psalmist who writes, "Take delight in the Lord, and he will give you the desires of your heart" (Ps. 37:4). We might hear this and think God is giving us a blank check. But the psalmist isn't saying we can have everything we want. He is commanding us to "delight in the Lord," to please the heart of God above all else, and not to get whatever we want. Why is this important? It creates a structure of order for our desires.

Parents live off this principle. When my son asks if he might go to his room and play, I say, "Yes, just make sure you clean up when you are done." There are always some general rules: no fire, no screens, no blood. So on and so forth. Off he goes, immersing himself in a world of Legos and Pokémon cards. Never have I dictated his desires when he asked to play. "Yes, you can go, but you must play with Legos and Pokémon cards." The parent establishes boundaries. The child enters into the delight of play. Truth be told, there's nothing more fun as a parent than seeing your child delight in the joys of their own desires—all in the boundaries you have established. The role of the rules, then, isn't to end desire. Rules make it possible for desire not to destroy the house.

For those in Christ, the delight of the Lord comes before the desires of the heart. The very structure of the psalmist's words reflects the relationship between identity and desire. Our identity as children of God gives structure to what our hearts want.

This frees us from the fear of thinking we have to figure everything out on our own.[24] Too often, we operate out of fear, convinced that God is a divine naysayer who enjoys giving us a perpetual no. Terrified to do anything wrong, we end up doing nothing at all. But this isn't the posture of someone rooted in a Father who adores and loves them. A good father lets his kids make decisions and make mistakes. God is no helicopter parent. So the endless fear that we're one wrong decision away from messing up God's sovereign plan both overestimates our own abilities and underestimates God's unimaginable sovereignty. He is a good composter who knows how to turn a pile of feces into soil. The weight of heaven isn't on our shoulders. And we can rest in the fact that God is more interested in helping us live out his will than we are.

To see this most clearly, consider that there are only two times in the entire New Testament when Jesus is recorded as hearing the direct words of his Father in heaven: at his baptism and at the transfiguration, when he reveals his glory. In both occasions, the Father's words are the same: "This is my son, whom I love, with whom I'm well pleased" (Matt. 3:17; 17:5).

The only two times we hear the Father speaking to Jesus, he isn't telling Jesus what he is to do. Rather, he is telling him *who* he is. The Father speaks identity over Jesus. He loves him, and he is pleased with him.

---

24. The humble words of Wendell Berry's Jayber Crow come to mind: "Often I have not known where I was going until I was already there. I have had my share of desires and goals, but my life has come to me or I have gone to it mainly by way of mistakes and surprises." Wendell Berry, *Jayber Crow* (Berkeley: Counterpoint, 2001), 133.

Every counselor in the world who undertakes the sacred work of serving their clients' needs can speak to the pain that comes alongside the haunting uncertainty of a father's love. They see it every day. What if that were resolved in our hearts? What if we knew that the love the Father has for Jesus is the love he has for those who are in Jesus? What if we started our day with that? It would free us from living in a constant sense of inadequacy, that we are one move away from disappointing God. It would free us from thinking we needed to conjure enough desire to love God. It would liberate us from the thought that God's love for us is only as deep as our desire to do our morning devotions.

The Father is pleased with you. That is the basis of your identity.

———

Christians throughout history have documented their own mysterious loss of spiritual desire. The writings of Teresa of Ávila intimately describe an unparalleled nearness to God in prayer and solitude. Early in her faith, Teresa desired Jesus so intensely that one scholar deemed it "reckless."[25] Our experiences may have been similar. But history reminds us that during adolescence Teresa's desire for God grew cold as she experienced temptations of vanity, love of others, and earthly joys. The fact that we continue reading Teresa witnesses to an important reality: her steadfast love for God transcended her waning desires. Through ups and downs, Teresa's relentless, resilient love for Jesus remained. As our love for God becomes seasoned, our desire matures as it mellows.

This can only happen so long as our love for God runs deeper than our attraction to God. In today's culture, we now bow almost

———

25. Constance FitzGerald, OCD, "A Discipleship of Equals: Voices from Tradition—Teresa of Ávila and John of the Cross," in *Desire, Darkness, and Hope: Theology in a Time of Impasse*, ed. Laurie Cassidy and M. Shawn Copeland (Collegeville, MN: Liturgical, 2021), 27.

blindly before the Almighty Attraction, one of our favorite gods. If someone is attracted, drawn, inclined, titillated, awakened to a desire for some person, thing, or experience but decides to resist that thing, then they are ridiculed for being "repressed," as though some eternal law of nature were being violated. This unspoken deification of attraction has become the eternal dictum of Western culture immersed in a consumer mentality. We're expected—even required—to pursue that which attracts us. We're defined by our attractions.

But attraction has its limits. Attraction hasn't always held the weight it does now. Take cultural expectations in marriage. In generations past, a marriage between a man and a woman wasn't entered into solely through the gates of attraction. Many ancient cultures practiced "arranged" marriages, where attractions bore little weight.[26] Nor did choice or desire. For all intents and purposes, attraction was peripheral—covenant, community, and character were far more central. Admittedly, this wasn't the perfect scenario. For a variety of cultural reasons, the marriage bond has all but shifted toward attraction as the grounds for covenant in our moment.

This is fine and dandy—and likely a healthy corrective. But perhaps it has gone too far. If attraction is the sole basis upon which covenants are built, then attraction must remain for the covenant to survive. Soon, a marriage lasts only as long as attraction remains. This provokes a potential problem: once attraction diminishes, does commitment follow suit?

Too often, the answer is yes. One young man I know struggling in his new marriage illustrates the dangers of basing a covenant solely on attraction. When Doug started dating Clara, they shared a high-intensity sexual connection that was fulfilling and

---

26. Stephanie Coontz, *Marriage, a History: How Love Conquered Marriage* (New York: Penguin, 2005).

intoxicating. It was all sex, all the time. It was like they were made for each other. They soon got married. Doug was surprised to find—just two years after the wedding—that his sexual desire for his wife began to atrophy. Attraction slowly waned. *Did I make a mistake? Why isn't she as attractive? Should we have gotten married?* These questions haunted Doug as he lay in his bed at night next to a woman who was incrementally becoming a stranger. In a moment of confession, Doug named his greatest fear to me. When the sex was good, so was their relationship. But he wondered if, in the afterglow of passion, it wasn't really her that he loved. Maybe, he feared, it was only the orgasm he had when he was with her that he loved.

When attraction becomes the sole basis of one's love for another, then it's not the person we love. We only love what they give us. This raises a question: Do we love God? Or do we love the feeling God gives us when we're with him? As biblical categories, covenant love and attraction are worlds apart. Thank God. A desire placed on attraction is a house built on sandy shores. As Patricia Stacey openly grieved in an article on desire in *O, The Oprah Magazine:* "Desire sets up a dynamic, a game with rules that seemed to be invented in some torture chamber of the heart—all devised to make seeking real love, real connection, quite simply painful. We want what we cannot have—that is the strange irony of desire, of passion. And when we have it, often we lose that wanting."[27] That is, indeed, the dark side of idolizing attraction. When attraction becomes an end in itself, we can't sustain love after the object of our love is no longer attractive. Many experience the loss of desire in marriage, friendship, vocation, or career path.

This translates, often, to our relationships with God. We love God as long as we are attracted to him. We find him pleasing to

---

27. Patricia Stacey, "Understanding Desire," *O, The Oprah Magazine* (blog), 2008, www
.oprah.com/relationships/Desire-in-Relationships-What-Really-Causes-Attraction.

our senses and wishes. We are into him. But the minute he's no longer attractive to us, we seek a better suitor. We often love God for his grace, but then run from him for his commands. This way of following Jesus will leave us wanting so much more. It is unfulfilling. It's astounding how the Bible admits about Jesus, "He had no beauty or majesty to attract us to him, nothing in his appearance that we should desire him. He was despised and rejected by mankind, a man of suffering, and familiar with pain" (Isa. 53:2–3).

Jesus wasn't attractive. He wasn't photogenic in his own time. The sinful heart wouldn't—nay, couldn't—desire him. Yet he is pure Beauty. We simply can't see it. For the followers of Jesus, attraction isn't how we relate to Jesus. We have a deeper way of relating. We come to learn that loving God faithfully isn't the same as being attracted to him. The problem isn't that he isn't beautiful. Our hearts have lost touch with what true beauty looks like.

Chapter 6

UNDESIRED DESIRE

In the late twentieth century, a neuroscientist by the name of Benjamin Libet undertook an array of groundbreaking studies exploring the relationship between the brain and one's decisions. In one project, Libet had his subject voluntarily flick their wrist while he recorded the brain's activity in the milliseconds beforehand. As expected, brain activity spiked as the wrist flicked. But Libet discovered that 350–400 milliseconds beforehand, there appeared a noticeable build-up of energy before the conscious decision to flick. What Libet's work suggested was that the individual's conscious decision to flick a wrist actually emerged from the unconscious part of the brain. That is to say, before a conscious decision, there appeared an unconscious desire that came just beforehand. As you might imagine, Libet's work brought him notoriety. But it also provoked a great debate.[1]

Libet's research provokes a variety of questions. Where do our desires come from? Do we choose them? Or do they arise from somewhere deeper than consciousness? On more than one occasion, I've binge-watched a gripping television program depicting real-life stories of individuals enmeshed in what the show dubbed

---

1. Benjamin Libet, "Do We Have Free Will?," in *The Volitional Brain: Towards a Neuroscience of Free Will*, ed. Benjamin Libet, Anthony Freeman, and Keith Sutherland (Thorverton, UK: Imprint Academic, 1999). For an argument that desire could not come from the unconscious, see D. Hulse, C. Read, and T. Schroeder, "The Impossibility of Unconscious Desire," *American Philosophical Quarterly* 41 (2004): 73–80.

"strange addictions." What most captures my attention is the sheer oddity of human addiction. Before discovering this show, I'd been keenly aware of more common addictions to drugs, sex, alcohol, and codependency. But the world of *strange* addictions took me to unknown places.

One notable episode described a young woman's lifelong struggle under a debilitating desire to eat the stuffing found in couch cushions. Day after day, year after year, the woman experienced an overwhelming and insatiable urge to ingest bite-sized pieces of cushion foam.

Did this woman choose this strange desire? Or did the strange desire choose her?

In the episode, the mystery surrounding the couch-eating woman is never fully resolved. Nobody (including the woman) could account for it. This was the central feature of her story—her inability to identify why she, or anyone, would desire to do such a thing. She admitted the irrationality of it all. She was keenly aware that there were no social or nutritional benefits to eating couch cushions. She didn't want this desire, which had consumed decades of her life. No amount of counseling, reading, conversation, or introspection could illuminate why this unwanted and embarrassing desire had such control over her. All that remained was a sense of oppression, enslavement, and entrapment to a desire she did not desire.

Odd? Yes. Even a little comical? Undoubtedly. But something at the heart of that young woman's story filled me with empathy. I found myself overwhelmed simultaneously with disgust at the thought of eating couch cushions and compassion for her predicament. Underneath this addiction is a story common to all of us. I found myself drawn toward introspection. Why do *I* have strange, unwanted desires that lurk inside of me?

We all have desires we wished we didn't have. Unwanted desires are a fundamental part of human experience—even if we rarely talk about them. Philosophers who study desire call these unwanted desires coming from mysterious places "fleeting desires."[2] These are those unchosen desires that seem to catch us unawares from some abyss within the depth of our being. Examples abound from our everyday existence. We see a car we fancy. Soon, our desire (wanted or not) is awakened at its very sight. I smell a fresh doughnut at the local bakery as I stroll down the street. I'm immediately moved by seemingly coercive, internal desires I know are hostile to my long-term health goals. Or one may find that a certain kind of person with particular bodily features arouses sexual desire. A fleeting desire is, above all, one that besets us apart from any decision of the will.

One way this has been considered is in the reflections of the revivalist and theologian Jonathan Edwards's in *A Treatise on Human Affections*.[3] Edwards is fleshing out the relationship between one's emotions and the work of the Holy Spirit. How do they overlap, even intersect? Edwards argues that there's a difference between one's emotions and what he calls "affections." Emotions are fickle, coming and going without our permission or will. But affections are parts of our internal being that have been reformed and remolded by the miraculous work of the Spirit. Emotions are like the weather: they come and go, day to day, hour to hour. But affections are like the climate: the systemic, long-term, meta nature of the weather. Emotions, like fleeting desires, do not reveal much about the deep, systemic nature of our hearts.

Similarly, fleeting desires are a central part of our lives. Scientific research on the topic suggests they take up much more of our lives than we may assume. One such scientist, Timothy Wilson,

---

2. Timothy Schroeder, *Three Faces of Desire* (New York: Oxford University Press, 2004), 150. Others, such as G. F. Schueler, distinguishes between "motivated desires" (desires we birthed in reason) and "unmotivated desires" (desires born apart from reason). G. F. Schueler, *Desire: Its Role in Practical Reason and the Explanation of Action* (Cambridge, MA: MIT Press, 1995), 28.

3. Jonathan Edwards, *The Works of Jonathan Edwards: Religious Affections*, ed. John E. Smith, vol. 2 (New Haven, CT: Yale University Press, 2009).

suggests in his book *Strangers to Ourselves* that we have an "adaptive consciousness." By this, Wilson means we have an internal set of interwoven desires that are more often than not subconscious. He contends that very few of our desires are actually wanted or even known. His research suggests that no more than 5 percent of our daily choices are the direct result of deliberate, chosen will.[4] That is to say that very few of our daily decisions are guided by conscious intent. It is fair to say: not only do we have unwanted desires; we are composed *mostly* of them.

Not all unwanted desires are bad. Paul didn't *want* to encounter Jesus on the road to Damascus in Acts 9. This would have meant an entire change in his life's orientation. Later, he would write about how he was "compelled to preach" (1 Cor. 9:16). In other words, he couldn't *not* preach. On that road to Damascus, God had awoken a desire within him that would make his life far more difficult. Even when he didn't want this to happen.

I've sometimes wished I could just shake my desire to love God. Lord knows, it would make my life easier. But God, in sheer grace, woke up a desire for himself even when I myself didn't desire it.

We all encounter a complex set of desires when we attend to our heart. Life after Eden is a world littered with "thorns and this-tles." We all have desires that we didn't plant in the garden of our lives. We seem unable to permanently rid ourselves of them. Jesus spoke plainly about this in the parable of the weeds in Matthew 13. Jesus tells of a farmer. At night, he goes to bed only to find that someone has "sowed weeds" (v. 25) throughout his land. He didn't put them there, but he must deal with them. That's the human experience around fleeting desire. While we may seek to cultivate the fruit of the Spirit and a life of virtue, it often feels as though weeds keep growing throughout our lives.

---

4. Timothy D. Wilson, *Strangers to Ourselves: Discovering the Adaptive Consciousness* (Cambridge, MA: Harvard University Press, 2002). I'm grateful to James K. A. Smith for including a section on Wilson's work in his *You Are What You Love*, 32–35.

The eighteenth-century revivalist John Wesley is said to have called himself and his band of followers *homo unius libri*, "men of one book." Wesley, of course, was nodding to their love of the Bible. In that vein, Christians have long been called "people of the book." Few traditions are as committed to reading as are Christianity and Judaism, who see their sacred texts as worthy of repeated reading, reflection, and consideration. God's people are bookish.[5] Yet, while revering these sacred writings, we fail to take into account exactly what it is that we're reading.

Picture yourself sitting down to read Colossians or Romans or 1 Timothy or Philemon. What are you actually reading? Truth is, we aren't reading polished thoughts of some ivory tower professor preparing a graduate seminar. No, we're reading the personal thoughts of people like Paul, Peter, and James who are experiencing immense travail, persecution, or jail time. Biblical writings aren't academic. They are inspired reflections of people struggling with life, waking every day to lay down their lives to serve Jesus, knowing they could face execution or marginalization. These are Jesus' activists laying down their lives to bear witness to the great spiritual revolution known as the kingdom of God.

Grit and struggle are on every page. To steep yourself in a New Testament epistle is to read personal correspondence about extremely personal circumstances. That's just one of the reasons they are so enduring. I often wonder if the writers believed their thoughts would have impact beyond their immediate audience.

As a genre, journals and letters have been generative for my

---

5. So many have instilled in me a love for reading, including Karen Swallow Prior, *Booked: Literature in the Soul of Me* (New York: T. S. Poetry, 2012); Terry W. Glaspey, *Great Books in the Christian Tradition* (Eugene, OR: Harvest House, 1996). For an academic examination on how reading shaped the culture of early Christianity, see Frances Young, *Biblical Exegesis and the Formation of Christian Culture* (Cambridge, MA: Cambridge University Press, 1997).

spiritual life. Years ago, a spiritual mentor challenged me to write a list of those (dead or alive) whose faith had shaped mine the most. I sketched out a list that included C. S. Lewis, Henri Nouwen, John Wesley, Flannery O'Connor, Eugene Peterson, Augustine, and Dietrich Bonhoeffer. Then I was asked to identify what they shared in common. An epiphany struck. My heroes were people who kept journals. The people who have most shaped me were real people with real problems who put those problems in writing.

Over the years, I've immersed myself in my heroes' journals. Flannery O'Connor's *Prayer Journal* is a compilation of posthumously published prayers written before the novelist became famous. In one raw, unvarnished prayer, O'Connor asks God to let her be a writer. She says she will do whatever God wants. But she would like it most to be a writer. She concludes her prayer with one simple caveat: "Help me to feel that I will give up every earthly thing for this. I do not mean becoming a nun."[6]

I can't help but find O'Connor's humorous self-knowledge endearing. She wanted to do what God wanted her to do. But she knew herself enough to know that she wanted to do anything but become a nun (and she never did). Little did she know, O'Connor's literary career would enjoy a meteoric rise. But it was short-lived. After publishing her first few works, which were met with near universal acclaim, the southern, Catholic writer was diagnosed with Lupus, and it eventually took her life. Her later writings are marked by raw clarity and cutting insight. In her own vocational Gethsemane, she wrote with a limp.

I've learned something about myself: those who have most shaped my spiritual journey are the ones who loved Jesus yet didn't get everything they desired on this side of death. Lewis's wife died a devastating death shortly after their marriage. Nouwen wrestled

---

6. Flannery O'Connor, *A Prayer Journal*, ed. W. A. Sessions (New York: Farrar, Straus and Giroux, 2013), 6.

with his calling and sexuality his entire life. Peterson struggled with alcohol much of his ministry. Augustine never fully escaped his self-centeredness and sexual desires. Bonhoeffer gave up a promising career as a theologian to stand up against the Third Reich. In not receiving everything they wanted, their hearts and minds turned to God. I think this is what the author of Hebrews describes about the faithful who walk with God: "These were all commended for their faith, yet none of them received what had been promised, since God had planned something better for us so that only together with us would they be made perfect" (Heb. 11:39–40).

The path to holiness goes through *not* getting everything we want. In the Puritan tradition, it's said that God makes us holy by giving us what they call the "strokes" or "crosses"[7]—by not giving us what we want. Now that I think about it, the opposite is equally true. The least mature and most self-centered people I know are those who get everything they want. What if God's brilliant design is to make us holy through disappointment?

Continuing my exercise in the reading of spiritual journals, my mentor challenged me not only to read the journals of my heroes but to read my own as well. Given that I've been journaling nearly twenty-five years, there are many entries to read. And I'm no C. S. Lewis, Flannery O'Connor, or Henri Nouwen, so there's a good deal of fluff. Still, these writings are a window into my soul. Like time-lapse photography, they help me see myself change over time.

Upon rereading my journals, I was struck by the endless repetition of a capital *X*. There are thousands of them. They appear on almost every page. The story of the *X* goes back to when I first

---

7. As described in Iain Duguid, *Ezekiel*, NIV Application Commentary (Grand Rapids: Zondervan, 1999), 295–96.

began writing out my thoughts and prayers to God. Over time, these journals became a confessional, a safe place for me to name what was going on inside of me. Many of these confessions are little frustrations throughout the day: thoughts about theology, people who are bugging me, or a coworker's idiosyncrasies. Having the space to name these issues liberated my soul. I became more and more vulnerable as I shed more light on what was really going on inside.

In my journals, I began talking to God about my own unwanted desires I'd wrestled with since my conversion to Jesus. I had always feared my journals would be found out or discovered. So my way of keeping things safe was to simply write a big X for my struggle. Reading them now, I'm struck at the consistency of the X. X here. X there. God, why do I have X? God, please forgive me for X. God would you please deliver me of my X. Jesus, can you still love me with X? Spirit, show me yourself through my X.

It's as though—even as I wrote these entries—there was deep shame in myself for all of these Xs. Why have the same struggles been with me for three decades? Why can't I just get over this? I am no longer ashamed of the X. I shared with my mentor this embarrassment; that all I talk about with him and write about in my journal are the same old struggles. He reminded me that these are the sign of God's grace. The object of my worship is Jesus, not my own spiritual growth. I can't accomplish spiritual growth. I can only receive it as a gift. And that when I survey my walk with Jesus over these decades, the X has marked the very spot where God has most intimately met me—and where I've most desperately needed him.

I'm not alone. Even Paul, giving language to the experience of following Jesus in the first generation of Christians, was perplexed by his own struggle with things within that he so wished were not there. "I do not understand what I do," Paul wrote in Romans 7:15–16. "For what I want to do I do not do, but what I hate I do. And if I do what I do not want to do, I agree the law is good." It is almost like Paul is putting a big X in the middle of his letter to the church of Rome. If Paul carried such heavy burdens on his walk to glory, isn't it likely we may as well?

More often than not, whatever X we find ourselves with marks the spot of God's grace and faithfulness. If we watch long enough, we'll begin to see that the very thorn in our side that creates the most pain is the place where God makes himself known to you. At the end of ourselves is the beginning of grace.

———

The most painful, difficult, angering parts of our lives are often the very location where we are most being formed into Christ's image. This isn't to sugarcoat or trivialize life's unimaginable difficulty. Nor should it make us want to chase or glorify suffering. Instead, it's a mindset that can very likely provide us with great hope.

Life is marked by frustration. In Romans 8, Paul describes the world as being "frustrated" by the corrosive power of sin. Three times, Paul uses the word *sustanezō*, or "groaning." Three things groan: the "whole creation" (v. 22) groans, "we ourselves" (v. 23) groan as we await our adoption as children of God, and the Spirit groans with "wordless groans" (v. 26). Creation, humanity, and God all groan together as one. For the fourteenth-century mystic St. Catherine of Siena, Paul's language here is meant to awaken our knowledge that the Spirit sheds tears *with* creatures in our anguish.[8]

Many New Testament scholars believe Paul's language about groaning in Romans 8 is a jarring image of a woman in the throes of giving birth. If so, then the gift of life is to be seen as being on the other side of the pain of groaning. We must remember that childbearing was particularly dangerous in antiquity because of

---

8. Catherine of Siena, *The Dialogue*, ed. Suzanne Noffke (Mahwah, NJ: Paulist, 1980), 168–69.

high mortality rates. There was nothing braver to do than give birth. In *Childbirth as a Metaphor for Crisis*, Claudia Bergmann demonstrates that, in ancient art, women giving birth were commonly portrayed as warriors.[9] Nothing could be more warrior-like than birthing life in antiquity. Indeed, giving birth is (I'm told) a profoundly painful and difficult experience. But the result of such great travail is intended to be life, a gift, and love. It seems that, in part, Paul wants us to see the difficulty, the frustrations, the groanings of life as the birthplace of life's greatest gifts.

In the midst of such unimaginable pain, there's a great gift. We could even say that pain itself can be a gift. Paul Brand and Philip Yancey once wrote a fascinating book entitled *The Gift of Pain*.[10] Brand, a physician, had spent years serving lepers. In his book, he explains that one of the main difficulties for a leper is that they do not have the capacity to feel pain. Why might pain be important, someone could ask? Well, if we could put our hand over a fire and not feel it, then we would run the risk of burning our hand off. Pain, in essence, is God's built in design to protect us from harm.

In the therapeutic West, we almost always see pain as an evil. What if pain can be a gift from God? The phrase *can be* is very important here. We must never valorize pain and suffering and make it a goal. If we do, we run the risk of needing to find someone to experience pain and suffering. That is to say in glorifying suffering, we need suffering to be perpetuated. But we can begin to see pain in a new, redemptive light. It is fascinating to consider the number of times in the New Testament Jesus is described healing a leper of their disease. If the New Testament is describing what we know as leprosy, then the healing of the leper was not only a healing of the person to well-being; it was equally the healing of

---

9. Claudia D. Bergmann, *Childbirth as a Metaphor for Crisis: Evidence from the Ancient Near East, the Hebrew Bible, and 1QH XI, 1–18*, vol. 382 (Berlin: de Gruyter, 2009).

10. Paul Brand and Philip Yancey, *The Gift of Pain: Why We Hurt and What We Can Do about It* (Grand Rapids: Zondervan, 2020).

the person to feel pain once again. Restoration is a return to the original human state, and humans were given a nervous system for a reason. The healing power of Jesus restores our capacity to feel pain once again. What a strange gift!

On more than one occasion, I've walked a new follower of Jesus through the waters of baptism. I've come to find that when someone is regenerated by the blood of Jesus, one of the first things they experience is a new kind of pain for the sin they have been living in. For the first time, they feel internal conviction for their struggle with pornography or excessive drinking or a harsh spirit or the way they've treated those close to them. Upon believing, they experience the pain of regeneration, like a leper learning to feel again. Before, we were people who "lost all sensitivity" (Eph. 4:19) and were "free from the control of righteousness" (Rom. 6:20). This is why Peter is so hurt when Jesus asks three times if Peter loves him after Peter's denial (John 21). Even reconciliation can lead us back to godly pain. Part of healing is learning to feel pain again. Numbness is not a Christian virtue.

Pain can be a gift. It is through the experience of pain that life is brought into the world. Wide-eyed in the arms of a new mother, a child has been given new life because a mother has been willing to pay the price of pain that brings newness. We need to remember this when we are put in places in life when the life that God is giving us is different than the lives we wanted. No mother wants the pain of childbirth. But a mother wants their child. Often, in God's enigmatic economy, we go through that which we do not want to receive what we do.

The painful experience of walking for decades with deep unwanted desires has had its effect on me. More than anything, it has produced within me an endless need to be desperate for God.

Without the hand of grace, without God's sustaining mercy, without the help I was made to need, I am inclined toward self-reliance. The testimony of people like Paul and C. S. Lewis and Henri Nouwen and the like is that the crucible of gnawing unwanted desires is that they force us toward dependence—dependence upon God, dependence upon others to walk with, and dependence on the work of the Holy Spirit. I'm grateful for my X. It has produced in me such a deep and unending need for God.

And the opposite of that has been true for me. Without struggle, I become stagnant. In *The Price of Privilege*, Madeline Levine shows that one of the most debilitating things we can do to our children is give them everything they desire. In providing every want, Levin argues, a host of developmental issues can arise, such as delayed maturity, loss of relationship, and even the absence of meaning and purpose.[11] This can make the task of parenting very difficult. True parental love entails withholding some desires for the sake of the child's formation. Too often, insecure in ourselves, we give our kids their every wish because we'd rather be their friends than their parents. We become what sociologists call "peerents."

Doctors know this principle well. I remember my father, a physician, quietly complaining how many patients came into his office having prediagnosed their own pain and expecting a specific drug to be prescribed. Often, a sign of addiction is a patient who can name the drug they desire. And, of course, in medical ethics, a doctor should be wary about giving a drug or treatment just because somebody wants it. We have an opioid epidemic on our hands, in part, because the work of saying no is so difficult.

The myth that true happiness results from fulfilled desire can be seen in nearly every realm of human existence. One may think happiness arises from getting everything we desire. But it can have

---

11. Madeline Levine, *The Price of Privilege: How Parental Pressure and Material Advantage Are Creating a Generation of Disconnected and Unhappy Kids* (San Francisco: HarperCollins, 2006).

the inverse effect. Being deeply formed isn't the same as getting every one of our desires. In fact, getting everything we want can transform us into the shrillest and shallowest of monsters. This does not mean we are called to be unhappy. The way of Jesus is about the call toward true happiness.[12] But it redefines what happiness is. In our world, happiness is getting everything one wants. In the kingdom of God, happiness is leaning fully into everything God wants.

———

Matthew's gospel details the final days of Jesus' life. Preparing for the cross, Jesus enters a garden called Gethsemane where he will pray. After finding his disciples asleep and unable to pray through the night, Jesus is alone, abandoned, and preparing for the task he alone can bear. There, in the quietness of his coming death, he prays, "My Father, if it is possible, may this cup be taken from me. Yet not as I will, but as you will" (Matt. 26:39).

The experience is so anxiety-ridden and traumatic that he begins to "sweat blood." Why does Jesus willingly subject himself to this pain? The location of this prayer is important: a garden called Gethsemane. In Hebrew, the word *gat shemanim* means "oil press." It describes a location where a first-century Jew would crush olives to harvest their oil. Matthew seems to be making a connection between the location of this prayer and what's happening to Jesus. As olives were crushed in this place to gain oil, Jesus is being crushed to the point of shedding his blood.

Jesus appears to be asking—if God willed it—to be relieved of his crucible of dying upon the cross. "The cup" to which Jesus is referring is the "cup of wrath" described at multiple points of the

---

12. This is the thesis of John Piper, *Desiring God: Meditations of a Christian Hedonist* (Colorado Springs: Multnomah, 2011).

Old Testament.[13] This was the cup of suffering that would be his
crucifixion. Naturally, Jesus does not want to die such a horrific
death. For the reader, it's worth noting that Jesus was alone when
these words were spoken. Thus, he would have had to pass along
the story of his request before the Father to those (the disciples)
who would eventually write down the account. All the possible
witnesses were asleep. So the fact that Jesus reported this after the
fact to the authors of the New Testament speaks to its importance.
Scripture wants us to see Jesus' anguish.

Here is the question: Was Jesus' request answered?

On more than one occasion, when I've invited someone to read
this story and answer whether Jesus' prayer was answered, it has
become clear that we have a big problem with prayer. More often
than not, people do not believe Jesus' prayer was answered. Jesus
died on the cross. He asked not to die on the cross. How was his
prayer answered?

We usually only believe a prayer is answered if we get what we
desire out of it. We see an answered prayer as a prayer that worked
out well for us. Of course, Jesus' prayer *was* answered. The answer
was no. Jesus would die on the cross. And he would do so out of
total abandonment to the Father's will in an act to save the world
from their sin.

There is no such thing as an unanswered prayer. Sometimes
God answers with a yes; other times with a no. Sometimes the
answer is "later." No prayer remains unheard or unanswered.

The entire account is one of a sinless man submitting his desire
to the will of another. The world is saved by a savior who willingly
put aside everything to do what his Father wanted him to do. He
put himself under his Father's will. The world is saved by someone
who not only was crucified but who crucified his desire in favor of
his Father's will. By being pressed, he gave us life. The reversal from

---

13. See Ps. 75:8; Isa. 51:17; Jer. 25:15–16.

the first garden is unmistakable. The first Adam said, in essence, "Not your will, God, but mine be done." Jesus, the second Adam, declared, "Not my will, Father, but yours be done."

The place Jesus submits his will to God is in the place of prayer. In our prayer, our desires are most purified. We get to lay them down before God. But we do not end there. We give the Father our desires and willingly receive his. Jesus is our model. The cross reveals, among other things, the abundant willingness of Jesus to pour himself out—all of himself.

This reframes everything we think about love. Love isn't getting what you want. Love isn't about winning. Love gives away. Sometimes love loses—and in so doing, paves a quiet way to victory through the pangs of death. In God's kingdom, winning isn't conquering. It is *being* conquered, being crucified.

Hard things are not always bad things. As we seek to lay our desires down—even those unwanted ones that haunt us around every corner—we find a savior who showed us the way. Our unwanted desires can, no doubt, make us frustrated, tired, and even resentful. But the glory these struggles bear and the life on the other side is simply unimaginable. As Paul would finish his reflections on the "groanings" of this world in Romans 8, he gives his reader hope: "I consider that our present sufferings are not worth comparing with the glory that will be revealed in us" (Rom. 8:18). Our lives have been subjected to frustration. It is, without question, a world of endless thorns.

But it is producing so much good in us.

God wants us to be revealed as glorious. This glory does not come without a price. What if, in the end, we can come to see that God actually loves us too much to give us everything we want?

Part 3

THE NURTURE OF OUR LONGINGS

Chapter 7

KILLING DESIRE

There are many things we can control. We can control our habits, schedules, and even decisions. But controlling our desires is not as easy. Our desires can often feel like the feral part of our hearts. Exhaustion at trying to control them can come about. It is not uncommon for me to have a deep sense of sadness and even fatigue having to battle desires within. "Why can't I get over this already?" "I've fought this for decades." "This is exhausting. Loosen up and enjoy life already." Perhaps, along the way, we can all feel overwhelmed with the idea that completely sanitizing our hearts of certain desires is like chasing a mirage on a desert skyline. I don't mean to make you feel hopeless; that's not my goal. I'm seeking to be realistic.

The human heart needs a dose of realism.

What is the heart? Western thought tends to separate the life of the mind (reason and intellect) from the heart (feelings and emotions). But this wall is erected by us, not by Scripture. A biblical theology of the heart doesn't neatly bifurcate emotions and intellect into mutually exclusive domains. In fact, the Greek word *kardia* is the same word used in the New Testament for both "heart" and "mind." Hebrew doesn't even have a word for the brain. *Kardia* is our internal reality. It is the part of us—which some have suggested should be translated more generally as "guts" or "innards"—from which we simultaneously feel and think and orient our lives.[1]

---

1. James K. A. Smith uses "guts" interchangeably with heart throughout *Desiring the*

The biblical authors don't isolate desire as part of either the heart or the mind. Desire is our entire inner orientation. This is at the heart of Ephesians when Paul writes that they are "being corrupted by [our] deceitful desires" and should be "made new in the attitude of your minds" (Eph. 4:22–23). Transformed desires parallel a transformed mind. This is why Paul writes of "setting the mind" on particular desires. Similarly, the prophets such as Ezekiel and Jeremiah declare that God would "circumcise" (Jer. 4:4) Israel's heart; cutting, slicing, and marking the desires of the flesh. The circumcision of the heart is the circumcision of desire; what some have called the "woundedness of desire."[2] This Spirit-accomplished miracle reorients our hearts, minds, souls, and spirits (our "guts") toward God and his kingdom.

This explains why we often experience new desires upon following Christ. The Spirit reorders our hearts' desires. Before conversion we have what Augustine called "disordered loves." Without the Spirit's work, we continue in these disordered loves: loving evil things over good things, good things over ultimate things, or created things over eternal things. Disordered desire is similar to the prophetic words of Hosea, who speaks of Israel as a prostitute who chases after many lovers (Hos. 2:5). Israel loves, but their love is disordered. The Spirit, then, reorders our desires into their original nature.

This catapults us toward a vexing question. Do we actually have the power to kill, crucify, and circumcise our desires? In other words, do we have will over our desires? This thorny theological

---

Kingdom: Worship, Worldview, and Cultural Formation (Grand Rapids: Baker Academic, 2009). For a terrific exploration of the biblical concepts of "head" and "heart," see Rick Nanez, Full Gospel, Fractured Minds: A Call to Use God's Gift of the Intellect (Grand Rapids: Zondervan, 2010), 23–24.

2. I encountered this phrase first in Ian Curran, "Mindful Desire: Contemplation and the Practice of Theology in Wendy Farley," in Erotic Faith: Desire, Transformation, and Beloved Community in the Incarnational Theology of Wendy Farley, ed. Mari Kim (Eugene, OR: Wipf & Stock, 2022).

debate has raged throughout Christian history. In the early church, for example, two leading figures named Pelagius and Augustine went toe-to-toe over the mysterious nature of will. For Pelagius, humans were free to choose willingly between sin, virtue, and desires. Augustine disagreed, believing humans lacked the ability to change desires through will. While Augustine believed we are free to sin, he also taught that we were *not* free from the corrupting powers of sin. As it relates to desire, the difference between Pelagius and Augustine could not hold more weight. Theologian Roger Olson writes,

> For Augustine, people are free to sin but not free *not* to sin. That is because they *want* to sin. The Fall has so corrupted their motives and desires that sinning is all they want to do apart from God's intervening grace. Thus they are sinning "freely." Pelagius and his followers would almost certainly reject this idea of free will and argue that a person is only truly free if he could either sin or not sin.[3]

The operating word here is *want*. One residual element of Augustine's theology is his idea that our sin nature has become wed to our desires. Our problem isn't merely that we sin. Our problem is we *desire* sin. Some of the most important books in Christian history wrestle with this, such as Jonathan Edwards's *Freedom of the Will* and Martin Luther's *Bondage of the Will*. It's also a central theme of John Calvin's theology. He described the heart as an "idol factory" that endlessly created idols for itself.[4]

God has, indeed, extended forgiveness through the cross and resurrection of Christ. But atonement doesn't magically disconnect

3. Roger Olson, *The Story of Christian Theology: Twenty Centuries of Tradition and Reform* (Downers Grove, IL: InterVarsity, 1999), 273.

4. For a full exploration of this theme, see Richard Keyes, "The Idol Factory," in *No God but God: Breaking with the Idols of Our Age* (Chicago: Moody Publishers, 1992).

our hearts from their disordered loves. In our rebellion against God, it wasn't merely that our behavior was unaligned with God; it was that we had a disordered desire to do what God commanded us not to do. Throughout Christian history, this has been called "concupiscence"—that pulsating desire in all of us for that which God does not want. This is the part of us that, upon being told not to do something, suddenly desires to do it. Paul describes this: "But sin, seizing the opportunity afforded by the commandment, produced in me every kind of coveting. For apart from the law, sin was dead" (Rom. 7:8). At the moment God voices a command, the sinful heart desires to violate it.

We are like children who play inside all day refusing to go out in the sun. And the minute the deluge begins to fall, we are angry and demand to run in the rain.

Dallas Willard suggests this is why it's critical we never call something evil if God calls it good. For example, sexual desire—in its God-ordained boundaries—is a *good* desire. But when sexual desire is itself deemed to be bad, our sinful hearts are awakened to want it at the wrong time or the wrong way. In so doing, Willard writes, we "make it more powerful in that what's forbidden has in itself a way of calling to action and desire."[5] Falsely labeling something good as bad bends the heart to desire what T. S. Eliot called the last great temptation: "to do the right thing for the wrong reason."[6]

For this reason, Willard reminds us of the difference between one's will (our ability to choose) and one's desire (our ability to want). The will makes decisions based on the good and the bad. The desire often wants without regard to moral metrics. Free from the formation of the Spirit, our wills become the servants of our desires. But by the Spirit's work, the will slowly becomes lord *over*

5. Dallas Willard, "Beyond Pornography: Spiritual Formation Studied in a Particular Case," *Journal of Spiritual Formation and Soul Care* 9, no. 1 (2006): 6.

6. T. S. Eliot, *Becket* (New York: Harcourt Brace, 1935), 44.

desire, as it should be. "The real danger," Willard warns, "[is when] our will has been captured by our desires."[7] Perhaps this is what Jesus has in mind as he teaches his disciples,

> Whoever wants to be my disciple must deny themselves and take up their cross and follow me. For whoever wants to save their life will lose it, but whoever loses their life for me will find it. What good will it be for someone to gain the whole world, yet forfeit their soul? Or what can anyone give in exchange for their soul? (Matt. 16:24–26)

No doubt, part of denying yourself (which is one of the only commands of Jesus that shows up in all four gospels) is consciously making the choice to subsume human desire under God's will. In so doing, it becomes the right reorientation of placing our hearts' wants and desires underneath the will, wants, and desires of God. There's a choice. We will either deny our own desires and follow the will of Jesus, or we will deny the will of Jesus to follow our own desires.[8]

This is a lifelong journey toward liberation. And it is a painful journey that entails choosing to give up one's false loves and letting them rest under a love for God. In *The Selfless Way of Christ*, Henri Nouwen said this narrow way of Jesus is hard for all of us. It confronts the false god of power that rules our hearts. Nouwen wrote,

> It seems nearly impossible for us to believe that any good can come from powerlessness. In this country of pioneers and self-made people, in which ambition is praised from the first moment we enter school until we enter the competitive world

---

7. Willard, "Beyond Pornography," 7.

8. This is what Søren Kierkegaard meant when he wrote about "the purity of heart is to will one thing." It is, in our case, to set our own wills under the will of God. Søren Kierkegaard, *Purity of Heart Is to Will One Thing* (New York: HarperOne, 1994).

of free enterprise, we cannot imagine that any good can come from giving up power or not even desiring it. The all-pervasive conviction in our society is that power is a good and that those possessing it can only desire more of it.[9]

I find Nouwen's words to be deeply realistic and healing. We all know the complexity of our insides. The heart is like a garden—able to flourish with the most exuberant, lush, beautiful, life-giving fruits. But the heart can also cultivate noxious weeds that crowd out eternal life. The heart is the soil from which our desire grows. When the heart is cultivated, good desires grow.[10]

The lifelong adventure of a maturing, growing love for Jesus requires not only that we pay close attention to the things that grow in our internal selves but also that we learn the skills to nurture God's desires and kill disordered desires. We will grow whatever we water in our gardens. This is the pastoral wisdom behind the words of A. W. Tozer: "The unattended garden will soon be overrun with weeds; the heart that fails to cultivate truth and root out error will shortly be a theological wilderness."[11]

———

The New Testament offers a realistic diagnosis of the human heart. On two occasions, in fact, the apostle James warns us that the desire for sin is born from inside a person's being: "Each person is tempted when they are dragged away by *their own* evil desire and

9. Henri Nouwen, *The Selfless Way of Christ: Downward Mobility and the Spiritual Life* (Maryknoll, NY: Orbis, 2007).

10. Curt Thompson similarly speaks of heart's desires as a garden, writing, "desire does not exist as some independent phenomenon to which we respond; it is also something that, like any good gardener knows, must be pruned." Curt Thompson, *The Soul of Desire: Discovering the Neuroscience of Longing, Beauty and Community* (Downers Grove, IL: InterVarsity Press, 2021).

11. A. W. Tozer, *Man: The Dwelling Place of God* (Chicago: Moody Publishers, 1997), chap. 37.

enticed" (James 1:14, emphasis mine). He does not end there. In short order, James argues that quarrels and arguments among even the regenerated result from "desires that battle *within you*" (4:1, emphasis mine). Indeed, we have evil desires. But those desires, often, are sourced locally—birthed within us.

How does this reframe the way we think about temptation? It might be easy to assume that all temptation is delivered by some little demon sitting on our shoulder with whispers of sex, chocolate, and murder. Temptation, indeed, *can* be the work of evil implanting thoughts, ideas, or desires into us. Often, though, evil simply needs to affirm desires already resident within us. It is perplexing: I've never once in my entire life seen an advertisement in a public space for pornography. But that is because this four billion-dollar-a-year industry needs no advertisement. Perhaps James helps us understand why. Pornography plays off the desires that humans already harbor in their hearts. Who needs an advertisement out there when the twisted heart is already doing seductive work in here?

One young man I mentored years ago experienced overwhelming unwanted sexual desires. He recounted his attempts at seeking a professional therapist who could support him in his struggle as he lived in Portland. He bordered on hopelessness because of the difficulty he faced finding a counselor who would willingly support him in his desire for celibacy, sexual holiness, and singleness. Time and again, he was warned that his "repressive" attitudes could lead to sadness, depression, and even suicide. This reveals a dark side of the enemy's tactics. The enemy won't force us into sin. He's subtler. Sometimes we're affirmed into sin by a thousand thumbs-ups. We become, too often, complicit by affirming in others what God may be inviting to be crucified. Evil doesn't always need to tempt us from the outside if it only needs to affirm what's on the inside.

At the same time, we must not be simplistic. Temptation comes in many forms. Some temptation does arise from our insides, some from the outside. But no matter how temptation comes to us, it's paramount that we reject any notion that temptation is in itself a sin. The temptation to do evil or darkness isn't a sin—just as encountering unwanted desires isn't a sin. To experience moments of fleeting desires for this or that isn't something we can control. How can we say this? Quite simply, Jesus, our sinless Savior, was tempted. He was *actually* tempted because he was fully human. Yet he was sinless at the same time. Either temptation is a sin and Jesus was a sinner, or Jesus was sinless and temptation is not a sin. This is liberating. Whenever we shame ourselves for experiencing temptation, we betray our identity as sons and daughters of God.

Our problem isn't temptation per se. The problem is in our response to temptation. Sin is what happens when we allow temptation to stay for dinner and then move in. Entertained temptation is the birthplace of sin. This is why the Bible often describes the connection between temptation and sin as a snowballing experience. In Psalm 1, the author describes the blessed life:

> Blessed is the one
> > who does not walk in step with the wicked
> or stand in the way that sinners take
> > or sit in the company of mockers,
> but whose delight is in the law of the LORD,
> > and who meditates on his law day and night.
> > (Ps. 1:1–2)

Notice the psalmist's idea of the progression of wickedness. The author speaks of the person who "does not walk in step with the wicked." Then they don't "stand" around the things that sinners do. Nor do they "sit" in the company of wickedness. Many biblical commentators have pointed out that there appears to be a clear progression of activity in and around wickedness. First we walk by. Then we stand with. Then we sit down.

What begins as a walk soon becomes immersion. One wonders

if the author of Psalm 1 is reflecting on the Cain and Abel story in Genesis 4. What concludes with the murder of one brother at the hand of another didn't begin that way. The story begins with religious jealousy. Cain resents that Abel's sacrifice was acceptable before God when Cain's was not. Things progress quickly. Cain soon takes Abel on a walk. And before we know it, he murders his brother. Cain is soon banished to be a wanderer. The result of misaligned desire, a walk ends in a murder. Unconfronted sin snowballs.

The psalmist employs similar language in Psalm 137. This psalm is an imprecatory psalm—one of anger and rage. The author is rightly rageful at the Canaanites for harsh treatment of him and God's people. And he soon declares to God about the Canaanites,

> Happy is the one who seizes your infants;
> and dashes them against the rocks. (Ps. 137:9)

We must rightly read this psalm in its entirety. This isn't God voicing a desire to enact violence. Inspired Scripture is giving voice to the psalmist's rage. We must simultaneously recognize that there's no evidence the psalmist went and acted out what he says. Let's be clear: this psalm isn't endorsing violence. This is describing the nature of sin. The psalmist is angry that the Canaanites grow up to kill God's people, so they must be dealt with early on. The message here has clear spiritual dimensions about sin. Sin must be killed early on. Why? Because if we don't kill it, it eventually grows up and starts killing us. In the words of Søren Kierkegaard, "Sin grows every moment one fails to get out of it."[12]

---

12. Søren Kierkegaard, *The Sickness unto Death*, trans. Walter Lowrie (New York: Penguin, 2004), 106. Or as La Rouchfoucauld would surmise, "It is far easier to stifle a first desire than to satisfy all the ensuing ones."

What are we to do with temptation toward evil desires? In too many instances in our modern situation, it's become an accepted religious axiom to simply apply a heavy dose of "stop it" or "be better" as a remedy for human imperfections. But humans need more than hollow prohibitions. Research shows that those who struggle with stuttering and speech impediments often do so because of anxiety around stuttering and speech impediments.[13] The fear of stuttering can trigger the stuttering itself. And telling someone to just "stop it" can make it worse. This same principle plays itself out in temptation. In prohibiting unwanted desires, we can easily become obsessed with those desires and unable to think about anything else. Samuel Perry calls this the "preoccupation hypothesis."[14] Tell a person to stop having a desire, and the anxiety they feel can end up being exacerbated.

Rules can fix behavior but not desire. One tool we have at our disposal in facing temptation is what sacred Scripture calls "confession." What is confession? And how is it undertaken? For most Protestants and Evangelicals, we tend to imagine a confession booth, a priest, a sinner, and the rattling off of some rote penance as a means of forcing God's hand at forgiveness. As a result, many in these traditions ignore the practice of confession as antiquated and useless. Broadly, there are two forms of confession contained in the New Testament. One is confession before God, and the other is confession before people. John describes the first kind—confession to God—in his first letter: "If we confess our sins, he is faithful and just and will forgive us our sins and purify us from all unrighteousness" (1 John 1:9). By speaking truthfully of our sin before God, we are assured a forgiving Father.

---

13. Timothy Schroeder, *Three Faces of Desire* (New York: Oxford University Press, 2004), 22–23.

14. Samuel Perry, *Addicted to Lust: Pornography in the Lives of Conservative Protestants* (New York: Oxford University Press, 2019), 34.

But there's a catch. John's word for "confess" is *homologeō*. It is a word bringing together *homo* ("same") and *logeō* ("say"). This little compound word literally means "to say the same" or "to say with one voice." Confession is agreeing with God. This kind of confession isn't informing God of something he is unaware of or does not already know. Quite the opposite. God already knows our sins intimately. Confession is acknowledging something before God he's keenly aware of. This is the spirit of Psalm 38, who cries out, "All my longings lie open before you, Lord; my sighing is not hidden from you" (v. 9). Confession is not us informing or teaching God. It is an act of agreeing with what God something he already knows and is witnessing to our hearts about. When we acknowledge our sin, John writes, we tap into a deep well of forgiveness and grace for those things we've done that have violated God's desire.

One form of confession is before God. The other form of confession—to each other—is mentioned at the end of James's letter: "Therefore confess your sins to each other and pray for each other so that you may be healed" (James 5:16). A few elements of James' admonition are noteworthy. For one, this is a command. Confession is an essential part of the Christian life. As such, we should not write it off simply because our imaginations have been falsely formed around it.

Also, notice that we are commanded to confess "to each other" in a way that is accompanied by "praying for each other." The "each other" is repeated, evoking a sense of mutuality between two people. This isn't about one person in power receiving a word of confession from another not in power. This evokes two equals mutually sharing their sins.

Confessing to God is easy. Confessing to each other is excruciating. Still, the careful words of James give us a key as to why confessing to one another is so critical. This kind of mutual, human-to-human confession to which he is speaking brings about what James calls "healing." Did you notice that? The result isn't forgiveness. The result is healing. When humans name their sins to one another, healing takes place. Research bears this out. Psychologist James Pennebaker has studied the effects of confession on the body and the mind and found significant "long-term health benefits" to people who regularly name their sins one another.[15] Confessing our sins to one another brings healing to our souls, spirits, and even our bodies. Why? Because humans need a safe relationship in which to take the difficult truth of their lives and hearts.

The problem, for Protestants, is that we have all but done away with the human-to-human expression of confession. This has created a vexing problem. The result is that far too many Christians experience the forgiveness of confession to God but miss out on the healing of confession to one another. We often go through our lives forgiven but unhealed. The preeminent psychologist Carl Jung believed this was one of the greatest problems of the Protestant Reformation—by doing away with the confessional, something was lost. He writes,

> Protestant theology, strangely deluded, . . . robs itself of the most effective means of combating man's insecurity—the confessional, which the Catholic Church has wisely appropriated for the benefit of mankind. . . . The decline of confession and absolution sharpened the moral conflict of the individual and burdened him with the problems which previously the Church had settled with him.[16]

---

15. J. W. Pennebaker, C. F. Hughes, and R. C. O'Heeron, "The Psychophysiology of Confession: Linking Inhibitory and Psychosomatic Processes," *Journal of Personality and Social Psychology* 52, no. 4 (May 1987): 781–93.

16. C. G. Jung, "Editorial," in *The Collected Works of C.G. Jung*, trans. R. F. C. Hull, vol. 10, Bollingen Series XX (New York: Pantheon, 1964), 549–50. For a comprehensive overview of Jung's thinking around confession, see Elizabeth Todd, "The Value of Confession and Forgiveness According to Jung," *Journal of Religion and Health* 24, no. 1 (Spring 1985): 39–48.

Following the Protestant Reformation, Jung believed, the confession booth of the Catholic church was jettisoned—along with it our confession one to another. In that loss, something of the healing power in the church was also lost. The baby was thrown out with the bathwater. Some have gone so far as to suggest that once Protestants stopped practicing confession in local churches, the human need for confession continued, resulting in what you and I now call a therapist's office. One scholar was even willing to deem the modern-day therapist as "the secular priest of society."[17]

By no means does this diminish the work of counseling. I've been paying one handsomely for years. Rather, this should help us appreciate why counseling has become so important in our moment. Every human needs a place to name the desires (good and bad) that they find in their heart. The meeting of this fundamental need is why Alcoholics Anonymous has been so wildly transformative. And it might explain why the revivals under John Wesley in the 1700s had such a lasting impact on countless lives. At a time when the church experienced rampant apathy and lethargy, Wesley developed a system of small groups broken up into societies, classes, and bands—the "method" of Methodism. Discipleship to Jesus, Wesley knew, must entail coming together to listen, confess, and investigate each other's spiritual journeys. Hear some of the questions Wesley outlined for group discussion:

Do you desire to be told your faults?
Do you desire that those around you should have permission
　to tell you what they see in your life?
Is it your desire to be open about your sin and repent
　appropriately?[18]

---

17. For more, see John G. Stackhouse, *Can God Be Trusted? Faith and the Challenge of Evil* (New York: Oxford University Press, 1998), 81–89.

18. Paraphrased from Keith Matthews, "Alone Together: An Epidemic in the Church?," *Conversations: A Forum for Authentic Conversation* 13, no. 1 (Spring and Summer 2015): 52–57.

Desire plays a central role in Wesley's questions. Why? He knew people needed a place to name their desires and experience healing through confession.

We can't always cut out our desires within. But we can *always* confess those desires to a trusted community in Christ. The result is transformative. Confession is telling God and others what's true. The key to dealing with unwanted desires is to shed light on them—to allow others into them in a safe, trusting, and loving relationship. Confession heals. By naming our desires to a trusted other, the power of that desire can lose its foothold over our hearts.

———

Another means by which followers of Jesus have cultivated their desires is through asceticism. Asceticism is the willful practice of self-denial and chosen abstinence from earthly enjoyment—of "cutting off" particular pleasures—as a means to sanctifying one's desires. When we withhold ourselves from the pleasure our desires seek, our true self becomes exposed. This is what Saint John of the Cross has in mind when he writes, "Deny your desires and you will find what your heart longs for."[19]

In recent years, asceticism has received increased attention in many Christian circles. This has broadly dovetailed with the church's renewed awareness of its idolatrous worship of opulence, political power, and wealth. Anglican theologian Sarah Coakley has sought to reintroduce healthy Christian asceticism into the church by contending that the intentional withholding of human pleasure can turn one's eyes from earthly to heavenly matters. In *The New Asceticism*, Coakley highlights celibacy (withholding from sexual oneness) as one form of asceticism that can restore our

———

19. See saying 15 in Saint John of the Cross, "Sayings of Light and Love," in *The Collected Works of Saint John of the Cross*, trans. Kieran Kavanaugh and Otilio Rodriguez (Washington, DC: ICS, 1991).

disordered desires. In turning from physical pleasures, hearts can be drawn *toward* satisfaction in God. To this end, Coakley writes, "The reflective, faithful celibate and the reflective, faithful married person may have more in common—by way of prayerful surrendering of inevitably thwarted desire to God—than the unreflective or faithless celibate, or the carelessly happy or indeed unhappily careless married person."[20]

No doubt, asceticism can be disastrously misused. Scripture never suggests that purity requires being a prude. But ascetic practices (such as celibacy) can have remarkable power to reorient our lives in a sex-crazed culture like our own. Others—such as Wesley Hill—have insightfully written about how celibacy can be seen as a blessing for the common good. Celibacy and marriage, Hill contends, are both gifts of God. But neither are owed to us by God. In our "throwaway culture," the gift and practice of celibacy reminds the church that sexual desire is never to be treated as a kind of "audition" for intimacy. Relational intimacy doesn't depend on sexual fulfillment. In fact, intimacy precedes sex in creation and survives it in new creation. True intimacy doesn't require an orgasm. True intimacy is a gift of grace to all humans.[21]

This is the logic of disciplines such as fasting and silence. Fasting, among other things, is a prophetic stand against the idea that we *are* our desires or that one's fulfillment or identity can be derived from bodily desire. In the way of Jesus, willingly withholding food or drink (or anything) has the intended effect of forcing our desires Godward. Be it food, alcohol, noise, internet, sex, or anything else, in restraining ourselves from compulsive desire fulfillment, we turn our eyes to God as our sustainer and lover. This is

20. Sarah Coakley, *The New Asceticism: Sexuality, Gender and the Quest for God* (New York: Bloomsbury, 2015), 39. Henri Nouwen also wrote about the power of celibacy as a means to deepen one's love for God. See part 2 of Henri Nouwen, *Lifesigns: Intimacy, Fecundity, and Ecstasy in Christian Perspective* (New York: Random House, 1989).

21. Wesley Hill, "Celibacy for the Common Good," *First Things* (blog), March 6, 2015, https://www.firstthings.com/blogs/firstthoughts/2015/03/celibacy-for-the-common-good.

the same rationale for contemplation and silence. Here, we sit with desires swirling within. But we choose not to follow them blithely or compulsively.[22] Silence becomes one's protest against the tyranny of impulse. Many in the early church wrote extensively on how acts of asceticism like these have immeasurable power to form the Christian both morally and ethically.[23]

But is asceticism rooted in the teachings of Jesus? Some might believe it is not. But when we visit Jesus teaching in the Sermon on the Mount, we find that Jesus instructs his disciples to undertake drastic measures in their pursuit of godliness:

> You have heard that it was said, "You shall not commit adultery." But I tell you that anyone who looks at a woman lustfully has already committed adultery with her in his heart. If your right eye causes you to stumble, gouge it out and throw it away. It is better for you to lose one part of your body than for your whole body to be thrown into hell. And if your right hand causes you to stumble, cut it off and throw it away. It is better for you to lose one part of your body than for your whole body to go into hell. (Matt. 5:27–30)

Is Jesus telling us to cut off body parts to follow him? There is a wrong way to read this. History reminds us that some have misapplied Jesus' teaching. Origen, of the second century, was one of the church's most brilliant preachers and thinkers. As his ministry grew, so did the group of beautiful young women who came to hear him preach. As they did, Origen was overcome with sexual temptation. He turned to Jesus's words. In what he believed would

---

22. See the final "coda" in Sarah Coakley, *God, Sexuality, and the Self: An Essay on the Trinity* (New York: Cambridge University Press, 2013), 340ff.

23. Gregory of Nyssa, for example, believed that the act of fasting was intrinsically connected to our ability to have moral strength to do God's will. See Raphael Cadenhead, *The Body and Desire: Gregory of Nyssa's Ascetical Theology*, vol. 4, Christianity in Late Antiquity (Oakland: University of California Press, 2018), 57.

dampen his sexual impulses, Origen took the words of Jesus literally and severed off his own testicles.

Is this the best way forward? Almost immediately after his death, the church collectively agreed that Origen's approach was not reflective of the spirit of Jesus's commands of Matthew 5. (One can hear the collective sigh of relief.) In fact, many of Origen's teachings were roundly rejected posthumously by the church. Some believe he eventually came to regret his decision to castrate himself. Still, Origen's method for dealing with desire has been replayed countless times through church history in one form or another. Rather than hearing the words of Jesus contextually with sensitivity to how his original audience responded, we conclude that Jesus is inviting us to self-mutilation. While few Christians would take such drastic steps, we often take a similar approach. We too often believe the absence of desire to be better option than the possibility of healed desire. Rather than working to cultivate good desires, we become desire*less*. We wrongly assume Jesus' goal for our lives is the absence of desire.

This plays out in how churches often address pornography. In our attempts to rightly name the evils of pornography, we too quickly move into the realm of hinting that *all* sexual desire is of evil origin. Sexual sin is soon seen to be the ultimate sin—something Samuel Perry calls "sexual exceptionalism."[24] The new goal becomes an absence of sexual desire rather than the cultivation of good and healthy sexual desire. Everything, here, is boiled down to little more than lust management. What results is a type of sexual anorexia. We kill what God wants sanctified.

Jesus' teaching in Matthew is not a teaching against sexual desire. God created sex. Nor does Jesus ask us to deal with our wayward desires by hurting the good bodies he created. So how do we read Jesus in Matthew 5? A few observations: First, Jesus

---

24. Throughout Perry, *Addicted to Lust*.

never demonizes sexual desire as a sin. As we've discussed, there's a radical difference between longing and lusting—we control the former, but the latter controls us.

Second, notice that Jesus is speaking to a group of men. There is no indication that women are present. In fact, Jesus specifically says, "If you look at a woman lustfully . . ." Jesus does not address how women clothe themselves. Jesus asks the men to address their own desires. Jesus allows no blame-shifting here. The problem here isn't the beauty of a woman's body. The problem is the sin of a man's heart. Jesus knows the heart of man. And he understands that men often blame women for their own disordered desire. Jesus doesn't do this. He confronts the man's desire head on. Of course, women can and do wrestle with the same issues Jesus raises here. And any follower of Jesus should wear clothing that brings glory to God. But Jesus is the Lord of history. And he is keenly aware that sexual sin in men has been used for power and violence against women at a disproportionate rate. Off-loading the sin of men onto the shoulders of women in the name of modesty isn't in his teaching here.

Third, Jesus *does* tell us to "cut off" and "gouge out" hands and eyes. How do we deal with that? In my New Testament class, I like to ask my students to raise their hands and look at me. Then I read this text out loud and ask them why they haven't followed the words of Jesus yet. They stare, terrified. There's no footnote in which Jesus says, "Just kidding." He commands us to do this.

The good news for us is that it is unlikely Jesus was being literal. How can we know? Two reasons. First, Jesus only mentions hands and eyes. If dealing with *sexual* desire was the issue at hand here, clearly Jesus has forgotten the one body part that for a man, were it cut off, would resolve the problem in short order. He never mentions that body part. Second, none of the disciples who were at this event are recorded as having literally done what Jesus instructed. Why? Because they were there. They read the room.

And saw the heart of Christ. They understood Jesus was speaking figuratively, not literally.

So what is Jesus speaking about if not body parts? He is speaking about the heart. His point is that the heart is controlled by dark sexual desires. Lord knows, if one were to cut off their right hand, they'd still have a left hand with which they could do the same thing. Or if the right eye were gouged out, a left eye would still remain to do with as one pleased. The problem isn't in the limbs. The problem is what lies in the depths of human desire.

We can confess and cut, but there's one more approach: filling ourselves up with the right desires. The problem of evil desires is creatively tackled in a series of sermons by Scottish preacher Thomas Chalmers. In *The Expulsive Power of a New Affection*, he proposes that the issue isn't just the cutting off of desires. Rather, it's being filled up with good desires. "The only way to dispossess the heart of an old affection," Chalmers wrote, "is by the expulsive power of a new one."[25] Think about a glass full of air. How would we get the air out of that glass? The glass must be filled with something else. The new substance displaces the old. Chalmers writes, "It is then that the heart brought under the mastery of one great and predominant affection, is delivered from the tyranny of its former desires."

The philosopher Dietrich von Hildebrand writes of this spiritual law in his book *Transformation in Christ*. He says, "A strong desire must fill us to become different beings, to mortify our old selves and re-arise as new men and women in Christ. This desire... to decrease so that 'he may grow in us,' is the first elementary precondition for the transformation in Christ."[26] To be filled, we must

---

25. This famous sermon can be found in its full form on countless websites.

26. Dietrich von Hildebrand, *Transformation in Christ: On the Christian Attitude* (1948; San Francisco: Ignatius, 2001), 5.

be emptied. What Chalmers and Hildebrand are getting at is that
there is no such thing as a spiritual vacuum. In Matthew 12, after
casting out a demon from someone, Jesus says,

> When an impure spirit comes out of a person, it goes through
> arid places seeking rest and does not find it. Then it says, "I will
> return to the house I left." When it arrives, it finds the house
> unoccupied, swept clean and put in order. Then it goes and
> takes with it seven other spirits more wicked than itself, and
> they go in and live there. And the final condition of that person
> is worse than the first. (vv. 43–45)

A spiritual house can't stay empty. It must be filled with something.
The cure for evil isn't spiritual absence.[27] It is the renewed presence
of God. We don't just cast *out* the demons; we also must be filled
by the presence, wonder, and desires of God. The cure for a demon
possession isn't merely exorcism; it's a new possession—being *filled*
with the Spirit above all.

When we purchased our home that we have turned into an
urban garden, we cut down a whole grove of Leyland cypress trees.
More or less, they were only taking up space and creating a natural
barrier with our neighbors. Upon leveling these trees, we found that
all this new space invited noxious weeds. We traded in one problem
for another. We came to find that the only way to keep the weeds
away is the growing of good ground cover. Nature abhors a vacuum.
So does the realm of our heart's desire.

Jesus is up to this very thing with Peter. Following the resurrection, Peter and the disciples are up in the morning fishing, back to

---

27. As Methodist preacher C. K. Barrett declares in his sermon "Living by Faith" on Gal.
2:20, "Nature abhors a vacuum and so does the self. Cast out one demon and if nothing powerful takes its place, it will return with seven more demons worse than itself. The only way not
to be self-centered, is to be God-centered. The only way to be free is to accept the rule of God."
Found in Ben Witherington III, ed., *Preaching Methodist Theology and Biblical Truth: Classic
Sermons of C. K. Barrett* (Nashville: General Board of Higher Education and Ministry, 2017).

what they did before they followed Jesus. Upon realizing Jesus stands on the shore, they return lakeside to discover he has made them breakfast. What happens next transforms Peter. Peter had denied Jesus three times. And in John 21, Jesus asks Peter three times, "Do you love me?" After Peter affirms his love, Jesus tells his friend,

> "Feed my sheep. Very truly I tell you, when you were younger you dressed yourself and went where you wanted; but when you are old you will stretch out your hands, and someone else will dress you and lead you where you do not want to go." Jesus said this to indicate the kind of death by which Peter would glorify God. Then he said to him, "Follow me!" (John 21:17–19)

Peter would build the rest of his life on these words. This calling moment for Peter represents the reversal of everything we have come to believe life should be about—especially in the American dream. For too long, we've been sold a vision of life promising more and more freedom the older we become: more money, more choices, more affluence, then retirement. What Jesus gives Peter—and us— is the opposite. The remainder of Peter's life will be marked not by going where he wanted to go but where Jesus wanted him to go. He won't even clothe himself. His future isn't marked by more freedom but by increased faithfulness.

Henri Nouwen called this "downward mobility." The American dream is a mirage marked by believing that everything will go up and to the right like a booming stock exchange. But Peter's future won't be up and to the right. He will spend the remainder of his life serving the church and suffering for the gospel. Jesus is reversing the American dream. In the kingdom, the more we progress, the more we bend our ways to Jesus. Nouwen continued,

> We are taught to conceive of development in terms of an ongoing increase in human potential. Growing up means becoming

healthier, stronger, more intelligent, more mature, and more productive. Consequently, we hide those who do not affirm this myth of progress, such as the elderly, prisoners, and those with mental disabilities. In our society, we consider the upward move the obvious one while treating the poor cases who cannot keep up as sad misfits, people who have deviated from the normal line of progress.[28]

To mark this occasion, Jesus tells Peter he will "feed my sheep." That is an odd command to give to a fisherman, isn't it? Peter didn't do sheep. He did nets and boats. Jesus shows that he understands the nature of Peter's heart—and our hearts. We need more than mere prohibitions. We need to be filled with something when something is taken from us. Jesus changes the metaphor of Peter's life. He isn't just removing Peter's old desires. He is giving Peter new desires, a new vocation. In killing one desire, he plants the seed of another.

---

28. Henri Nouwen, *The Selfless Way of Christ: Downward Mobility and the Spiritual Life* (Maryknoll, NY: Orbis, 2012), 27.

Chapter 8

NURTURING DESIRE

In 1992, a team of neuroscientists led by Joaquim Brasil-Neto undertook an experiment. They sought to discover if one's desires could be changed. To accomplish this, they placed magnetic stimulators on a group of subjects' heads while tapping small clicking sounds. They simultaneously sparked a small electrical burst that stimulated one of the sides of the subject's brain. Subjects were then instructed to turn their heads to one side or the other. The outcome was remarkable. With near total predictability, the subjects would turn their head in the opposite direction of the side their brain that was being stimulated. Though the subjects believed they followed their own will, some 80 percent of the time they turned their heads in the predictable direction. A robust debate ensued. Had scientists actually discovered a way to manipulate their subjects' desires?[1]

The debate over where and how we get our desires isn't new. In Eden, God created a world of resplendent delight marked by virtually boundless freedom for the humans who inhabited it. One tree—the "tree of knowledge of good and evil"—was off-limits for human consumption. Oddly, only *after* the serpent's discussion with the woman is the prohibited tree described as "desirable for gaining wisdom" (Gen. 3:6). Then and only then is the fruit

---

1. J. P. Brasil-Neto et al., "Focal Transcranial Magnetic Stimulation and Response Bias in a Forced-Choice Task," *Journal of Neurology, Neurosurgery, and Psychiatry* 55, no. 10 (1992): 964–66.

called "desirable." Like the electrical stimulation from Brasil-Neto's experiment, is the deceiver awakening human desire? The serpent's words certainly twisted human desire. In the very garden where God's word had once been trusted and contentment reigned, the serpent's words became trusted, and discontentment awakened. Desire turned toward the only spoken prohibition.

Biblically, human desire is malleable, flexible, even fluid. We change our minds. Our attitudes *need* changing. Similarly, desires can be remolded and awakened. Human desire isn't eternally transfixed, free from manipulation from external forces. Desire, in fact, is the component of human nature the serpent first seizes upon and weaponizes.

The manipulation of human desire is arguably the basis of Western capitalism. What is advertising but the simple reeducation and awakening of novel desires? The thinking behind modern advertising is predicated on the notion that well-crafted images and arguments can nurture within the consumer what we might call unnecessary desires. Advertising is an industry that seeks more than anything to create "a desire for desire."[2] In 1927, Paul Mazur of Lehman Brothers famously wrote what would become the mission statement of the modern Western advertising industry: "We must shift America from a needs to a desires culture. People must be trained to desire, to want new things, even before the old have been entirely consumed. We must shape a new mentality. Man's desires must overshadow his needs."[3]

On a rudimentary level, advertisement is the commodification and monetization of human desire—the engine of capitalism that

---

2. Rodney Clapp, "The Theology of Consumption and the Consumption of Theology," in *Border Crossings: Christian Trespasses on Popular Culture and Public Affairs*, ed. Rodney Clapp (Grand Rapids: Brazos, 2000), 126–56.

3. Quoted in Jeremy Lent, *The Patterning Instinct: A Cultural History of Humanity's Search for Meaning* (Amherst, NY: Prometheus, 2017). I'm grateful to my friend John Mark Comer for this reference in his fabulous book *The Ruthless Elimination of Hurry* (Colorado Springs: Waterbrook, 2017).

seeks to "convert desire into money."[4] This became the focal point
of social critic Herbert Marcuse, who believed consumer culture
creates a person who becomes increasingly oppressed by novel and
exotic desires. Humans, Marcuse said, have what he called "true
needs." But consumer culture solidifies a belief that unneeded goods
(or "pseudo-needs") can fulfill us. Marcuse called this "the creation
of false needs."[5] Humans need food, shelter, and relationships.
Advertising sells something else altogether. It awakens desires for
the endless unnecessaries: entertainment, boundless sexual pursuit,
and an endless assortment of products.

And advertising has been effective. It has reeducated our
desires to the tune of the 4,000–10,000 advertisements we enter-
tain every day. It's almost impossible (if not dizzying) to discern
which desires are from God and which are merely the algorithms
messing with our brains.[6] Whether we want it or not, our desires
are being discipled and educated.

The question, in part, isn't *if* our desires will be educated but
how they are being educated.[7] They are either being formed into
Christ's image or the serpent's. Indeed, Jesus was a "teacher"—a
rabbi, an instructor in the way. But the New Testament says that
demons teach as well (1 Tim. 4:1). Everyone follows some rabbi.

No doubt this is part and parcel of what Paul called being
"transformed by the renewing of your mind" (Rom. 12:2). Human
desire is often downwind from what we put in our heads. Yes, part
of sanctification is the external parts of our lives being changed:

---

4. Moshe Sluhovsky, "Review of David Bennett, The Currency of Desire," *Psychoanalysis and History* 13, no. 3 (2017): 429–31.

5. Herbert Marcuse, *One-Dimensional Man: Studies in the Ideology of Advanced Industrial Society* (New York: Routledge Classics, 2002).

6. On how neuromarketers manipulate the pleasure center of our brain associated with desire, cravings, and sex, see Christopher West, *Fill These Hearts: God, Sex, and the Universal Longing* (New York: Image, 2012), 35.

7. Christianity is, above all, an education in desire. See T. J. Gorringe, *The Education of Desire: Toward a Theology of the Senses*, John Albert Hall Lecture Series (London: Bloomsbury T&T Clark, 2001).

actions, good deeds, the tongue, our public lives. But God's invitation is never to sanitize the outside while leaving the inside untouched. Reflecting on holiness, John Wesley described transformation as the "purity of intention, dedicating all life to God. It is the giving God all our heart; it is one desire and design ruling all our tempers."[8] Notice Wesley's emphasis on desire. Transformation, first and foremost, is an inside job.

The same desires that have been formed by God and *de*formed by Satan must also be *trans*formed by the Spirit.[9] This is the process of "disciplined desire"[10]—or what Augustine called a "holy longing." He believed "that is our life, to be trained by longing . . . in the measure that our longings are severed from the love of the world."[11] Without having a discipled or educated desire around the person of Jesus, then the desires themselves become the guiding force in our existence. Rather than following Jesus, we follow what Paul called "the cravings of our flesh" (Eph. 2:3) and what Jude called "ungodly desires" (Jude 18). As William Cavanaugh writes, "We desperately need not to be left to the tyranny of our own wills. The key to true freedom is not just following whatever desires we happen to have, but cultivating the right desires . . . we must consider the end toward which the will is moved."[12]

8. John Wesley, *Containing a Plain Account of Christian Perfection*, vol. 8, *The Works of the Rev. John Wesley* (Philadelphia: D. & S. Neall and W. S. Stockton, 1827), 66.

9. Used here is the paradigmatic language of Dallas Willard, *Renovation of the Heart: Putting on the Character of Christ* (Colorado Springs: NavPress, 2021), 6.

10. John Mark Comer, *Live No Lies: Recognize and Resist the Three Enemies That Sabotage Your Peace* (Colorado Springs: Waterbrook, 2021), 113.

11. Quoted in Augustine, *Later Works* (Philadelphia: Westminster, 1955), 290. Thanks to James K. A. Smith for pointing this out in *Desiring the Kingdom*.

12. Cavanaugh, here, sums up Augustine's view on desire. William T. Cavanaugh, *Being Consumed: Economics and Christian Desire* (Grand Rapids: Eerdmans, 2008), 11–12.

What is the "end" (borrowing from Augustine) toward which our desires are aimed? Why do we want? Articulating the goal of one's desire isn't always easy to discern. In March of 1981, President Ronald Reagan visited the Washington, DC, Hilton Hotel. The hotel had become a favorite for presidents to host fundraisers and deliver policy speeches at. Exiting the hotel, a young John Hinckley Jr. shot five bullets in under two seconds, attempting to assassinate the sitting president. Reagan and three others were shot, although nobody died that day from their wounds. Soon afterward, Hinckley's motivation became evident. He did not shoot the president primarily to kill him. Hinckley, rather, had succumbed to an erotomaniacal obsession with eighteen-year-old actress Jodie Foster, whom he believed would be impressed by his brazen actions. What at first appeared to be a desire to kill the president was, at a deeper level, a stunt to win the attention of a beautiful actress.

What are our ultimate desires? In the journey toward maturity, we must increasingly be in touch with the desires that propel our actions. Philosophers of desire have pointed out that human desires appear to be interlocking and interconnected—rarely, if ever, existing in isolation from one another. Our desire for one thing is likely connected in some unseen way to a desire for something else. William Irvine calls this the "chain of desires."[13] This chain connects our presenting desires with our base, bedrock desires. In *On Desire*, Irvine illustrates this with his students' comical responses to his question, "Why are you taking this class?"

> A typical response: "So I can pass your class." And why does he want to pass? "So I can graduate." Why graduate? "So I can get into law school." Why go to law school? "So I can become a lawyer, obviously." And why become a lawyer? "So I can buy an

---

13. William B. Irvine, *On Desire: Why We Want What We Want* (New York: Oxford University Press, 2006), pt. II.

Arrest-Me Red Dodge Viper RT / 10, with a 415 horsepower
engine that will go from 0 to 60 in 5.0 seconds."

The chain of desire shapes the whole of our existence. Do we
desire to be physically fit and healthy, or are we seeking something
else? Do we desire more money, or is there some lifestyle money
provides? Do we desire a good meal or the romance that may be
sparked over the meal? Is it really the car keys we are looking for or
the thing the keys can start?

Our presenting desires aren't always identical to our ultimate
desires. Let me illustrate. Think about holding a wad of paper
money in your hand. What are you holding? Money is government-
issued paper that we all agree (almost on faith) holds some particular worth at a given historical moment. Money, in itself, is
little more than paper. But the pursuit of money is not the pursuit
of paper. No, the desire for money is always a pursuit of some
other desire.

Irvine distinguishes between what he calls "terminal" and
"instrumental" desires.[14] Terminal desires are bedrock desires that
motivate and orientate our other desires. These are what we *really*
want. Instrumental desires, however, are those in service of deeper,
terminal desires. Back to Hinckley. His instrumental desire was
shooting the president. His terminal desire was a celebrity's attention. The intimate relationship between instrumental and terminal
desires has been explored by many in Western philosophy, including Plato, who believed all desires connected to base appetites, such
as a need for food, water, and shelter.[15]

The pursuit of money is a perfect example of an instrumental desire. Few desire money because they enjoy the way the

14. Irvine, *On Desire*, 55–57.
15. On Plato's view of desire, see the insightful Diogenes Allen and Eric Springsted, *Philosophy for Understanding Theology*, 2nd ed. (Louisville: Westminster John Knox, 2007), chap. 2.

government-issue paper smells or feels in their hands. The desire for money is instrumental because it opens the door for other desires: purchasing power, homes, cars, status, early retirement, relationships, clothing. Instrumental desires aren't inherently bad.[16] Money can also provide things everyone needs, like shelter, food, clothing, and medical care. But whether it's meant for good or bad purposes, money is rarely an end goal. Deeper desires are always afoot.

Scripture picks up on this. The Old Testament word for "money" (Heb. *kasef*) is the same as "desire" or "languishing over something."[17] The biblical tradition, in its wisdom, is keenly aware of money's disproportionate power to capture human desire. To that end, Paul would instruct Timothy that "the love of money is the root of all kinds of evil" (1 Tim. 6:10). Money isn't evil. Instead, one's insatiable pursuit of money can ruin the soul—what Paul would call a "trap" that leads to "temptation . . . and harmful desires that plunge people into ruin and destruction" (1 Tim. 6:9). Jesus even equates "thorns" with the "deceitfulness of wealth and the desire for other things" which choke out the good seed God has sown (Mark 4:18–19). Nothing diminishes our human glory more than pursuing misdirected desire.

This is why religion can be dangerous. It easily provides cover for nefarious desires that betray Christ and his kingdom. Jesus often critiqued the motivations of the religious leaders of his day, warning against the desire to please the crowds, seek money, and attain power that can pervade toxic religion. Jesus sternly warned the Pharisees who fronted with piety but were "full of greed and self-indulgence" (Matt. 23:25). Desire hidden in toxic religion can devastate; it hides behind robes and theological

---

16. To be sure, earning money isn't evil. The philosopher Diogenes Allen susses out the necessary human need to work and earn money in Diogenes Allen, *Quest: The Search for Meaning through Christ* (New York: Walker, 1990), 114–15.

17. Os Guinness, *The Call: Finding and Fulfilling the Central Purpose of Your Life* (Nashville: Nelson, 2003), 130. Similarly, the Latin word *cupere* is the origin of our word *cupid*, the namesake of the Greek god of love. West, *Fill These Hearts*, 20.

rigidity. Michel Foucault, a twentieth-century postmodern philosopher, believed that religious truth claims were often merely a "desire for power."[18] Awkward bedfellows as they may seem, Jesus and Foucault shared similar critiques of the possible dangers of religiosity.[19]

An inescapable part of Christian maturity is learning what truly motivates us. Parker Palmer is a Christian educator whose work has helped many understand the craft and vocation of teaching. In *Let Your Life Speak*, Palmer tells the story of a time when he was asked to become president of a major university. Honored by the opportunity, Palmer struggled to discern if he should leave the classroom for the role. He sat on the question with his Christian community. Along the way, a friend asked, "What, Parker, would you like most about being president?" Palmer answered in complete candor, "I guess what I'd like most is getting my picture in the paper with the word president under it."

Palmer had his answer. He turned down the job and kept teaching. Later, a friend reminded him that there are "easier ways to get your picture in the paper."[20] Being in touch with our true desires can help us understand how best to make decisions with our lives.

▬▬▬▬

18. Quoted in an interview with Foucault and Giles Deleuze: "Intellectuals and power: A conversation between Michel Foucault and Gilles Deleuze," libcom, September 9. 2006, https://libcom.org/article/intellectuals-and-power-conversation-between-michel-foucault-and-gilles-deleuze. This transcript first appeared in English in the book *Language, Counter-Memory, Practice: Selected Essays and Interviews by Michel Foucault*, ed. Donald F. Bouchard (Ithaca, NY: Cornell University Press, 1980).

19. I'm a product of sermons. I won't soon forget Dr. Tim Keller's sermon "Absolutism" preached at Redeemer Presbyterian Church in New York in which he contended Jesus and Foucault share a similar critique of religion. I owe this thought to the seed Dr. Keller planted years ago.

20. Parker Palmer, *Let Your Life Speak: Listening for the Voice of Vocation* (New York: Jossey-Bass, 2000), 44–46.

This dialogue about instrumental and terminal desires can reshape our lives if we let it. The Bible has a stock word to capture this idea of one's terminal desires: worship. We worship what we expect will give our lives ultimate meaning and value. Put another way, what we seek, want, and spend our lives pursuing is intertwined with what we worship. And worship, in the end, is what gives our lives a structure, ultimate meaning, and purpose.

When we look at Matthew's infancy narratives, we find that it juxtaposes the Magi and King Herod, who are both "searching" for Jesus. The Magi, magicians from the East, follow celestial stars in search of Jesus bearing gifts of gold, frankincense, and myrrh.[21] The Magi search for Jesus to worship him. Herod also searches for Jesus, but not to worship him. Herod wants the child dead. This baby represents a threat to Herod's power, prestige, and rule. In a way, the Magi and Herod represent two paradigms for living. Are we searching for Jesus as the center of our existence? Or are we the center of our own story, searching to get rid of Jesus our threat?[22] Searching for Jesus is not enough. Searching for Jesus with the right intent is what is most important.

This juxtaposition evokes something important. The Gospels don't invite us just to be seekers of Jesus. Herod did that. We are called to seek Jesus in a particular kind of way for a particular purpose. We can hear this in Jesus' call, which inevitably exposes the true desires and motivations of those being called. Jesus says, "Whoever *wants* to be my disciple must deny themselves and take up their cross and follow me" (Matt. 16:24, emphasis mine). Jesus isn't seeking groupies. The call is to a unique form of following that

---

21. *Desire* comes from a Latin word *desiderare* meaning "to long for," "to wish for," or "to expect." Interestingly, *de sidere* meant "from the stars" or "awaiting what the stars brought." West, *Fill These Hearts*, 16.

22. Marva Dawn describes worship as a "royal waste of time"—it should never be "useful" for adjacent purposes such as church growth or emotional manipulation. Marva Dawn, *A Royal Waste of Time: The Splendor of Worshiping God and Being Church for the World* (Grand Rapids: Eerdmans, 1999).

includes self-denial, the cross, and a life of displacement for the kingdom.

Even a desire to follow Jesus must be shaped by his being. The mark of this kind of pursuit is to seek God for God's sake, not for our own sake. The Christian Frenchman Francois Fénelon described this kind of love:

> The first effect of a sincere love is an earnest desire to know all that we ought to do to gratify the one we love. Any other desire is an indication that we love ourselves under a pretense of loving God. It shows that we are seeking an empty and deceitful consolation in him and that we want to use God for our pleasure, instead of sacrificing that pleasure for his glory. God forbid that his children should love him that way! No matter what it costs us, if we truly want to love him, we must know what he requires of us and try to do it without reservation.[23]

This is cruciform, or *cross-shaped*, desire. Jesus' rubric of true discipleship isn't merely to follow. It is to follow in a certain way. Some, it turns out, followed Jesus for the free lunches and miracles. In the end, they walked away. The teachings were too difficult. Others followed Jesus to top off their already perfect life that they might inherit the kingdom as some kind of spiritual 401(k). They too walked away sad.

It's not enough to desire Jesus. Our desire for Jesus must be cross-like. Christian psychologist Richard Beck calls this "cruciform desire":

> The sanctification of our desires is a process of making them cruciform. This occurs in the context of covenant. Covenant is

---

23. Francois Fénelon, *The Complete Fénelon*, ed. Robert J. Edmonson and Hal L. Helms (Brewster, MA: Paraclete, 2008), 88.

a "school of desire" akin to a spiritual discipline, even a monastic discipline given the relationality of the process, where *eros* is shaped by fidelity and self-emptying servanthood (*kenosis*). The daily practices of covenant lead to the divinization of desire, where eros is made chaste, holy, and a participation in the Triune love of God.[24]

Embarking on the path toward cruciform desire requires that we integrate into our existence the reality that Jesus sits at the center of our lives.

Life has two paths. Either I'm the center of my universe, and everything bends to the gravity of my desire. Or God is the center of the universe, and we bend to the gravity of his desire. These are fundamentally different paths, but they remain the spiritual architecture for all Christian formation. "The spiritual life," Dallas Willard contended, "is a life organized around God."[25] This represents a stark contrast to the way of the world, which sees the self as the center—what Martin Luther was fond of calling *homo incurvatus in se* ("humanity curved in on itself").

Self-centeredness rules our day. Ours has become, in the words of David Brooks, a culture encouraging people to see themselves as the center of their universe.[26] This is why the digital revolution has been so devastating to the human person. It gives us a set of tools and devices that place us at the center of our existence. A life mediated through the internet allows us to do this with excellence. In the book *The Rise and Triumph of the Modern Self*, Carl Trueman suggests that social media and the digital revolution allow us to create, "A world in which it is increasingly easy to imagine that

---

24. Richard Beck, "A Theology of Desire, Love and Marriage," *Experimental Theology* (blog), December 9, 2014, http://experimentaltheology.blogspot.com/2014/12/a-theology-of-desire-love-and-marriage.html.

25. Willard, *Renovation of the Heart*, 31, 41.

26. David Brooks, *The Road to Character* (New York: Random House, 2015), 6.

reality is something we can manipulate according to our own wills and desires, and not something that we necessarily need to conform ourselves to."[27]

Being self-centered ruins everything about us, including our thoughts of God. Jesus is the center *or* I am the center. Self-centeredness disfigures our theological imaginations. While we may undertake rigorous theological study, this doesn't ensure we're doing it rightly. Sometimes our way of controlling God is by studying him, what Calvin would call "senseless curiosity."[28] Even theology can be self-centered.

Worse yet, we arrange our ethics, truth, and beliefs around our own feeble reasoning and fickle desires. We bend God's words around our desires. Before we know it, we think about God the way Marie Kondo organizes: if it sparks joy, we keep it; otherwise, we chuck it. Christ and his Word and his glorious cross are soon displaced and replaced by feeble and whimsical human preference. All truth is now *my* truth.

God, forgive us.

━━━━━

During a particularly fruitful season of public ministry that took me around the world to teach, preach, and minister, a nagging sense arose within me: God was inviting me to lay down my preaching gift. I wouldn't have concocted such a plan on my own. Yet there it was. For as long as possible, I resisted the whisper. But I couldn't

27. Carl Trueman, *The Rise and Triumph of the Modern Self: Cultural Amnesia, Expressive Individualism, and the Road to Sexual Revolution* (Wheaton, IL: Crossway, 2020), 41.

28. John Calvin, *Ezekiel I (Chapters 1–12)* (Grand Rapids: Eerdmans, 1994), 57. Theologians call sins impacts on the mind the noetic effects of sin. "When loving the truth is quite out of fashion," writes James Sire, "the very mention of the word can call up hatred. *Veritas odium Parit*, said the Roman poet Terence—truth engenders hatred. The desire to flee truth is deep . . . and that fact is not obscure to anyone." James Sire, *Habits of the Mind: Intellectual Life as Christian Calling* (Downers Grove, IL: InterVarsity Press, 2022).

neglect the gentle voice indefinitely. I didn't know for how long, but I knew I had to let preaching go. "Come away," the voice said. "Come and *be* with me."

I underwent discernment with those closest to me. I spent late nights talking with my wife. My spiritual director prayed alongside me. And I had countless conversations with my friends. I'd long held Henri Nouwen's definition of discernment as gospel truth: "listening and responding to that place within us where our deepest desires align with God's desire."[29] Nouwen's wisdom now made little sense to me. Nothing within me desired what God wanted. I wanted what *I* wanted—to teach, preach, and minister. No part of me wanted to walk away.

Eventually, I submitted—a sudden shift that required me to cancel countless engagements on the upcoming calendar. With each cancellation, I had to rethink the family budget. People called worried I was having some neurotic break or midlife crisis. Nobody knew what to do with me. I didn't know what to do with me. And I certainly didn't know what to do with God. The confusing experience rendered me nearly obscure overnight. I felt naked. Useless. Aimless.

God was making me lie down beside streams of grace (Ps. 23:2). There, in the quiet, is where we often discover what we truly love. I faced a year of quiet obscurity. In the silence, an idol surfaced in my heart. I loved preaching. But somewhere along the way I'd fallen *more* in love with how preaching made me feel, how useful I felt when people connected with God as I preached, the joy of being used by God, the feeling of being needed by the church. When I preached, I was wanted, I was loved, I was seen. Without a pulpit, my identity was unclear. Did God still love me? Was I needed by the church? Did people still want me? My emotional supply chain

---

29. Henri Nouwen, *Discernment: Reading the Signs of Daily Life* (New York: HarperOne, 2013), 150.

had broken down. In my own eyes, I was only someone when I was wanted, seen, and listened to. The Spirit was gently and lovingly purging me of *lesser* desires.[30]

The Father's invitation back to preaching wouldn't happen until I settled in my own heart that I was first a beloved child loved by God. If that didn't happen, I couldn't return. The path Jesus was leading me on would no longer allow public ministry to replace the joys of deep friendship, prayer, the disciplines, and being in the arms of my Beloved. No longer could I use the pulpit to share vulnerably with strangers while side-stepping the work of intimacy with people closest to me. No longer could I use the pulpit to forge one-way vulnerability without doing the work of being known by God.

We are creatures made to be desired. "God longs for us to be aware that he longs for us," writes Curt Thompson, "that he was thinking about us forever before we even became a zygote, let alone a newborn or adult."[31] In failing to see ourselves as children desired and noticed by the Father, we end up needing others to desire and notice us to feel fulfilled.[32] Only when we know we are first and foremost desired by the Father can we freely offer our gifts to others.

When we fail to begin at the place of our belovedness, we place an invisible yoke on others to fill our emotional debts. "Let no debt remain outstanding," Paul would wisely command in Romans 13:8. But this cuts two ways. We must forgive the debts others have toward us. But we must also resist putting others under the yoke

---

30. Sarah Coakley defines this purgation of desire as the "Father . . . through the Spirit . . . stirs up, and progressively chastens and purges, the frailer and often misdirected desires of humans, and so forges them, by stages of sometimes painful growth, into the likeness of his son." Coakley, *God, Sexuality, and the Self: An Essay on the Trinity* (New York: Cambridge University Press, 2013), 5.

31. Curt Thompson, *The Soul of Desire: Discovering the Neuroscience of Longing, Beauty and Community* (Downers Grove, IL: InterVarsity Press, 2021), 63.

32. In his explosive commentary on Matthew, Frederick Dale Bruner writes, "We were made to notice and to be noticed by God, to imag(e)-ine and image his pleasure. In Jesus' vocabulary in Matthew's Gospel the desire to be noticed by the Father is what later Christian tradition calls 'faith.'" Frederick D. Bruner, *Matthew*, vol. 1 (Grand Rapids: Eerdmans, 2007), 283.

of emotional debt to our bankrupt hearts. Only in the Father's love can all debts be canceled.

I came back to preaching. Just differently. Same task, different spirit. I'm still a fisher of men. I've just learned how to fish off the other side of the boat.

———

How do we forge our desires around the cross? Without doing this work, we run the risk of equating our desires with God himself. In 2015, Oprah Winfrey's television studio produced a new show called *Belief* as an exploration of spirituality from one of America's most inspiring women. During a promotional tour, Oprah was interviewed about her favorite Bible verse. Oprah said she loved Psalm 37:4, which reads, "Delight thyself also in the Lord: and he shall give thee the desires of thine heart" (KJV). She then explains who the Lord is:

> Now what that says to me, "Lord" has a wide range [of meaning]. What is Lord? Compassion, love, forgiveness, kindness. So you delight yourself in those virtues where the character of the Lord is revealed. Delight thyself in goodness, delight thyself in love, kindness, and compassion, and you will receive the desires of your heart. It says to me, if you focus on being a force for good, good things will come.[33]

As inspiring a reading of Psalm 37 as this may be, it fails to capture the heart of God's voice in the text. In a world that purports to give us what we want—a world that offers us what Eugene Peterson called the "new trinity" of "holy needs, holy wants, and

---

33. Megan Garber, "How Stephen Colbert Is Bringing Religion to Late Night," *The Atlantic* (blog), October 16, 2015, https://www.theatlantic.com/entertainment/archive/2015/10/stephen-colbert-is-bringing-religion-to-late-night/410959/.

holy feelings"[34]—we need an environment where desires are given parameters, not full reign. We need a form of desire that is not shaped around us but around God.

Many have written about how religious symbolism and liturgy can disproportionately "orient our desire" in the right direction.[35] One first step we can take is to place ourselves willingly in a community where our desires and wants aren't given full reign. Perhaps in the marketplace we might get what we want how we want it. But the church should be a counterformative environment, where the message is not merely what listeners want to hear. There is wisdom in being in a Jesus-seeking church in which I must submit myself to things I don't wish to hear and that I can't shuffle my way out of. I must submit myself to a message I may not like and can't wiggle my way out of. There, I must lay down my personal preferences and love people who are nothing like me. It's an environment where we run the risk of being disciplined for our sin and, Lord willing, come face to face with the teachings that have been handed down from generation to generation. Individualism is the womb of heresy.

Indeed, we need a worshiping community for our desires to be molded. But we must not limit our understanding of the nurture of desire solely to our religious spaces. If we do, we run the risk of stymying our transformation. What if our liturgies included activities we undertook every day? James K. A. Smith writes about what he calls "cultural liturgies" (and what Eric Jacobson calls "common grace liturgies"[36]) as those things humans do with regularity that shape their internal desires. Yes, we should pray, go to church, take communion, and confess sin. But what if everyday liturgies like

---

34. Eugene Peterson, *Eat This Book: A Conversation in the Art of Spiritual Reading* (Grand Rapids: Eerdmans, 2006), chap. 3.

35. Wendy Farley, *The Wounding and Healing of Desire: Weaving Heaven and Earth* (Louisville: Westminster John Knox, 2005), 14.

36. Eric O. Jacobson, "The Ballet of Street Life: On Common Grace Liturgies," *Comment* (blog), December 13, 2013, https://comment.org/the-ballet-of-street-life-on-common-grace-liturgies/.

doing the dishes, walking through the woods, and cleaning the garage could have equal transformative power.[37] We become our everyday habits.

Second, we discipline our desires through the practice of simplicity. The sociologist Jonathan Haidt has argued that humans are far less rational than they like to believe. In *The Happiness Hypothesis*, Haidt uses the image of an elephant with a rider as a way of describing our emotions and our reason. The elephant represents the emotions, desires, and feelings of the rider. The rider represents the rational part of the human. We can often see ourselves as rational beings in charge of our emotions. But Haidt believes the elephant of our emotions often drives the rider. He argues that we tend to rationalize our feelings and desires rather than being purely rational beings. Our desires are often internalized habits.

I believe Haidt's point here has explosive value in how we think about cultivating right desires. More often than not, our lives are driven by desires that march forward like an elephant. We buy new toys, endless products, and novel experiences without much thought. This gives more and more power to those desires. Practicing the ancient way of simplicity—buying less more thoughtfully and more justly—undercuts this often-uncontested desire. We may assume that if we just change our desires, our lives will change in turn. But often the opposite is true. We must change how we live in order that our desires might be remade.

Third, another critical discipline that nurtures our desires is to read the Gospels. What does reading the Gospels have to do with our desire? Desire needs a trellis, a framework, and boundaries for us to live appropriately and flourish in holiness. Thus, marrying as intimate partners the commands of God and our desires is the essence of biblical faith in the way of Jesus. Human desire needs lines in

---

37. No doubt, the most explosive treatment of this topic comes in the form of Tish Warren, *Liturgy of the Ordinary: Sacred Practices in Everyday Life* (Downers Grove, IL: InterVarsity Press, 2016).

which to color. God's commands serve as that structure. Only when those boundaries are in place can human desire be released from its enslavement to self-centeredness. What else could Jesus have meant by saying, "If you remain in me and my words remain in you, ask whatever you wish, and it will be done for you."? (John 15:7). Or when John restates the teaching he had heard from his master: "If we ask anything according to his will, he hears us. . . . We know that we have what we've asked of him" (1 John 5:14–15). In some mysterious way, when our desires are structured around God's Word, they take on a potency that can move the heart of God.

Jesus' and John's words are not, as some have thought, some ancient trick for wish fulfillment. They are expressly clear: we receive what we ask for only when the "words of Jesus" remain in us and "we ask according to his will." This teaching is profound. When our desires have first been shaped by God's desires we will only ask for that which God would want. No wonder we receive. We are praying God's will back to God. This is what it means to pray "in the name of Jesus." We are praying through the character and cross of Jesus.

The relationship between how we live and our desires cannot be overstated. Our desires are shaped profoundly by our character.[38] When the way of Jesus becomes the boundaries of our desire at the core of our being, we only ask for those things we know God would want. A request in prayer will be heard and received and given *within* the boundaries of a person submitted to and living in faithfulness to Jesus and his word. I've heard it said that if your prayer isn't answered, this may tell you more about your prayer than it does about God. Indeed. When our prayers are mere wish fulfillment, we walk away wildly disappointed. But when you ask God for that which God wants, God delivers. Always.

---

38. For an interesting recent publication that explores the relationship between ethics and desire, see Gregory Ganssle, *Our Deepest Desires: How the Christian Story Fulfills Human Aspirations* (Downers Grove, IL: IVP Academic, 2017).

Chapter 9

ORDERING DESIRE

In the last chapter, we took time to examine a cruciform desire—the work of forming our desires around the life, death, and resurrection of Jesus. The goal of doing so is the pursuit of a life of godliness, but it also helps us order our loves in a way that reflects God's priorities. We're made into more than just lovers. We're made to love rightly. We all have disordered loves, be it loving something too much, loving something not enough, loving things we shouldn't, or neglecting to love things we should. In *On Christian Teaching*, Augustine describes the ordering of love:

> The person who lives a just and holy life is a person who has ordered his love, so that he does not love what is wrong to love, or fail to love what should be loved, or love too much what should be loved less, or love too little what should be loved more, or love two things equally if one of them should be loved either less or more than the other, or love things either more or less if they should be loved equally.[1]

And Augustine defines sin as "the immoderate urge towards those things at the bottom end of the scale of good [whereby] we abandon the higher and supreme goods, that is you, Lord God, and your truth and your law."

---

1. Augustine, *On Christian Teaching*, 1.27.28.

We are all people of disordered loves. I often experience great
dissatisfaction with my garage. It can't be conquered. No matter
the time I give it, it always reverts back to its primordial state of
chaos. It makes me feel like a failure. On my evening exercise,
I run through a nice neighborhood where garage doors are often
left open. I regularly return home simmering with jealousy at
my garage's state compared to theirs. Then I remember my place
in life. Life, right now, is being a present father and a loving husband. I simply can't be as loving and present as I want *and* have my
sanctified garage. I'm limited. Somewhere down the road, my son
will grow up and move out. Then—and likely only then—will my
garage get saved.

Nobody can love everything equally. Nor should they. As we
acknowledge our limits, fleeting time, and priorities, certain desires
must take the backseat. Imagine the insanity of having a clean
garage while having a child unsure of their love. Indeed, holiness
demands that we prioritize certain desires over others. As the wisdom of the medieval world dictates, every choice is a renunciation.
"By choosing one road," Antonin Sertillanges wrote, "I am turning
my back on a thousand others."[2] Every choice closes a thousand
doors and opens up countless others. Will we order our loves in
such a way that we put our most important love over others?

Years ago, I visited the Tunisian city of Tunis, known in antiquity as Alexandria. At one archeological site we visited, we happened upon what was believed to be an early Christian home from
the third century. How did they know it was a Christian home?
The front room was filled with Christian relics and symbols. But
in the back of the home, a secret room full of Roman idols was discovered. Those in charge of the site had one theory: they believed
the home housed a family that had converted to Christianity

2. A. G. Sertillanges, *The Intellectual Life: Its Spirit, Conditions, and Method*, trans. Mary
Ryan (Washington, DC: Catholic University Press of America, 1998), 121–22.

but resisted letting go of their former idols. They wanted both. I described it in my journal as a religious mullet—Jesus in the front, idolatry in the back.

That little home represents disordered love. We may desire and love God. For many of us, that isn't the problem. Rather, our problem is that we hide some other lovers in the back that we refuse to give up. So much of Jesus' teaching was aimed at people torn between these kinds of loves. Listen to Jesus teach on loving God and money: "No one can serve two masters. Either you will hate the one and love the other, or you will be devoted to the one and despise the other. You cannot serve both God and money" (Matt. 6:24).

Jesus teaches that God and money cannot be served equally or on equal terms. Decisions are required. By putting off ordering our loves, we end up hurting ourselves.[3] The results can be disastrous. By way of spiritual law, we tend to form our lives around our deepest loves and in turn, as the psalmist writes, "will be like them" (Ps. 115:8). We are and become what we love.[4] On an elementary level, this is first seen in the man and woman's immediate response to eating from the tree of knowledge of good and evil. They make clothes from a fig tree. Though the text doesn't clearly articulate what the forbidden fruit was, one could reasonably conclude they ate from a fig tree.[5] I own a fig tree. Their leaves are like sandpaper. There's no other rationale for putting such uncomfortable leaves on such vulnerable body parts. They are grasping for the leaves that were within reach. Why? Shame seeks to cover up fast.

---

3. In his confrontive "Temple Sermon," Yahweh instructs Jeremiah that those who "follow other gods" do so "to your own harm" (Jer. 7.6). Above all, idolatry harms most those who embody it. Idolatry is a form of spiritual self-harm.

4. The thesis of James K. A. Smith, *You Are What You Love: The Spiritual Power of Habit* (Grand Rapids: Brazos, 2016).

5. Victor Hamilton, *The Book of Genesis: Ch. 1–17*, NICOT (Grand Rapids: Eerdmans, 1990), 190–91. The fig tree tradition goes as far back as the Talmud (*Sanhedrin* 70b). While Hamilton acknowledges the tree's species is omitted, he suggests the size of fig leaves could provide the making of clothing.

Don't miss this. What do the man and woman do with the thing they desired and ate? They start looking like it. They wear it. Soon, they run into a tree grove. The progression is almost comical. They ate what they desired. Then they looked like what they desired. Finally, they hid among those things which looked like their desire.

Before long, our unconfronted desire becomes our identity. In other words, we define ourselves by our wants, desires, and longings. This has become, in part, the way identity in our modern, secular, Western culture is increasingly conceived. No longer is identity shaped externally by a creator God or a community that brought us into the world. Identity is what we want. Desire is the last controlling narrative in this context. We can hear echoes of this all over our world. We "fall in love." We are "captivated" by someone. We have "crushes." All such metaphors, more than anything, speak to a desire we have no control over. It takes over our lives. Without the critical work of structuring our desire around God's, we become oppressively bound to following our desires, which, Dallas Willard argues, make for "terrible masters."[6] Rather than people *with* desire, we become our desires. This is the secular ontology of our time. Really, it is just another way for humans to hide among the trees.

Throughout his letters, Paul writes about how disordered love shapes our being. In Ephesians, for instance, Paul lists a set of godly qualities for the person following Jesus. New Testament scholars call these "virtue lists," and Paul offers a number of them. In Ephesians, he pairs his list of virtues with a list of vices that includes sexual immorality, impurity, obscenity, and coarse joking. Right in the middle, Paul includes greed. Immediately upon mentioning greed, he continues, "No . . . *greedy* person—such a person is an idolater—has any inheritance in the kingdom of Christ and

---

6. Dallas Willard, *Life without Lack: Living in the Fullness of Psalm 23* (Nashville: Nelson, 2018), 131.

God" (Eph. 5:5, italics mine). The precision of Paul's language suggests a particular danger for those who have been enmeshed with greed. They don't have greed. They are *greedy*. Paul doesn't say those who experience momentary greed or temptation with greed forfeit their kingdom inheritance. Rather, the "greedy person" forfeits the kingdom.

For Paul, there remains a fundamental difference between an experience of overloving money and one who has been given over to a love of money. Lord knows, it is a normal part of fleshly human experience to encounter moments of disproportionate love for anything good, money being one of them. But this isn't the same as becoming a "greedy person." Idolatry, one could say, is a life *given over* to a particular false love.

The Christian witness, in contrast, separates desire from identity. Our essence is not bound by our desires. We are people with desire. Notice that Paul commands Christian communities only twice to flee something. He tells followers of Jesus to "flee from sexual immorality" (1 Cor. 6:18) and "flee from idolatry" (1 Cor. 10:14). That's it. But the gravity of this is as important today as it was two millennia ago. Paul knew our sexuality and our worship were not two different conversations. Nothing, for Paul, revealed more about what we love and the ordering of desire than how we embody our sexual selves. Does our sexual life reflect the worship of one true God? Or does it reflect the worship of many gods of our making?

As people seeking to order our love, we must accept that not everything gets to be ours. Look at the Ten Commandments through the lens of desire. It has been said that, in the first half of our life, we struggle with the sixth commandment ("do not commit adultery"), but the second half of life is learning to obey the fifth ("thou shalt not murder"). The first commandment for Israel was to worship God above all. Yet when Moses descended the mountain to Israel, they were worshiping a golden calf. There is a

long-standing tradition in Jewish theology that says this is intended
to be a critique of Israel. The law can't even be delivered without
it being broken. That is, before we receive God's word, we've
already rebelled.

The people of Israel were told not to be jealous of other people
for their things. But look at the second commandment: "You shall
not make for yourself an image in the form of anything in heaven
above or on the earth beneath or in the waters below. You shall
not bow down to them or worship them; for I, the Lord your God,
am a jealous God" (Ex. 20:4–5). Then the final commandment is
about not being jealous of your neighbors: "You shall not covet your
neighbor's house. You shall not covet your neighbor's wife, or his
male or female servant, his ox or donkey, or anything that belongs
to your neighbor" (Ex. 20:17). For the reader, there should be just
a little bit of head-scratching. God is described as a jealous God,
but we are commanded not to be jealous. Why does God get to be
jealous but we don't?

Humans desire that which is missing, absent, or misplaced.
We want out of lack. As James wrote, "You desire but do not
have" (James 4:2). This is one of the fundamental differences
between human desire and God's desire. We desire out of lack.
God, on the other hand, desires out of love. This is why the Ten
Commandments can simultaneously forbid human jealousy *and*
describe God as a jealous God. Simply put, humans get jealous for
that which is not theirs. God gets jealous for what's already his.

Loving rightly reorients everything about our lives. René Girard
famously argued in his book *I See Satan Fall Like Lightning* that
while it is true that the last commandment is against jealousy, it is
ultimately the commandment that speaks to why we break the rest
of them.[7] The central motif of jealousy in the Ten Commandments

---

7. René Girard, *I See Satan Fall Like Lightning*, trans. James G. Williams (Maryknoll, NY: Orbis, 2001), 7–18.

is important for our discussion about desire because jealousy often represents the place where our desires and our idols become one. Contentment, we must remember, is not the absence of desire.[8] Rather, it is a desire rightly ordered to that which we are given by God.

———

Our inner world shapes our outer world. As Jesus said, "Out of the abundance of the heart the mouth speaks" (Matt. 12:34 NKJV). To know our inner lives is to love others. Unspoken desires and unnamed expectations can mangle relationships. Nothing can harm a relationship more than holding another person hostage to desires we've never given language to. When someone brings a set of unhealthy and unrealistic expectations into a marriage, it can wreak havoc for years to come. The problem often isn't the marriage but what we expected the marriage to be like. Taking time to interrogate our own desires helps us come to others with healthier and more honest intentions. Everything—from relationships to homes to schedules—is shaped most by the desires within. Every last bit of architecture, city planning, and technological ingenuity is, on some level, a result of human desire. History is the story of human desire. "History is," Thomas Merton affirmed, "unthinkable without man's desire [and] initiative."[9]

Human desire can shape the world for good or bad. Observers of Russian culture often point out that there seem to be bright and sunny skies in Moscow whenever a public parade or national day of observance is held. It is generally held as common knowledge that

———

8. "Contentment is not freedom from desire," writes John Eldredge, "but freedom of desire. Being content is not pretending that everything is the way you wish it would be; it is not acting as though you have no wishes. Rather, it is no longer being ruled by your desires." John Eldredge, *The Journey of Desire: Searching for the Life You've Always Dreamed Of*, expanded ed. (Nashville: Nelson, 2016), 192.

9. Thomas Merton, *Disputed Questions* (New York: Farrar, Straus and Giroux, 1965), 59.

Putin has the technological ability to spread chemicals in the sky to remove clouds. Many wonder if Russia is weaponizing weather to make his parades great—and display power.[10]

Apocrypha or not, this is the essence of what has led to the ecological crisis. God made a good world. But sinful, rebellious people have refused to see God as the center of all of creation and increasingly seek to place themselves on the throne. This attempt at dethroning God as the Lord of creation, in the end, causes tremendous suffering to the entire created world. God clearly indicated this would happen; he *curses the ground* after the fall of the humans (Gen. 3:17). Gil Bailie writes, "We are creatures in whom has been implanted and to whom has been entrusted a world-consuming desire, and if misdirected, it will sooner or later lay waste the world."[11]

One could arguably say that any kind of human-made devastation is, first and foremost, a crisis of desire. We want more than we should have and take what isn't ours. We reject boundaries and limits. A simple look at mountaintop removal in Appalachia reveals heartbreaking images of spaces ravaged by human desire. Our desire can literally destroy mountains, removed for minerals and coal.

We should have listened to Jesus. He was clear. Our inner worlds can shape our outer worlds: "Truly I tell you, if you have faith as small as a mustard seed, you can say to this mountain, 'Move from here to there,' and it will move. Nothing will be impossible for you" (Matt. 17:20). The faith within—small as it may be—can be the kind of saving faith that restores relationship with God. And the same internal powers can accomplish the literal moving of a mountain. The lesson? We order the world around our desires.

10. Fiona Macrae, "Can Russia Control the Weather?," *Daily Mail*, February 15, 2022, https://www.dailymail.co.uk/news/article-2954933/Can-Russia-control-weather-Climate-researcher-says-CIA-fears-hostile-nations-triggering-floods-droughts.html.

11. Bailie, *God's Gamble: The Gravitational Power of Crucified Love*, 37.

Our desires give shape to the world. Indeed, it is okay to want things and realities outside of God. Just as Adam wanted human companionship even while he had a unilateral relationship to the glory of God, we will want and desire things other than God. That is not only okay—it is the way God designed us. Much has been written about how Augustine often had a rather hostile view toward desire. But recent thinkers have concluded that Augustine actually saw human desire as what ordered the world. He believed human desires most played themselves out in the realm of politics and a just society.[12] As humans desire, there goes their society.

In recent years, I've watched as many of my students have become infatuated with the concept of "manifesting." As inspired by books and writings like *The Secret*, this pseudoscientific movement claims that when one names their desires to the universe, it will provide them. When asked what I think about this, my response is simple: "Be careful because it works." This has been the move of sinful humanity since the beginning. If Putin can change the weather and we can remove mountains, then the inner terrain of our desires can accomplish just about anything. The secular prosperity gospel of manifesting has been very popular—and lucrative. Not that the universe as some force has power to provide these things. Rather, it speaks to the simple power of the desire residing in all of us to reorient the world around ourselves. Though our desires might be manifested, they are not always good.

As the horrors of World War II raged on, the literary critic and converted Christian C. S. Lewis delivered a series of radio addresses

---

12. See John von Heyking, *Augustine and Politics as Longing in the World*, The Eric Voegelin Institute Series in Political Philosophy (Columbia: University of Missouri Press, 2001).

on issues ranging from God, worship, church, evolution, and even desire for the British public. These addresses were compiled into a book we now know as *Mere Christianity*. Bombs were literally reigning down over London as Lewis spoke. Swirling around these addresses were a variety of cultural shifts Lewis believed were insidious and dangerous. Slowly, Lewis's world was shifting away from the supernaturalism of the Christian narrative to a reductionistic and naturalistic understanding of the world. Lewis, in one poignant excerpt, asks how one can "find themselves" in a world devoid of God. The task, he believed, wasn't possible. As such, the goal of the Christian life isn't self-discovery; it is self-displacement to follow Jesus. Lewis says,

> The more I resist Him and try to live on my own, the more I become dominated by my own heredity and upbringing and surround and natural desires. In fact what I so proudly call "Myself" becomes merely the meeting-place for trains of events which I never started and I cannot stop. What I call "My wishes" becomes merely the desires thrown up by my physical organism or pumped into me by other men's thoughts.[13]

Lewis's comment is acerbic and pointed: a life without God creates a vacuum of desire. Without a center, humans devolve into a mishmash of narrative happenstance (what Lewis calls "trains of events") and "natural desires," which are in us "by other men's thoughts." Without God, Lewis believes, we are left to choose our desires from the buffet of our genetics or whatever experience has been placed on the schedule this week. And the result is a palpable emptiness. In the words of Sylvia Plath, "I am afraid. I am not solid, but hollow. I feel behind my eyes a numb, paralyzed cavern, a pit of

---

13. C. S. Lewis, *Mere Christianity* (New York: MacMillan, 1960), 189.

hell, a *mimicking nothingness.* . . . I do not know who I am, where I am going."[14]

We, Lewis believes, can be shaped by other people's desires. Just as our inner worlds can shape our outer worlds, the outer worlds around us can profoundly shape our own inner worlds. We can become—borrowing from Lewis—merely the desires "thrown up" or "pumped into" us by relationships and environment.

No one has written more about this phenomenon than Christian philosopher René Girard. Single-handedly reshaping the study of human desire, Girard believed the basic idea that the cross is God's way of exposing human desire. In *Things Hidden Since the Foundation of the World*, Girard suggests that in the cross God unveils hidden desires of humans. The gathering crowd would rather a prisoner (named Barabbas) be free and God (Jesus) be killed. By doing this, God—in the words of Edmund Waldstein— "saves humanity by unveiling the secrets of mimetic desire and the scapegoat."[15]

Girard's theory of "mimetic desire" has gained significant academic traction. In his book *Deceit, Desire and the Novel*, Girard explores how we are impacted by other people's desires.[16] We don't create our own desires, Girard argues. Rather, we reflect and borrow them from others. We mimic other people's desires just as we learn to speak as children. As a result, we are forced to project ourselves into the world as desirable from an early age. Girard believed that all desire was "triangular"—a three-way relationship between a subject, model, and an object. For example, when I look at someone else's life, I see something I want. But it isn't the person we desire.

---

14. Sylvia Plath, *The Journals of Sylvia Plath* (New York: Ballantine, 1991), 59–60.

15. Edmund Waldstein, "Desire, Deicide, and Atonement: René Girard and St. Thomas Aquinas," *Sancrucensis* (blog), May 12, 2016, https://sancrucensis.wordpress.com/2016/05/12 /desire-deicide-and-atonement-rene-girard-and-st-thomas-aquinas/.

16. René Girard, *Deceit, Desire and the Novel: Self and Other in Literary Structure* (Baltimore: John Hopkins University Press, 1976).

Rather, we desire their state of being or something they possess. Girard calls this "mimicry." Gil Bailie describes mimetic desire in the following terms:

> Human desire . . . is always aroused, redirected, and intensified by the desire of another. We desire what we see another desiring, striving to obtain, or enjoying. Two children in a room full of toys inevitably want the same toy, and the more emphatically each expresses a desire for it, the more the other desires it and the more heated the rivalry between the two becomes. . . . Every reaching for a desired object or gloating over its possession amounts to a public declaration of the object's desirability.[17]

In other words, desires are sticky. We tend, by law of nature, to pick up the desires of those around us. As I write this, the church is slowly beginning to reemerge from nearly two years of isolation and lockdown as a result of the COVID-19 outbreak between 2019 and 2021. Something has changed in us. Nearly every pastor in my circle of relationships is reporting nearly word-for-word similar experiences. "It is as though," a number have observed, "people are coming back *radicalized*." In many cases not only have people undergone a great deal of great personal trauma and pain, but it is also as though their entire inner worlds have been reoriented. What happened?

At the same time we were returning from the lockdown, I was shown a heartbreaking series of videos of Uyghur Muslims being sent off by railway to distant reeducation centers in China. There is, for lack of a better term, a genocide taking place right now in China. Two things happen to the detainees at these reeducation centers. First, people are separated from those they love: family, friends, acquaintances. Then, they are forced to watch nearly nine

---

17. Bailie, *God's Gamble: The Gravitational Power of Crucified Love*, 12.

hours a day of reeducation videos. The combination of isolation and endless propaganda videos are expected to change the hearts and minds of an entire people group.

As we reflect on what happened during COVID, much scholarly work will be done to understand the cultural and relational ramification of what took place. But one wonders if we came back different for similar reasons. We spent two years isolated from our communities and in front of our screens at home. Have we been reeducated?

Many (if not *most*) of our desires are learned. Consider the rise of "suicide clusters," people committing suicide because someone in their circle did. Or copycat violent crimes, where something violent is done for the attention. Or the "twitching" phenomenon of kids on TikTok.[18] When a viewer of conservative news is paid to watch progressive news for a little more than a month, studies show that their politics and ideology make major changes.[19] We reflect what we look at. Indeed, God made us that way.

Mimetic desire can be seen in Scripture. Look at Israel just after their freedom from Egypt. Coming to Mt. Sinai, where Israel would remain for a year, Moses descends the mountain with God's law only to find that Israel is now worshiping a golden calf. Why a golden calf? All evidence points to the fact that Egypt worshiped golden cows. Where had Israel just been? Israel is reflecting the worship they saw in Egypt. It would take time for this desire to be exposed.

Many years later, when Israel was divided, the Northern Kingdom was led by Jeroboam, who had been exiled in Egypt by Solomon before his death. The Northern Kingdom didn't have the

---

18. Helen Lewis, "The Twitching Generation," *The Atlantic*, February 27, 2022, https://www.theatlantic.com/ideas/archive/2022/02/social-media-illness-teen-girls/622916/.

19. Adam Gabbatt, "What Happens When a Group of Fox News Viewers Watch CNN for a Month?," *The Guardian*, April 11, 2022, https://www.theguardian.com/media/2022/apr/11/fox-news-viewers-watch-cnn-study.

temple of Jerusalem. Still, they needed a place for worship. To that end, Jeroboam set up two alternative temples in Dan and Bethel. Inside, he set up two idols in the form of golden calves. The author of 1 and 2 Kings called this "the sins of Jeroboam" (2 Kings 3:3). Why two golden calves? Again, look where Jeroboam had been. He had been exiled in Egypt.

Our desires are shaped by our world. Is this very thing happening to us? Our desires are always being rewired.[20]

As I mentioned earlier, we love others by having ordered desires.[21] Take the work of parenting. In nurturing a child, the caregiver must constantly identify the greatest good for a child at a given moment. What may seem like sternness may actually be the loving discipline a child needs at their life stage. If, as caretakers, we quietly determine that our child's happiness is the highest desire worth pursuing, then our parenting will reflect it. Leonard Sax, a physician and psychologist, has written on the dangers of making the oft-used parental mantra of "I just want my child to be happy" the goal of parenting. He writes, "Unfortunately, when you let contemporary American kids do whatever makes them happy, the result is likely to be teenage girls who spend all their time on Instagram or Snapchat, and teenage boys whose favorite pastimes are video games and pornography."

Sax isn't demeaning happiness. Instead, he's saying that happiness is elusive and arbitrary. In concert with a biblical theology of

---

20. The best exploration on the relationship between screens and desires is Doug Smith, *[Un]Intentional: How Screens Secretly Shape Your Desires and How You Can Break Free*, 2nd ed. (Grand Rapids: Credo House, 2021).

21. "To love oneself rightly," writes Bradley Holt, "is neither to grab from others to satisfy one's desires, nor to neglect the care which we all need physically, psychologically, and spiritually." Bradley Holt, *Thirsty for God: A Brief History of Christian Spirituality*, vol. 3rd (Minneapolis: Fortress, 2017), 36.

desire, we should say happiness is a fine goal so long as it's educated and nurtured around the character, virtue, and truth of Christ. Happiness is a great servant but a horrendous master. For Sax, there remains an unignorable connection between character, virtue, and our desires:

> It is no use letting kids do whatever they desire unless you have first *educated their desire*. The first job of the parent is to educate the child's desire: to instill a longing for something higher and better than video games or pornography or social media, whether that something be found in science, in music, in the arts, in nature, or in religion.[22]

Bernard of Clairvaux (1090–1153) is remembered by church historians for his passionate and, some would say, zealous desire to see the church reformed and purified. To that end, Bernard wrote a piece known as "On Loving God" (Lat. *de diligendo Dei*) exploring how to order love around God. Bernard saw four "degrees" (or "steps") in deepening intimacy with God through loving rightly. We move from loving ourselves for our own sakes, to loving God for our own benefit, to loving God for the sake of God, to loving ourselves for God's sake. This final stage is the most transformative as we learn to see ourselves exclusively through God's life and love.

For Bernard, the purest form of devotion and love of God was learning to love God for God's sake—not in loving him for how he makes us feel, what he gives us, or because he is everything we wish him to be. This serves as a great contrast with our time. One of our greatest difficulties is that we conflate love with want. More than once, I've caught myself declaring as I come home that I "love" my wife and son, only to sit at the dinner table and declare that I "love" pizza. How confusing this must be to a child. Our language reveals a distortion. We rarely distinguish in our language between love and desire, so we end up loving what we desire. But love transcends desire. When someone says, "I love chocolate cake," the last thing they should want is for someone to take a knife out to cut it, as Dallas Willard once quipped.[23] Loving and desiring are very different activities.

If love isn't primary, desire malforms. Even God has a hierarchy of desires. Take, for example, God's revelation through the prophets when he says, "I desire mercy, not sacrifice" (Hos. 6:6). Does this mean God did not desire sacrifice in the Old Testament? Of course not. In fact, we have virtually an entire book in Leviticus dedicated to the place of sacrifice in the covenant community of Israel. God desired sacrifice. But not at the expense of mercy toward the poor, vulnerable, orphan, and widow.[24]

Old Testament scholar Jeremiah Unterman points out that this is one of the distinctive features of the Old Testament in the ancient Near East. Like other religions, Israel was supposed to sacrifice. But the God of Israel never made that the bottom line. Sacrifices were to be done rightly, in a way that honored God and honored people. They shouldn't just go through the religious motions. Sacrifices must be done mercifully. God had desires other than just sacrifice for sacrifice sake.[25] God had other desires that were to shape Israel's call.

This gives us insight into God's emotions. And in some way it explains why and how God gets angry in the biblical story. For many modern individuals, God's anger is a stumbling block.

---

23. Dallas Willard, "Beyond Pornography: Spiritual Formation Studied in a Particular Case," *Journal of Spiritual Formation and Soul Care* 9, no. 1 (2006): 9.

24. This list is derived from Zech. 7.9–10 and has been called by philosopher Nicholas Wolterstorff the "quartet of the vulnerable." Nicholas Wolterstorff, *Justice: Rights and Wrongs* (Princeton, NJ: Princeton University Press, 2008), 75–79.

25. Jeremiah Unterman, *Justice for All: How the Jewish Bible Revolutionized Ethics*, JPS Essential Judaism Series (Philadelphia: Jewish Publication Society, 2017), chap. 4.

"Modernity expected God to be disinterested," writes Robert Jenson, "and if a judge, then a disinterested judge, on the model of one behind the bench of a British or American courtroom." Too many want a wrathless God. But the so-called god of modernity's imagination isn't found in Scripture.

A God of rightly ordered love must get angry, judge, and protest human iniquity. A God who doesn't could hardly be considered loving. It has become permissible to passionately protest injustice while rejecting God for doing the same. Is God expected to be silent? The hypocrisy of modernity is that we demand God to be all generous while we stand against injustice. God won't comply. Jenson continues, "But the biblical God is precisely not disinterested; his boundless personal investment in his creatures is his most determining characteristic."[26]

———

Jesus taught the priorities of love (ironically) through the virtue of hatred. His words are pointed: "If anyone comes to me and does not hate father and mother, wife and children, brothers and sisters—yes, even their own life—such a person cannot be my disciple. And whoever does not carry their cross and follow me cannot be my disciple" (Luke 14:26–27).

No doubt, Jesus' teaching on hate may come across to us as strict—if not entirely unsettling. Hate? Really? We need to recognize at the onset that whatever negative impression we may have about this teaching says more about us than Jesus. On a cultural and church level, we've tended to marginalize hatred as categorically evil. It isn't uncommon to hear Christian sermons or teachings cast all negative emotions (anger, lament, and hatred) as the opposite of

---

26. Robert Jenson, *Ezekiel*, Brazos Theological Commentary on the Bible (Grand Rapids: Brazos, 2009), 63.

the Christian way. I observe the same hatred of hatred in neighbor-hood yard signs, which regularly declare, "No hatred is allowed in this neighborhood," and "In *our* America, there's no hate."

Admittedly, our resistance to hatred may be grounded in admirable intentions. Still, it fails to account for Jesus' teaching. Stanley Hauerwas has criticized the uncritical belief that hatred is always bad. In reality, hatred is a sign of validation. Hauerwas tells the story of a pastor who asked him if hell was a place where God hated everyone. Hauerwas rejected the claim. He said, "I responded by saying that is surely wrong. If I know I am hated by God, I at least know I exist."[27] Hauerwas is saying that God's hatred must actually be understood as part of God's love—which is good because God is often described as "hating" (see Pss. 5:5; 11:5; Prov. 6:16–19; and Rom. 9:13). Our understanding of hatred is different from that of Jesus. Biblical hatred isn't the absence of love. Quite the opposite. Hatred is a form of love. As Amish Tripathi's character Veerbhadra says in the *Secret of the Nagas*: the actual opposite of love is apathy.

Hate is an essential part of discipleship. We aren't invited to hate. We are *commanded* to hate. Failure to do so can, in the words of Jesus, keep us from God's kingdom. Still, context is important. Jesus' teaching on hate must be read in light of the previous section of Luke 14, where Jesus has sternly warned against earthly dis-tractions to discipleship to Jesus. He tells a parable about a great banquet that a ruler has thrown. But the invited guests have other priorities. They would rather look at their fields or attend to their oxen or be with women. These desires aren't for evil things. They are reminders that the greatest obstacle to following Jesus is overly desiring good things.

Jesus warns that one could have every material possession yet fail to inherit God's kingdom. But not just material wealth.

27. Stanley Hauerwas, *A Cross-Shattered Church: Reclaiming the Theological Heart of Preaching* (Grand Rapids: Brazos, 2009), 85.

Anything—things, people, events—can distract us from God's kingdom. In this context, Jesus says that a disciple must "hate their mother and father." The point is simple but confrontive: just as an inordinate love of things or events can distract from God's kingdom, so can the inordinate love of people.

The cultural context of this teaching is just as important as the literary context. When we hear Jesus tell us to "hate," we are likely tempted to think of hate the way we, as Western readers, think of hate. But this creates a problem. In the modern West, hatred is almost always tied to realities such as racism, homophobia, Islamophobia, sexism, emotional vitriol, rejection, or murder. But for a first-century Jew like Jesus, hate wasn't about animosity.

"Hate," New Testament scholar F. F. Bruce contends, is an ancient biblical idiom basically meaning "to love *less*."[28] That is, Jesus is teaching about having set priorities in one's love. Hatred is love with priorities. If the best commentary on the Bible is, indeed, the Bible, then we cannot separate what Jesus is teaching here from everything else the biblical text teaches us. So the words of Jesus must be as true as the fifth commandment to honor one's mother and father. Jesus, as any good Jew, wouldn't have taught a thing that violated the tradition he sought to fulfill. So Jesus' commandment to "hate" parents most certainly can't mean to treat parents with disdain.

Hate is a biblical way of speaking about priorities. That interpretive key unlocks those pesky texts that talk about the hatred of God. For example, what does the text in Genesis mean that reads, "I have loved Jacob, but Esau I have hated" (Mal. 1:2–3)? Does this mean God had disdain for Esau? No. God doesn't *hate* Esau the way we hate. Malachi is describing God's choice of Jacob's as the Messianic line that leads to Jesus. God was choosing to work through Jacob, not Esau.

---

28. F. C. Bruce, *Hard Sayings of Jesus* (Downers Grove, IL: InterVarsity Press, 1983), 120.

How does this affect us? It is about ordering love. Jesus is instructing his disciples to order their love in a prioritized, righteous way. In the ancient Christian community, the church fathers saw Jesus' commandment to hate one's parents as the way to honor them. That is, the way to truly love your parents was to love God the most. To borrow from St. Augustine, "You see, you only love your parents properly and devotedly when you do not put your parents before God."[29]

Underneath Jesus' teaching is a lesson about love and the prioritization of desire. Even the love of a parent can reach further than it should. What if the command to love God with the most fervent fire is the way we guard our love for people. When our love for God either dies out or takes on a subsidiary role, then our exaggerated desire for others does great harm. Peter Waldstein once argued that "desire (especially in its modern form) is the desire to be God. God is therefore the ultimate rival, and desire includes an implicit hatred of God."[30] In other words, to love a human more than God is the hatred of God.

Yes, God hates. While that may offend our modern sensibilities, it is critical that we recognize that there's one thing God is never described as in the Bible: apathetic. He never *doesn't* care or love. God is a desiring God. As such, God hates.

Desire gets angry. Desire gets hurt. Desire rages at injustice. Desire and love protest. We find moments in the Bible where God exhibits these emotions! But what we never get, thank God, is an apathetic God who goes on retirement to watch the world burn away. Ours is a God who desires, wants, longs, and pursues.

Our problem is that we don't hate enough. We love everything and everyone the same. And as a result, we fail at our human vocation. It is not Christian to dismiss, condemn, or write off any human being. That is not what Jesus is commanding us to do. What Jesus is inviting us to is one of the most difficult—and pressing—invitations of the Christian way. It is to subsume all loves (even the love of our "loved ones") under and for a love for God. Only in loving God ultimately can we love anyone appropriately.

Part 4

THE REVIVAL OF OUR PASSIONS

Chapter 10

RESURRECTING DESIRE

One final time, we revisit the creation story. In and around the tragic event of the fall, the author twice mentions "desire" in Genesis 3. In the first, the woman is said to see the fruit hanging from the forbidden tree as "desirable for gaining wisdom" (Gen 3:6). The second occasion pops up just after the dust has settled on humanity's rebellion. The deed's been done. The fruit's been eaten. Consequences await. God's word to the woman is gentle, direct, and clear: "I will make your pains in childbearing very severe; with painful labor you will give birth to children. Your desire will be for your husband, and he will rule over you" (Gen. 3:16).

Set squarely between these two references is the fall. Desire's placement before and after the fall can be no mistake. In the second reference to "desire," the Hebrew word used is *t'shuqah*. Given how rare the word is in Old Testament literature, paying good attention here is wise and necessary. The double use of "desire" in Genesis 3 raises an unsettling set of questions for the reader. Did something in the realm of human desire lead to the fall? And did something in the realm of human desire become distorted because of the fall?

From this point forward in biblical history, something in the realm of the woman's desire was uniquely impacted by the traumatic events of Genesis 3. In some noticeable way, the woman's desire became malformed and twisted in a dangerous direction. God is no longer her primary desire. The man will take God's place in her eyes. The scent of idolatry wafts through the narrative.

The results are catastrophic. Rather than loving and caring for (and alongside) the woman, the man now resorts to "rule over the woman."[1] The language here is critical—and abusive if misread. God is in no way commanding the man to rule over her. Nor does God celebrate this. God weeps, observing the travesty that awaits. God isn't prescribing a world he desires. God is quivering with grief at knowing how his daughter would suffer in the land of sinful men. The dream of the garden where man and woman would work together morphs into a nightmare. The man is taking over. And the woman will be ruled. God's ways are quickly being left behind.

The woman isn't the only one limping out of Genesis 3. The fall uniquely changes the man's relationship to work. "You will work the ground," God tells Adam, "and it will produce thistles and thorns for you" (Gen. 3:18). A subtle, dangerous shift has happened. Rather than worshiping the Lord as a priest in Eden, Adam will now find his primary identity in his work. A distorted desire is born around the worship of production, acquisition, and accumulation. For Adam, the Lord of the Harvest is replaced by the harvest.

Taken together, the devolution of the man and woman led us into a dark world of cataclysmic heartbreak, unending pain, and avoidable suffering. This dual distortion of the woman and man's desire has, sadly but predictably, produced for us too many stories of misunderstanding, pain, and abuse between the two sexes that God meant to flourish together. It's a story too many know too well. The woman will desire the man. The man will desire his work. History bears the scars of this trauma. And it's part of the reason why therapists have so few openings for new clients.

But the biblical author isn't finished with that word, *t'shuqah*. At the beginning of Genesis 4 we're whisked into a story about brothers named Cain and Abel, humanity's second generation.

---

1. Derek Kidner argues that the phrase "rule over her" is synonymous with "domineering" over her. Derek Kidner, *Genesis* (Downers Grove, IL: InterVarsity Press, 2008), 76.

The downfall continues. Cain and Abel both make sacrifices to the Lord, only one of which (Abel's) pleases God. There's nothing suggesting that Cain couldn't have taken his sacrifice back or made a different one to rectify the situation. God doesn't cut him off or close the door to repentance. But rather than do what's right, Cain plots to kill his brother in a fit of jealousy.[2] Desire is now in full corruption. Before murdering his brother, God warns Cain, "Sin is crouching at your door; it desires [t'shuqah] to have you, but you must rule over it" (Gen. 4:7).

The literary progression transpiring between Genesis 3 and 4 is instructive. God is telling Cain, "Kiddo, you must rule over your desires. If you don't, your desires will rule over you." In the language of a popular modern theological cliché: kill your sin or your sin will kill you. Sometimes clichés can be true. The downward-spiraling de-evolution of desire over these two chapters signals a major problem for humanity. In the beginning, God gave humans good desires. Satan then weaponized those desires. Human desire turns humans against God. Evil desire then seeks humans out. That's where we find ourselves today. Suffice it to say, Cain doesn't listen, killing his brother and further exiling himself from God's presence.

Then something peculiar happens.

Basically, t'shuqah disappears. After its noticeable flurry in Genesis 3 and 4, t'shuqah goes dormant, fading into the background of biblical imagination for centuries. Forgotten. For such a central word in the earliest chapters of Scripture, it is striking that it drops off the face of the biblical landscape. Among scholars and commentators alike, this has fed quite the biblical debate.

Why does t'shuqah disappear? And where does it go?

---

2. Tremper Longman isolates Cain's sin in the realm, primarily, of desire: "There is no question but that the desire that sin has for Cain is a desire to control him." Tremper Longman III, *Genesis*, The Story of God Bible Commentary (Grand Rapids: Zondervan Academic, 2016), 87.

In 2022, I taught one of the most gratifying and terrifying courses I've ever taught: an undergraduate seminar-style course called Bible, Gender, and Sexuality. The syllabus mapped out the immersive experience. We would navigate ancient contexts, relevant biblical texts about human sexuality, and the history of biblical interpretation around the topic—with dollops of hot takes and biting cultural commentary along the way. Brimming with excitement that the course was approved for the academic calendar, I finally got to teach the class I'd been preparing for two decades. Then course registration began.

Names began populating the roster. As I perused the list, it became increasingly clear the course would pose a unique set of unforeseen problems. The people who I thought would be most interested in the class were not the people signing up. I had assumed our Bible and theology students would be the first to enroll. But I found myself bracing as the student makeup presented more wide-ranging diversity than I could've ever imagined. There were Christians. There were non-Christians. A couple agnostics and atheists made it in. It had equal parts conservatives and progressives. There were straight, gay, and questioning students. All of this, of course, was complicated by the fact I'm conservative ("old-school" in one student's words) on the topics we would wade through. I soon trembled with fear as the pressure mounted. What I had expected to be my best class I now feared could be my last.

Then the class met.

For the next sixteen weeks, we did our work. In the first session, I presented a lecture about how to talk about thorny theological issues without killing each other and how loving your enemies includes your theological enemies. What happened next was a miracle. In subsequent class sessions, there were times we cried. We yelled. I apologized on more than one occasion.

Students apologized to me on more than one occasion. We confessed. Sessions went too long because no one wanted to stop. We forgave each other. We held to our convictions. We respected each other. We wrestled with the Bible. We refused to make the ancient authors say what we wanted them to say. We prayed. We sat silently. But mostly, we all chose to listen and love one another.

The healing in that class was palpable. It healed *me*. As a Christian educator, I've been deceived into believing that the best thing I can do in the classroom is dance around hard things, keep it shallow and wimpish—don't rock the boat. The flesh tempts us to illegitimate peace-keeping rather than peace-making.

The class also healed some students. I learned that today's students are all-too-often oppressed by the condemning eye of social media and cower in silence rather than be fully present. The class broke all the rules. I saw a whole new world in which conservatives and progressives brought conviction but compassion with open ears. A world in which gay and straight people respected and honored one another. A world in which a confession didn't lead to cancellation. Where the benefit of the doubt was extended to all and dignity was assumed.

I swear it: the kingdom of Jesus fell in that classroom.

So much of that class lives in me as I write. Some of it was just darn fun. In one lecture, for example, I presented some emerging research in the field of sexuality around the nature of female orgasm. It turns out (this is no joke) that biologists can provide zero anatomical explanation as to *why* the female body can climax with an orgasm from an evolutionary perspective. I tried to bring theological clarity where science was scratching its head. I argued that scientists have uncovered what is perhaps one of *the* most compelling argument for God's existence. Could it be that we worship a God who gives the gift of pleasure just because? In nearly two decades of education, I've never seen more students interested in becoming theology majors.

Other days haunt me. Near the end of the semester, a male student approached me after class. His countenance said it all. He was in great pain. He had a question: If sex could be so misused to do so much harm to so many people, why would God make it so enjoyable? His honesty was breathtaking. After listening, I offered a thought. What if the problem was not sex itself nor the pleasure it brings? What if the problem is the way we abuse it and use it in ways God never intended? I rattled off one of my favorite C. S. Lewis quotes about how the abuse of a thing never nullifies its original use. Just as alcohol isn't to blame for the alcoholic, sex shouldn't be blamed for its abuse. Then I asked him the source of his question.

As he began crying, it hit me. So much of life includes being hurt by good things that have been misused. The good is the easiest to abuse. We are hurt by good things done wrongly. We all know this. It is in all of our stories. Even something as glorious as sex with all its potential joys and pleasures can be so co-opted for evil and darkness and ill-intent. The work of evil is never original. Evil is the abuse of the good. This is why Joseph can say to his brothers at the end of Genesis, "You intended to harm me, but God intended it for good" (Gen. 50:20).

God intended the good to bless, never to curse. Only evil uses good to curse. And only God can take evil and use it to bless. My student never invited me into his whole story. He didn't need to. His closing words that evening ring as loud in my heart today as they did on that rainy Oregon evening on my drive home after class: "If I rid myself of desire," he confessed, "then maybe I'll never hurt or be hurt again."

This is the human story. Satan found a way to weaponize our good desires against us. He uses blessings to curse. Our good desires get us into a lot of pain, trouble, and heartache. To survive, we start crucifying those good desires, thinking they are the problem. We often succeed. We kill the good desires within and lay them gently in the tomb, untouched, forgotten, lost. Lord knows, in a world still limping out of Genesis 3, we sometimes hope the Sunday of our desires never comes. When our desires keep hurting us, we turn against ourselves and do away with them.

I suspect that is what happens to *t'shuqah*. Humanity was deeply harmed by its desire. And desire just keeps on hurting us. So it's natural to want it to disappear. More or less, *t'shuqah* disappears from the biblical story for the same reason. Old Testament scholar Ellen Davis captures what appears to be happening after Genesis 4: "The word *t'shuqah* stands . . . in Genesis as a red flag warning: 'Caution, danger for women! Love may be hazardous for your health, to your *shalom*, your peace of mind and body.' Evidently the word *t'shuqah* was so laden with bad associations that no one touched it again for centuries."[3] No wonder we eventually subvert and kill our own desires. We believe they led us to the greatest heartaches of our lives.

When our own good desires have been weaponized against us, causing great pain and damage, killing desire is often a path of survival. Somewhere deep in the recesses of our primal being is a drive compelling us to run away from that which creates pain. I call it "survival fear," fear that can save your life. This is a healthy fear.

Try and remember, for example, that last restaurant that gave you food poisoning. Does it still make you nauseous? Hopefully. Why? Because, by God's grace, the body does keep the score.[4] Just as fear protects the stomach, it also protects the heart. When a fiery relationship ends up singeing our sense of self—leaving us

---

3. Ellen Davis, *Getting Involved with God: Rediscovering the Old Testament* (Lanham, Maryland: Cowley Publications, 2001), 72–73.
4. Bessel A. Van der Kolk, *The Body Keeps the Score: Brain, Mind, and Body in the Healing of Trauma* (New York: Penguin, 2015).

languishing and hopeless—our natural response is to run away from romance. When a community of Christians hurts us, who can question our decision to walk away? When we love God, serving faithfully, giving our all—never receiving those things we thought we had coming to us—disappointment (founded or not) can lead us to reject the One we trusted. I'm not valorizing this. I'm naming it. The heart keeps the score as a survival mechanism.

Lost desires can be our greatest teachers. It's there, in those places where desire has died, where God longs to do his greatest healing. So much of Christian ministry is about meeting people in their lack of desire for God. Often we can't go further than wherever someone desires to go. I've learned this as a teacher. One of the first assignments I give freshmen in the Introduction to Biblical Literature course requires them to reflect on the following question: If there were a God, would you even want to know him?

I usually get one of three responses. Some exhibit a kind of spiritual apathy—shrugging a dismissive "meh"—to ignore the whole question. I can do little about them. Others give an emphatic yes. These are usually my Christian students. It's hard to tell if they would *actually* want to know God or if they feel like they're *supposed* to want to know God. But that's not for me to know.

Then there are the nos. These are the students who honestly and passionately declare to their Christian Bible professor that, were there a God, they would have no desire to know him. Of all the reflections, these are always the most passionate. And I'll confess, these are my favorite responses—not because I agree with them, but because they have become the kind of people who are deeply in touch with their lack of desire. They see it. They name it. They aren't afraid of it. Time and again, I've found that these students are the ones sitting in my office most interested in faith at the end of the semester.

Here's my theory. When my students are honest about the absence of desire, they'll be equally passionate when they *do* desire.

The honest awareness of a lack of desire for God can often be the place where God enters in. This was one of the very things that led the great C. S. Lewis toward the Christian faith. He began to notice his passionate nondesire for God. Before his conversion to Christianity, he found himself struck by an "unrelenting approach to Him who I so earnestly desired *not* to meet."[5] Little did he know, the honest nonbeliever Lewis was well on his way to becoming an honest believer. The same is true of many of my students who express a disdain or anger at God in their first assignment. There is always something to be learned from those nondesires.

One of the nos I received for this assignment was from a young atheist. Meeting over lunch, I named something I had observed from our conversations. Whenever God came up, his blood pressure seemed to follow suit. God made him angry. I told him I thought it was odd he could become so animated over somebody he didn't think was real. We both agreed by conversation's end that an odd paradox had risen to the surface. It wasn't that he didn't believe in God. It was that he was deeply angry at and hurt by God. It's impossible to be mad at somebody who doesn't exist.

It's not that my students who answer no don't desire God. It's that the God they've been presented with isn't desirable. We weren't made to worship a monster. Time and again, the entire world of the nos crumbles and opens up at the same time when I get their heads and hearts into the stories of Jesus. There—in the sacred, verdant, and electric pages of Scripture—all of the naive, half-baked falsehoods we've used to judge God fall to the ground. When people actually take the time to gaze upon Jesus, their desire is resurrected.

---

5. As noted in the stage production of *The Reluctant Convert* by Max McLean. The same sort of thing is reported in Sheldon Vanauken's book about the passing of his wife. He writes, "Though I wouldn't have admitted it . . . I didn't want God aboard. He was too heavy. I wanted Him to approve from a considerable distance. I didn't want to be thinking of him." *A Severe Mercy* (New York: HarperOne, 1980), 136. Thanks to Domonic Done for this in his *Your Longing Has a Name: Come Alive to the Story You Were Made For* (Nashville: Nelson, 2022), 31–32.

Always. There's a reason a few of my students get baptized every year. It's because I make them read the Gospels and the stories of Jesus and then grade them on it. It's brilliant. They always thank me for it later.

———

How do we wake up our desire?

As I've shared along the way, I have a unique job as a professor of the Bible at a school where students do not have to be Christians. Many of my students are decidedly *not* Christians. This has created a difficulty. How do I teach students who may not want to learn the Bible? Is there a way to awaken their desire for the Bible? Sadly, many of these students come to the class with a kind of spiritual aposia.[6] In medicine, aposia (lit. meaning "nonthirst") is a condition wherein someone experiences a near to total loss of the sensation of thirst. In a spiritual sense, many of my non-Christian students come to the Bible with no sense that there's anything outside of themselves that they may need.

Yet I've seen key moments in a student's life when they all of a sudden awaken to thirst in the spiritual realm. These are moments when a student experiences loss, transition, death, heartbreak, or broken trust. Rarely, if ever, do my students whose lives are going according to plan desire to follow a God who calls them to something they are not currently doing. In the dark shadows of loss, students often find their way into my office hours to discuss spiritual matters. When the world lets us down, we must find something to sustain us. The French Christian Fénelon writes about this very thing: "The more we drink the impure and poisoned waters of this age, the thirstier we are for them, and the more we plunge into the

———

6. Discussed in Michael John Cusick, *Surfing for God: Discovering the Divine Desire Beneath Sexual Struggle* (Nashville: Nelson, 2012), 26–27.

world. Desires come to life in our hearts . . . enjoying the world's pleasures only makes the soul thirsty and weak. The soul becomes corrupted. It can never be satisfied."[7] When the waters we have been drinking are no longer filling us, we must turn somewhere to be satiated.

One of the core descriptions in Scripture of a holy person or saint is one who does *not* have their desires met. Listen to Psalm 42:

> As the deer pants for streams of water,
>   so my soul pants for you, my God.
> My soul thirsts for God, for the living God.
>   When can I go and meet with God? (vv. 1–2)

The author of this biblical poem has not yet experienced fullness. Their soul is "panting" the way a deer longs for water. Their soul is "thirsty," not yet having had its fill. They have yet to meet with God. They are asking when they will get to. The distinctive language of spiritual life here is not of one who has arrived, had their fill, or found what they are looking for. The narrator is still looking. More broadly, it is important to see how the language of "thirst" is connected to the life of holiness, blessing, and righteousness. In Matthew 5:6, for instance, Jesus instructs his disciples, "Blessed are those who hunger and thirst." Notice his language. Jesus does not say, "Blessed are those who drink." Blessed is the one who has yet to drink.

We are to be like the woman in the Gospels who is desperate, bleeding, and hopeless, who reaches out her hands in desperation to touch the hem of Jesus' robe. She didn't even reach out to touch Jesus—just his outer garment. Her desperation makes her special. "It is this very poverty," David Bennett reflects on the woman, "that leads [her] to reach out for God, longing for him. In this place of

---

7. Fénelon, *The Complete Fénelon*, 181.

trust, we are lifted up, made whole, and brought into the compassionate embrace of Jesus."[8]

This invites us to see the virtue of coming to God empty. Two times, in fact—Revelation 21 and 22—God celebrates those who are "thirsty" and invites them to approach and drink. The invitation to drink of "the water of life" is the final commandment in the entire Bible (Rev. 22:17). Oddly, it's the thirsty ones who are welcomed into the divine space, not the good and filled. The Bible ends depicting a well where all can come and drink for eternal life.

The entire story of Scripture can be understood along these lines. The beginning of humanity's existence comes with the commandment to "eat from the trees" in the garden. The last commandment given to humans is "drink from the wellspring of life." As my friend Leonard Sweet often says in his classes, the Bible is not primarily a book as much as an open table to come and dine with God.

In the pursuit of God, thirst and hunger are virtues—thirsting, longing, hungering, desiring, asking, seeking, knocking. This is the posture of the heart God is looking for. I always remember this as I come to the Lord's Supper. Walking away from the table, I wish I could have eaten more. It never fills me. The taste leaves me wanting so much more. The church is wise in this. We don't get the full meal yet. We just get a foretaste. The bread and wine can't fill us. These elements—as beautiful as they are—are signposts for a greater feast where all will be filled at the supper of the Lamb. For now, only appetizers are available.[9]

A true saint is the thirstiest person in the world.

---

8. David Bennett, *A War of Loves* (Grand Rapids: Zondervan, 2018), 102.

9. As Simon Tugwell would write, "The gift which God makes of himself in this life is known chiefly in the increase of our desire for him. And that desire, being love, is infinite, and so stretches our mortal life to its limits. And that stretching is our most earnest joy, but it is also our most earnest suffering in this life. So those who hunger and thirst are, even now, truly blessed; but their blessedness is that of those who mourn." Tugwell, *The Beatitudes: Soundings in Christian Traditions* (Springfield, IL: Templegate, 1980), 81.

———

Does *t'shuqah* ever return?

A sinful existence causes us to separate from what we were created to desire. As we saw, humanity covered themselves (Gen. 3:7) with fig leaves after being deceived. Their immediate reaction is both profound and inhuman. Humanity begins by covering their essential bodily differences. The man and woman had different bodies. Soon these differences are hidden. Rather than celebrating and loving one another's God-given differences, they cover them up. Sin hates difference. It eventually devolves into a culture free of God's handmade difference. Sin hides God's glorious diversity into a fake homogeneity where everyone's the same.

In so doing, they cover their desirable parts. They were meant to desire each other's bodies. This raises an interesting question. Will humans return to nakedness in the new creation? It is true: Jesus wore clothing after his resurrection. And few would disagree that it would have been awkward had he walked around naked for forty days postresurrection. Again this is taken up in John's Apocalypse—the book of Revelation. There we find heaven described as earth renewed. So earthy will it be that it is described with "crops" needing farming, "fruit" to be eaten, and "months" of harvest cycles (Rev. 22:2). This new heaven will have trees, edible gardens, and time.[10] Jesus, in his forty days of resurrection existence before his ascension, eats food (the activity recorded more than any other), has memory (remembering his friends who betrayed him by name), bears scars on his body, and walks around—and walks through walls to surprise his disciples. Part of resurrection life will be like this existence. And part will not.

Christians such as Augustine have long debated this question. Some have held that heaven will be entirely like this existence

---

10. Revelation 22:2.

(called the "continuous" view), and others believe the new heaven will be entirely different from this existence (called the "discontinuous" view). Those who have studied Augustine see this as a central theme of his writing—a topic to which he devoted great attention.[11] So, then, will we still have desire in heaven? Will we continue to want in heaven? Or will all our desires and wants be fulfilled?

A hint comes in 1 Corinthians 13. Paul is talking about when we will see Jesus face-to-face. Then we will shed our ignorance and partial knowledge. Yet Paul writes, "These three remain: faith, hope and love. But the greatest of these is love" (1 Cor. 13:13). Hope will remain. There, in new creation, we will continue hoping in our creator God, who saved us. Love will remain. That eternal city— where Christ is on his throne—will be as though Jesus the Lamb of God were the mayor administering love, justice, and only goodness. But faith? Why, in God's presence, would anyone need faith still? This seems to be at the heart of a hymn penned by Christopher Wordsworth about heaven:

> Faith will vanish into sight;
> hope be emptied in delight;
> love in heaven will shine more bright;
> therefore give us love.

> Faith and hope and love we see
> joining hand in hand agree;
> but the greatest of the three,
> and the best, is love.

> From the overshadowing
> of thy gold and silver wing

11. Alexander H. Pierce, "Augustine's Eschatological Vision: The Dynamism of Seeing and Seeking God in Heaven," *Pro Ecclesia* 29, no. 2 (2019): 217–38.

shed on us, who to thee sing,
holy, heavenly love.[12]

For Paul, faith, hope, and love will continue. Forever. Indeed, there's much to debate about Paul's language around faith, hope, and love. Many in Christian history—like Wordsworth—believed faith and hope will vanish into new creation's sunset, no longer needed. Will this be the same as desire? Will we no longer need it?

An appetizer of our future is found in the Song of Songs. As you'll recall, *t'shuqah* had disappeared from the biblical landscape almost as a kind of "red flag" (according to Ellen Davis) of desire's danger. Then something transpires in the wisdom literature of the Song of Songs. There a word comes back into use:

I belong to my beloved,
    and his desire [*t'shuqah*] is for me.
Come, my beloved, let us go to the countryside,
    let us spend the night in the villages. (Song 7:10–11)

T'shuqah is back, this time, in the context of a young woman's marriage night. What transpired in Eden is slowly being healed. A resurrection of desire is beginning to happen.

Notice what's happened. As God had said, the woman's desire would be for her husband, and he would rule over her. But now, in the marriage of the Song of Songs, the man isn't ruling. He is *desiring* her. Desire, as it was intended, is beginning to sprout. Healing is taking place. As Ellen Davis writes,

The line the poet is drawing stands out clearly. This is an intentional echo and reversal of the ending of the idyll in Eden.

---

12. Christopher Wordsworth, "Gracious Spirit, Holy Ghost," hymn 28, in *Holy Year; or, Hymns for Sundays and Holidays: And for Other Occasions*, 1st ed., (London: Rivingtons, 1862).

No longer, the poem declares, are desire and power unequally distributed between woman and man. The woman proclaims here true partnership of unrestrained self-giving and mutual advocacy: "I am for my darling and he is for me" (6:3). A rose replaces the red flag. The word now marks a new beginning to sexual history, a place of healing for women and men alike.[13]

The author of Proverbs hints at the same thing: "Hope deferred makes the heart sick, but desire fulfilled is a *tree of life*" (Prov. 13:12, emphasis mine). As we come nearer to our God, nearer we come to desire's intent. It is a proverbial return to Eden's tree of life. Certainly, the Song of Songs isn't merely describing a marriage between a man and a woman. No, this is a foretaste of the great marriage between Christ and his people to which we are all invited. There, as God's people, restored to her beloved, desire starts her resurrection.

---

13. Davis, *Getting Involved with God*, 72–73.

Chapter 11

LONGING DESIRE

While its origin remains unknown, there's a well-traveled tale of two missionaries returning from service on the same ship as President Teddy Roosevelt on route from an overseas safari. Bands play and well-wishers applaud as the massive vessel docks in a New York City harbor. Observing the crowds, the missionary comments to his wife. "See," he says enviously, "from a single hunting trip, the president returns to . . . parades and marching bands; but when we come home there's no one here to meet us." Turning to her husband, his wife whispers, "My dear. We're not home yet."[1]

This likely apocryphal anecdote represents a penetrating theological truth for the Christian. Ours is a journey of homesickness. We haven't reached our final destination. Philosopher Martin Heidegger once called this existential experience *unheimlich*, or "not-being-at-home."[2] The German word *Sehnsucht* describes that innate human desire each of us have that can't be satisfied by anything earthly.[3] Homesickness even serves as a recurring theme in the *Epic of Gilgamesh*, as a heartbroken Gilgamesh chases what biblical scholar Nahum Sarna called "an overwhelming desire for

---

1. As retold in week 6 and day 4 of Calvin Miller, *Fruit of the Spirit: Faithfulness* (Nashville: Nelson, 2008).

2. Martin Heidegger, *Being and Time*, trans. John Macquarrie and Edward Robinson (Albany: State University of New York Press, 1996), 189.

3. *Sehnsucht* is a theme throughout C. S. Lewis's writings about which Marva Dawn has penned an entire chapter in Marva Dawn, *To Walk and Not Faint* (Grand Rapids: Eerdmans, 1980), 33–37.

immortality" after his friend Enkidu dies.[4] If humans are at home, why don't we feel like it?

For the Christian, this homesickness isn't some glitch in evolutionary history. We were created for another world. In *Lost in the Cosmos*, Christian thinker Walker Percy observes how even after seemingly endless technological advances making human existence more manageable and comfortable, we, ironically, increasingly feel like foreigners on earth.[5] Others, like Ronald Rolheiser, have called this unsatiated longing for some other world our "fundamental disease."[6] C. S. Lewis considered this homesickness evidence for God's existence, writing, "If I find in myself a desire which no experience in this world can satisfy, the most probable explanation is that I was made for another world."[7]

Still, this homesickness has a tension. In a very real sense, we aren't home yet. Yet we *are* home. How could both be true? If I allowed someone to peruse the books in my office library, they would discover a mishmash of texts from a variety of disciplines, including biblical studies, theology, ecology, biology, and literature. They would also find a number of books from my earliest years of faith. Many transformed me. Others serve as little more than relics from a distant past. Even to this day, I'm struck by how many of those books that shaped me early on seem singularly obsessed with escaping life down here on this planet to go to heaven up in the sky. My earliest Christian imagination was disproportionately shaped by a goal of leaving. In one of these books, I jotted down the first definition of the Bible I'd been given: "Basic Instructions Before Leaving Earth."

4. Nahum Sarna, *Understanding Genesis: The World of the Bible in the Light of History* (New York: Schocken, 1966), 41.

5. Walker Percy, *Lost in the Cosmos: The Last Self-Help Book* (New York: Farrar, Straus and Giroux, 1983).

6. Ronald Rolheiser, *The Holy Longing: The Search for a Christian Spirituality* (New York: Doubleday, 1999), chap. 1.

7. C. S. Lewis, *Mere Christianity* (New York: Scribner, 1952), 106.

I mustn't condemn the old me. Still, I've come to see that much of this escapist outlook betrays what the Bible says about life. The goal of the Christian life isn't fleeing from a dying world on fire. Rather, it's to be lit on fire by the Spirit of God *in* and *for* a dying world. My entire imagination has been reoriented by the Bible—such is the case when I read John's vision of the future in Revelation:

> I saw the Holy City, the new Jerusalem, coming down out of heaven from God, prepared as a bride beautifully dressed for her husband. And I heard a loud voice from the throne saying, "Look! God's dwelling place is now among the people, and he will dwell with them. They will be his people, and God himself will be with them and be their God." (Rev. 21:2–3)

Heaven will come down here. To earth. As a husband. The goal, then, isn't escaping earth to go to heaven. The goal is heaven coming here. Jesus taught us to pray, "Your kingdom *come*, your will be done" (Matt. 6:10). His prayer will happen. The kingdom *will* come—here, in this place, as it is in heaven. This reframes everything for the Christian. No longer can God's people treat Jesus' return as some hall pass to destroy the very garden we were called to care for. No longer can we see justice as a distraction from preaching the gospel. No longer can I do with my body as I please. This isn't my body. This is God's body. Again, it changes everything.

That's the tension. We're home, and we aren't home—at the same time. The earth we find ourselves in is different from the one we were created for. In that future day, this entire "divorce court" (as Chesterton calls it) that marked life after the fall will be undone. Just as humanity's departure from Eden ended with a divorce from Eden, Eden's restoration is described as a wedding. The two will become one.

"Desire is wanting something," reflects Gerald May, "longing for some satisfaction."[8] Our desire for that remarriage (what Ecclesiastes 3:11 calls "eternity [set] in the human heart") is what leads us into this future. Humans long for an apocalypse, a future, an in-breaking restoration of heaven and earth. Even if it isn't anchored in the coming rule and reign of Christ, this innate longing remains. We still need an apocalypse. As have others, I can't help but notice the cultural tsunami of apocalyptic movies and writings in our time. Stephen O'Leary has chronicled four primary types of apocalyptic media that have surged in quantity: monster movies, alien films, postapocalyptic films, and dramas of nuclear destruction.[9]

Why are we so obsessed with the apocalypse? I'd suggest this sudden rise in zombie apocalypse and dystopian fantasy is directly tied to the vacuum created by the surge of secularism. Without God's future, the human heart still needs a reference point for the future. Apocalypse and dystopia, as genres, are more or less a cultural attempt at filling the vacuum of longings Richard Mouw describes as "deeply embedded in the human spirit."[10]

My doctoral research explored a biblical theology of caring for the earth as it relates to the Holy Spirit.[11] After finishing, I set out to build partnerships between the church and the environmental community of Portland. I wanted to learn. But I also wanted to be a witness of Jesus to them. It struck me how eager the top nonprofit leaders, environmentalists, and activists in the city were to meet with

---

8. Gerald May, *The Awakened Heart: Opening Yourself to the Love You Need* (New York: HarperCollins, 1991), 45.

9. Stephen D. O'Leary, "Apocalypticism in American Popular Culture: From the Dawn of the Nuclear Age to the End of the American Century," *The Encyclopedia of Apocalypticism*, ed. Stephen J. Stein, vol. 3 (New York: Continuum, 2000), 392–426.

10. Richard Mouw, *When the Kings Come Marching In: Isaiah and the New Jerusalem* (Grand Rapids: Eerdmans, 2002), 43. In another important work, Randall Rosenberg argues that our desires are ordered particularly toward the supernatural. See his Randall Rosenberg, *The Givenness of Desire: Concrete Subjectivity and the Natural Desire to See God* (Toronto: University of Toronto Press, 2017), 23.

11. For the three people interested in reading, it can be found at A. J. Swoboda, *Tongues and Trees: Toward a Pentecostal Ecological Theology*, Journal of Pentecostal Theology Supplement Series, vol. 40 (Blandford Forum, UK: Deo, 2013).

me, a conservative Christian. One well-known activist was not a religious person. Still, over breakfast, she shared about waking up every day to care for the planet. She cried sharing with me how many of her environmentalist friends had taken their own lives having given up hope. I asked her why she kept fighting. She told me she didn't know. "It's like," she confessed, "I was *made* to do this. It consumes every breath in my body. It feels like there's no hope anymore."

She longed for a future day when all would be made well. We shared that in common. This was when I shared my faith with her—the hope of glory, the future, God's promise of restoration. She politely listened. But then she shared with me that many of the Christians she knew didn't seem to care. I walked home sad. This woman was doing God's work without hope. The church, too often, has God's hope but fails to do the work. That breakfast changed me. I see now that *everyone* (Christian or not) has an innate longing for some future where all will be made right. Where does that come from? Could we say it comes from God himself?

My friend Matthew Sleeth, a doctor, has a theory about this. He tells me that when God breathed into Adam's nostrils, he did so through the part of the body that travels closest to the part of our brain where memories are kept. This is why we smell something and are immediately whisked back into some obscure moment from our childhood. Smell unlocks memories. It's as though every human being has a deep memory of the way things were. And the way they *should* be.

We all have a distant memory of God's desire for things, and we all have a longing to go back there. "The Spirit is the constant overflow of life of God into creation," writes Sarah Coakley, "alluring, delighting, inflaming, in its propulsion of divine desire."[12] This future is where the Spirit of Jesus leads us.

---

12. Coakley, *God, Sexuality, and the Self: An Essay on the Trinity* (New York: Cambridge University Press, 2013), 23.

Longing leads us home. But what will happen to our desire once we've arrived? In his allegory about hell *The Great Divorce*, C. S. Lewis tells of a man taken on a bus ride through hell with a guide, Virgil (representing Lewis's hero, George MacDonald).[13] Many details of Lewis's depiction of hell are striking. Everyone in hell, for one, continues moving further and further apart as if in an ever-expanding suburb. By the end, everyone is so spread out they can't see or hear any of their neighbors. Additionally, everyone encountered is hellbent on blaming someone else for their plight. No one takes responsibility. Perhaps most importantly, Lewis portrays those in hell as desiring to live there. The people in hell get what they desire.

I once heard someone say that as they get older, people don't change; they just become extra.[14] We become who we are becoming today. In Christ's passion scene, he is ridiculed by one criminal and loved by another. This raises a question: What were these criminals like before their death scene? As is often the case, we become our truest selves in our death. For Lewis, hell serves as an extension of the kinds of people we were in our earthly lives. Hell is a destination, but it is also the continuation of our life forever. Every moment is a precedent. Lewis's description of one character in hell captures this:

> It begins with a grumbling mood, and yourself still distinct from it: perhaps critiquing it. And yourself, in a dark hour, may will that mood, embrace it. You can repent and come out of it again. But there may come a day when you can do that no longer. Then there will be no you left to critique the mood, nor even to enjoy it, but just the grumble itself going on forever like a machine.[15]

---

13. C. S. Lewis, *The Great Divorce* (New York: MacMillan, 1946).
14. Attributed to David French as quoted in one of many of his interviews.
15. Lewis, *The Great Divorce*, 75.

We shouldn't build all our theology on fictional allegory. But so much of Lewis's vision resonates with Scripture. In Scripture, for example, an operative word for separation from God is "wrath." When one ceases worshiping God, God does something generous. In Paul's language, "God gave them over in the sinful desires of their hearts" (Rom. 1:24). Wrath doesn't often include lightning, curses, or earthquakes. It is usually described as being given over to one's desire.

The great biblical scholar Frederic Godet used the image of a boat to describe wrath. The river's current pulls at the boat, but a rope ties it to the dock, keeping it from flowing downstream. Wrath, for Godet, is "God ceas[ing] to hold the boat as it was dragged by the current of the river."[16] Wrath is God letting go, letting our desires have the final say. Lewis alludes to this as the evil witch in *The Magician's Nephew* gets the apple she desired: "She has won her heart's desire; she has unwearying strength and endless days like a goddess. But length of days with an evil heart is only the length of misery and already she begins to know it. All get what they want; they do not always like it."[17]

The Bible has a word for getting what we want: wrath. Heaven, on the other hand, isn't described as a place where we get everything we desire. Heaven, rather, is the place where we trust everything that God desires. Listen to some of the apocalyptic imagery of the prophet Isaiah describing what would happen when the Spirit-anointed Messiah would come and restore the world:

> The wolf will live with the lamb,
>   the leopard will lie down with the goat,
> the calf and the lion and the yearling together;
>   and a little child will lead them.

---

16. Frederic Louis Godet, *Commentary on Romans* (Grand Rapids: Kregel, 1977), 107.
17. C. S. Lewis, *The Magician's Nephew* (New York: Collier-MacMillan, 1955), 174.

> The cow will feed with the bear,
>> their young will lie down together,
>> and the lion will eat straw like the ox.
> The infant will play near the cobra's den,
>> and the young child will put its hand into the
>> viper's nest. (Isa. 11:6–8)

Isaiah's description of a coming Messiah includes the healing of relationships. The reader must note Isaiah's list of creatures. These are predators and prey. In the natural world, wolves eat lambs, leopards eat goats, lions eat calves, and so on. These victims wouldn't be caught dead in the presence of their predator. However, when the Spirit-anointed Messiah appears, relationships of predation will be healed. In the new creation, the lion will lie down with the lamb.

Reading this may evoke feelings of anger or frustration for some. Many of us do not want a world with that kind of restoration. Would a lamb really want to lie down with a lion? I think not. John's vision of heaven where Jesus is worshiped by every "nation, tribe, people and language" (Rev. 7:9) would be terrifying news for communities and nations that have been killing each other. Heaven will apparently be a place where God can bring together all those who in the natural world would run from each other in terror. As theologian Miroslav Volf reflects, this future new creation will be a place where Cain would no longer need to avoid looking his brother Abel in the eye. And Abel would no longer need to run from his brother in fear.[18] This is captured best by Karl Barth's response to the question, "Will I see my loved one's in heaven?": "Oh, not only your loved ones!"[19]

All of this is said with a great deal of irony. Hell will be the place where humans get what they want. Heaven, on the other

---

18. Volf, Miroslav, "The Final Reconciliation: Reflections on a Social Dimension of the Eschatological Transition," *Modern Theology* 16, no. 1 (January 2000): 94.

19. As quoted in Volf, "The Final Reconciliation," 91.

hand, is the place where we live at peace under everything God wants. In hell, our desires become our gods. In heaven, our every desire bends its knee before the God of desire.

━━━━━

If we were made to desire this future, then why does it take so long to get there? What's with God's delay? In the realm of eschatology, this is known as the *parousia* (or "return") of Jesus. He promised to come and restore the world. Since you are reading this, reason suggests we are still waiting. So we tarry. But why? What is God accomplishing in this delay? In a set of reflections on Jesus in the boat with the disciples during a storm, Martin Luther asks a simple question: Why is Jesus sleeping in the back? What, Luther asks, does God accomplish in taking a nap in a storm? Luther believes that it was what gave birth to the disciples' desire:

> It is well with those who find water breaking into their ship, for this moves them to seek help from God. Wherefore, observe how Christ is seeking our profit and is serving us even while he sleeps. . . . Indeed, he wants to arouse in us a desire for him, so that we may continue to cry out to him; he wants us to cry out to him in order that he may hear and answer us.[20]

For Luther, Jesus' nap was his way of cultivating the right desire in his disciples: a desire for him. Christopher West has called Jesus' delay "stretching desire."[21] Why does Jesus not come immediately? For the same reason Jesus naps in the boat. The intentional delay of God accomplishes in us the cultivation of right desire that can only be fulfilled by his arrival. Delay is the birthplace of desire. And it

---

20. *Luther's Works*, 51.24.
21. Christopher West, *Fill These Hearts: God, Sex, and the Universal Longing* (New York: Image, 2012), 82.

is how God matures our desire. In the delay, our desire is being perfected, seasoned, prepared. Only mature desire can maturely receive. Just as God accomplished what he wanted by making Adam wait for his marriage to the woman, God is accomplishing what he wants by making us wait for the remarriage of heaven and earth.

Just as parents must teach their child the principle of delayed gratification, God is preparing us to receive heaven in fullness. If we received it immediately, it would destroy us. We need preparation. Delay, then, is a feature and not a bug. It is awakening and maturing our desire.

Delay is also a great revealer of our false gods. It's only as Moses is delayed in coming down the mountain that Israel forms and worships their golden calf. Delay reveals our idols, and it's usually the time when we form them. In the waiting, we get tired and start to worship something we can place our hands on.

We are waiting. What we wait for—the hope of glory that is to come—is long in coming. Waiting is often treacherous. And it both reveals our hearts intent and prepares it for what is to come.

━━━━

On that day, we will see God's face.

As I wrote this book, I encountered the work of a Serbian conceptual artist named Marina Abramović. Her works generally include performance art—often with the artist herself—and evoke a sense of humanity in her observers. At the height of her fame in 2010, Abramović curated a show titled "The Artist Is Present." The masses bought tickets and awaited the show at the show Museum of Modern Art in New York, unaware of what they were about to see. Arriving, onlookers and admirers found two wooden chairs facing each other separated only by a table. The viewers were to enter the performance and sit, staring Abramović in the eyes. No words. No gestures. Just two people face-to-face. The responses of people ranged from awkward laughter, to discomfort, to downright confusion as they stared their hero in the face. For many, there was overwhelming emotion and tears.[22]

Earlier, we discussed ways in which humans are like animals. But there are also ways in which we are different. Humans are the only land creatures that have sexual intimacy face-to-face. We were made to be face-to-face. In the post-COVID era, it feels as though we have lost part of that face-to-face intimacy. During the pandemic years, we had to cover our faces with masks. We spent our time looking at our phones. When we had facetime, it was often through digital media. Humans were made to look each other in the face. And the fact that, even after quarantines were lifted, we still don't look at each other very much anymore has created an environment where it's an act of artistic expression—as Abramović showed us—simply to behold another's face.

Neuroscientists have shown us how, upon birth, human babies immediately look for some face that is looking back at them. In the last fifteen or so years, we've learned that the mirror neurons in a baby's brain seek connection and attachment to others within seconds. Babies often mimic the face of their mothers or fathers within the first thirty minutes of their lives. As Christian neuroscientist Curt Thomson wrote, "Every baby comes into the world looking for someone who is looking for him or her."[23] This is the beginning of what we call "attachment." Without attachment, a baby will experience difficulties and even begin to die.

The psalmist was prophetic in declaring that people should always seek God's face (Ps. 105:4). Without the face of God, we die. The face of God becomes the entire storyline of the Bible. In the

---

22. Michael Zhang, "Sitting, Staring, and Crying with Marina Abramović at MoMA," *PetaPixel*, April 23, 2010, https://petapixel.com/2010/04/23/sitting-staring-and-crying-with-marina-abramovic-at-moma/.

23. Curt Thompson, *The Soul of Desire: Discovering the Neuroscience of Longing, Beauty and Community* (Downers Grove, IL: InterVarsity Press, 2021), 21.

Old Testament, when sinful humans look into God's face, they die. But something changes with the incarnation of Jesus Christ. Jesus was the face of God—divine in human flesh. Now humans *can* see God's face, and the shift is profound. Humans first lived face-to-face with God. That was lost. After the fall, sinful humans would die if they looked at God's face. Then they saw God's face, and he died on a cross. But because of that, our future is glorious. As Paul writes, "We see only a reflection as in a mirror; then we shall see face to face" (1 Cor. 13:12).

Heaven might as well be called "The Artist Is Present." Until then, our hearts remain unfulfilled. They *can't* be fulfilled. We were born to behold God's face. Until then, something is missing. Still, we can't help but lovingly long. Perhaps this helps us understand anew Psalm 105. "Look to the Lord and his strength," the psalmist writes, "seek his face always" (v. 4). Indeed, we will seek his face always, forever, on eternity's doorstep. As Augustine wrote in *Exposition of the Psalms*, "But what is meant by *seek his face always*? I certainly know that it is good for me to cleave to God, but if he is always being sought, when is he ever found? . . . May we think, perhaps, that even when we do see him face to face, we shall still need to search for him, and search unendingly, because he is unendingly lovable?"[24]

Our desire will be resurrected. It will find what it has always sought. It still won't be satisfied. For the face it has always sought will take endless time to take in. At the end of *City of God*, Augustine says when we enter the presence of God in heaven, when new creation is established, we will keep on reading, and not just books. Forever in wonder and ceaseless joy, we will read the glorious face of God. For Augustine, we will keep seeking after seeing his face because it is eternally lovable, more and more and more.[25]

---

24. Augustine, *Expositions of the Psalms 99–120*, trans. Maria Boulding, vol. III (Hyde Park, NY: New City Press, 2004), 185–86.

25. Pierce, "Augustine's Eschatological Vision: The Dynamism of Seeing and Seeking God in Heaven."

As we come to a close, we finish with an image from Christian history. Count Nicholas von Zinzendorf (1700–1760) lived as German nobility. His childhood and early adult years were marked by ease as he was raised in wealth and exuberance. Zinzendorf is remembered for many things: being a musician and hymn-writer, being emotional, and caring about the poor. But it was his hand in the development of what would be called the Moravian church that sets him apart in history. When Nicholas was a teenager, he traveled to a number of major European cities to visit their artistic creations. In one such museum in Dusseldorf, Nicholas saw the famed *Ecce homo* by Domenico Fetti. The picture changed him forever, and he gave the rest of his life in service of God afterward.

What did Nicholas see?

This existence is more difficult than we often like to admit. But it is a story—God's story—that will be completed. It is a story that God began to reverse almost immediately. He won't give up. This is his creation. We are his creations. God told the man, "You will work the ground and it will produce thorns *for* you."

Yes, they are for you. What did Nicholas see in the *Ecce homo*? It is a painting of Jesus wearing a crown of thorns, preparing to die on the cross. While we can only surmise as to what this experience did within him, we know it changed him forever. Near the bottom of that painting appear these words in Latin: "All this I did for thee; what doest thou for me?"[26]

And it changes us. The King of Glory, the God of the universe, the Maker of heaven and earth—God has chosen, in his final act,

---

26. A. J. Lewis, *Zinzendorf, the Ecumenical Pioneer: A Study in the Moravian Contribution to Christian Mission and Unity* (Louisville: Westminster, 1962), 28. As a fitting tribute to Tim Keller, I acknowledge his inclusion of this story in his *The Kings Cross: The Story of the World in the Life of Jesus* (New York: Dutton, 2011). Keller passed away during the writing of this manuscript, and his work and ministry have inspired me on countless levels.

to wear a crown of thorns. Not accidentally. But with intention. On the cross, the one with the thorns on his head is dying to set us free.

One unknown twelfth-century priest once reflected in his journal what paradise would be like. He believed new creation would be a place without thorns. I cannot help but agree.[27] On the cross, Jesus wears the burden of our sin's weight. We were given a world of thorns upon our fall. Our lives become painful, difficult, tempestuous, and frustrated. Life leaves much to be desired. Still, that is not the end of the story. Love has let us know we are desired. And those thorns that were ours have been put on another.

Indeed, the one who bore those thorns is God's greatest gift.

---

27. From the ancient text *Elucidation*, quoted in McDannell and Lang, *Heaven*, 70–72.

ACKNOWLEDGMENTS

A pen," once wrote H. Hendricks, "is a mental crowbar." It's true: the writer gets the privilege of having their name emblazoned on the cover of their writing. But be not deceived—behind any writer is an incognito team of individuals and communities who have helped them find and pick up the crowbar they hold in their hand. My team is worthy of such deep gratitude. From the overwhelming support and faith the team at Zondervan Reflective has lent to me—Kyle Rohane, Lex De Weese, Liz England, Matthew Estel, and Ryan Pazdur. You have been outstanding to work with. Let's do it again. To Bushnell University and its faculty and staff who instrumental in forming my own craft and vocation, you are a gift. To the Doctor of Ministry team at Friends University that I'm privileged to lead, you are second to none. I cannot begin to adequately thank the attentive editorial assistance of Tony Scarcello, Gregory Coles, and Christy Rice, who each gave a hearty review of the manuscript in its formation process. And my agent, Tawny Johnson, this would not have become a reality were it not for you. In addition, the magnanimous work of the one and only Jared Dodson, who serves as my research assistant has proven as valuable as gold. I have the best friends in the world—brave souls who have walked with me through so much. Thank you, Trevor, Nijay, John, Nic, Andy, Brooks, Cameron, Josh, and George, for showing me the bright gift of companionship. And to my friend David, who entered glory as this manuscript was completed, keep writing worship songs, friend. You have so many songs to sing. All this alongside my humble gratitude toward my wife, Quinn, and son, Elliot, who have walked with me every step of the way. This has been a team effort. Whatever this book does to build the kingdom, may you reap the rewards. And whatever doesn't, that's on me.